Lecture Notes in Artificial Intelligen

Subseries of Lecture Notes in Computer Science
Edited by J. G. Carbonell and J. Siekmann

Lecture Notes in Computer Science
Edited by G. Goos, J. Hartmanis and J. van Leeuwen

Springer
Berlin
Heidelberg
New York
Barcelona
Hong Kong
London
Milan
Paris
Singapore
Tokyo

Brij Masand   Myra Spiliopoulou (Eds.)

Web Usage Analysis and User Profiling

International WEBKDD'99 Workshop
San Diego, CA, USA, August 15, 1999
Revised Papers

Springer

Series Editors

Jaime G. Carbonell, Carnegie Mellon University, Pittsburgh, PA, USA
Jörg Siekmann, University of Saarland, Saabrücken, Germany

Volume Editors

Brij Masand
Director of Knowledge Discovery and Intelligent Agents Technology
Redwood Investment Systems Inc.
Boston, MA 02110-1225, USA
E-mail: brij@redwood.com
Prior affiliation: GTE Laboratories, Waltham, MA, USA

Myra Spiliopoulou
Humboldt Universität zu Berlin, Institut für Wirtschaftsinformatik
Spandauer Str. 1, 10178 Berlin, Germany
E-mail: myra@wiwi.hu-berlin.de

Cataloging-in-Publication Data applied for

Die Deutsche Bibliothek - CIP-Einheitsaufnahme

Web usage analysis and user profiling : international workshop;
revised papers / WEBKDD '99, San Diego, CA, USA, August 15, 1999. Myra
Spiliopoulou ; Brij Masand (ed.). - Berlin ; Heidelberg ; New York ;
Barcelona ; Hong Kong ; London ; Milan ; Paris ; Singapore ; Tokyo :
Springer, 2000
    (Lecture notes in computer science ; Vol. 1836: Lecture notes in
    artificial intelligence)
    ISBN 3-540-41517-3

CR Subject Classification (1998): I.5, H.2, H.4.3, H.3, H.5, K.4, K.5, I.2

ISBN 3-540-67818-2 Springer-Verlag Berlin Heidelberg New York

Springer-Verlag Berlin Heidelberg New York
a member of BertelsmannSpringer Science+Business Media GmbH
© Springer-Verlag Berlin Heidelberg 2000
Printed in Germany

Typesetting: Camera-ready by author, data conversion by DA-TeX Gerd Blumenstein
Printed on acid-free paper   SPIN: 10722002   06/3142   5 4 3 2 1 0

Table of Contents

Preface

1   Data Mining for the Web

The web has revolutionized our conception of communication and interaction. It offers new ways of business-to-business and business-to-customer transactions, new mechanisms for person-to-person communication, new means of discovering and obtaining information, services and products electronically. The volume of web data increases daily and so does its usage. Both *web contents* and *web usage data* are potential bearers of precious knowledge.

Some years ago, Oren Etzioni questioned whether the web should be observed as a quagmire or a gold mine [Etz96]. Indeed, the web grows freely, is not subject to discipline and contains information whose quality can be excellent, dubious, unacceptable or simply unknown. However, a carefully designed vehicle for the analysis of data can discover gold in the web [Etz96]. More recently, Richard Hackathorn proposed a methodology called "web farming" for acquiring business-related information from the web, maintaining it and turning it into useful and actionable knowledge [Hac99].

After the advent of data mining and its successful application on conventional data, web-related information has been an appropriate and emerging target of knowledge discovery. Depending on whether the data used in the knowledge discovery process concerns the web itself in terms of *content* or the *usage of this content*, we can distinguish between "web content mining" and "web usage mining" [CMS99]. However, the two areas overlap, as is shown in Fig. 1.

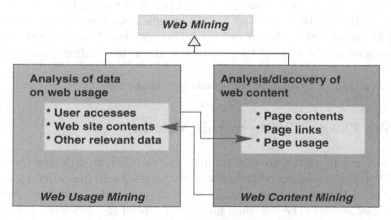

Fig. 1. Data mining for the web

Web content mining concentrates on discovering useful information in the web and on analyzing, categorizing and classifying documents. For document analysis, not only the document contents are taken into account, but also the

M. Spiliopoulou and B. Masand (Eds.): WEBKDD'99, LNAI 1836, pp. 1–6, 2000.

links connecting the web pages and potentially reflecting semantic relationships among them. Moreover, the access to the pages reflect how people conceive and interrelate them.

In contrast, web usage mining focusses on the discovery of knowledge about the people using the web, their interests and expectations, the problems they face and the implicit requirements they carry with them. Knowledge about the users forms the basis for dynamically adjustable sites, navigation assistants, customizable search engines, recommender systems and any other personalized services that seek to optimize the interaction between the person and the web. This knowledge is acquired by combining information on the page accesses, as recorded by the site servers, with information on page contents and with external data, such as user demographics, warehouse data on company customers etc.

2   Web Usage Mining at KDD'99

The 1999 ACM/SIGKDD International Conference of Knowledge Discovery and Data Mining hosted its first workshop concentrating on the challenges posed by mining the usage data from the web. WEBKDD'99, the Workshop on Web Usage Analysis and User Profiling brought together the communities of mining researchers, tool vendors and web usage data holders. The establishment of user profiles from anonymous web usage data, the extraction of knowledge from the navigation behaviour of the users and the assessment of the *usefulness* of this knowledge were the main axes of investigation identified during the workshop. Open issues concerning data quality, scalability and privacy were vividly discussed during the panel session.

A report on the activities of the WEBKDD'99 workshop can be found in [MS00]. Briefly, WEBKDD'99 had 23 submissions, from which 10 were accepted for presentation after refereeing by 3 reviewers. The accepted workshop contributions, in the form of long abstracts, are in the on-line archive of ACM under
http://www.acm.org/sigkdd/proceedings/webkdd99/.

3   Web Usage Mining in this Volume

The collection of papers in this volume was established as follow-up of WE-BKDD'99. The workshop contributions were revised and expanded to incorporate some of the open issues brought forward during the workshop, especially in the panel session. The following provides a tour of the different contributions organized roughly according to the workshop sessions.

3.1   User Modelling

The assessment of user profiles is an issue of major interest for web applications. User modelling is being investigated for a long time in different contexts and for a variety of domains, ranging from intelligent tutoring systems to recommendation agents in e-commerce. As merchants and service providers shift from mass products/services to customized offerings, the demand for knowledge about the individual interests and needs of each potential customer becomes paramount. The preferences of and further information on web site visitors can be obtained either by requesting input from the users or by drawing conclusions based on the users' observed behaviour.

The second approach fits ideally to the domain of data mining and is the subject of the first three papers in this chapter. Murray and Durrel investigate the issue of inferring demographic attributes, like gender and age, for users anonymously accessing a web site. The data on their activities are preprocessed and summarized using the the Latent Semantic Analysis vector space model and then classified by a neural network. Pre-classified data from demographic surveys are used to train the network, so that the demographics of the anonymous users can be derived with a certain degree of accuracy.

Fu, Sandhu and Shih investigate the discovery of user groups characterized by similar access patterns. They apply attribute-oriented induction to generalize from the concrete page accesses into concepts describing the page contents. Then, user groups are formed by hierarchical clustering on the concepts appearing in the sessions.

While these two studies focus on the acquisition of user profile data by the site provider, Philip Chan considers user profiling in the context of building a personalized browser of web documents. His adaptive personalized web browser forwards the user's queries to multiple search engines. It analyzes the result pages actually read by the user and ranks them according to an "interestingness" measure. From this ranking, themes interesting the user can be assessed; they form her profile. When the user issues a new query, the browser applies this derived profile to rank the results.

The gathering of personalized information and the establishment and exploitation of user profiles by the site providers is raising privacy concerns. The juxtaposition of privacy and data mining in the web is the subject of Alan Broder's invited paper. HTTP services do not preserve identity and can thus blurr the mining results on web usage. Hence, web site providers apply more advanced techniques, such as smart cookies, to acquire reliable data on the site visitors. At the same time, anonymization services emerge to better shield the user against unwelcome knowledge acquisition. So, the user can exploit modern technology to protect her privacy, albeit both engagement and effort are required.

3.2   Extraction of Knowledge in the Form of Rules and Patterns

The papers in this chapter discuss data mining algorithms that can extract rules or more general patterns from web usage data. Researchers in web usage analysis mostly take one of two approaches. In the first approach, data are analyzed using general-purpose algorithms, mainly for discovery of association rules, sequence mining and clustering, whereby the research concentrates on appropriate data modelling and preparation and on measures to evaluate the results for a particular problem setting. The second approach contributes to web usage mining with algorithms dedicated to cope with the particularities of knowledge discovery in the web.

Baumgarten et al adhere to the second approach. They propose M*i*DAS, a sequence miner for the discovery of navigation patterns. Taking web marketing as an example application domain, they investigate how the background knowledge of a company can drive the process of knowledge discovery. This knowledge is reflected in the establishment of the web site topology, in the construction of concept hierarchies over the data being mined and in the formulation of query templates that guide the mining process performed by M*i*DAS.

A mining algorithm for the discovery of navigation patterns is also proposed by Borges and Levene. Their approach is based on probabilistic grammars, whereby highly preferred trails are modelled as strings with high probability values. The theory of probabilistic grammars is combined with a new measure: entropy is used as an aggregate estimator of the statistical properties of each result grammar. Since the set of all grammar strings with probability above a threshold can be quite large, the authors investigate heuristics that compute a selected high-quality subset of the result set.

Lan, Bressan and Ooi adhere to the first approach of web pattern analysis. They use discovery of association rules for effective document pushing in a two tier (web server/browser) and a three tier (web server/proxy/browser) architecture. The conventional miner returns rules describing the support and confidence with which one document will be requested immediately after another one. The challenge lays then in devising measures and heuristics that select which document should be pushed among those suggested by a set of association rules. The authors propose a weighting scheme for the rules taken into account by the prefetching mechanism, derive heuristics based on this scheme and apply them on different two-tier and three-tier settings.

3.3   Determining the Interestingness of Knowledge Findings

The articles in the last chapter propose mechanisms for identifying *interesting* findings from the data. Lee et al investigate the domain of web merchandizing. They first distinguish among different areas of analysis in this domain. They then propose a set of metrics, called *micro-conversion rates*, with which they measure the effectiveness of merchandizing policies in real applications. For the analysis of merchandizing data with the new metrics, they use a grouping & visualization mechanism, with which they model data on promotion, offerings and on-line purchases of products across different dimensions and project them into a two-dimensional trajectory for display.

Spiliopoulou, Pohle and Faulstich address the problem of assessing the effectiveness of a web site in turning its users into customers. They generalize the concept of "customer" from web marketing and study the contribution of each web page into the overall *contact and conversion efficiency* of the site, as reflected in the navigation patterns of its visitors. The navigation patterns of customers and non-customers are discovered by the web utilization miner WUM. Then, selected customer patterns are juxtaposed to comparable non-customer patterns, in order to identify differences and detect pages that are responsible for the different behaviour among customers and non-customers. Such pages should be redesigned, either statically for all users or on-the-fly by dynamic links. A mechanism assessing such links is suggested in the last part of the paper.

Cooley, Tan and Srivastava study the general problem of interestingness in the context of web usage mining. They consider a set of beliefs and propose a quantitative model based on *support logic* to determine the interestingness of a pattern. They assert that important domain information on the web is encapsulated in the content, structure and usage of the web pages, and exploit the last two factors to derive the evidence provided by a discovered pattern for or against a belief. Their quantitative model is embedded in the WebSIFT system, which is comprised of tools for data preprocessing, pattern discovery and pattern analysis. Pattern discovery is undertaken by conventional mining algorithms, while pattern analysis concentrates on identifying interesting patterns among the results of the miners.

4 Open Issues

Knowledge discovery using web data is an emerging research area with still many open issues. E-commerce is a motivating force in this area, since companies place high investments in the electronic market and seek to maximize their revenues and minimize their risks. Further applications, like tele-learning and tele-teaching, service support and information dissemination for the citizen, are also flourishing in the web. In all these application areas, there is a need for understanding and supporting the user, by means of recommender systems, dynamically adjustable information findings and personalized services. Knowledge about the user is indispensable for the design of such services.

In web usage mining, the discovery of patterns is not the sole issue to be addressed. The data acquisition itself is not a universally acceptable activity; it raises privacy concerns and active resistance from users and institutions. The acquired data are often noisy and must be preprocessed in special ways to preserve validity. Access logs can grow by gigabytes daily and become outdated soon, due to factors internal and external to the site. The web usage findings are also large in number, partly due to the large amount of quickly changing data. They require new innovative solutons to detect and summarize important findings. Hence, further new issues emerge, including: the validation of the reliability of the data, the scalability of the mining algorithms, the volatility of data and the short life expectation of patterns derived from them, the interpretation of the discovered patterns. Also, the issue of compatibility between data acquisition and privacy remains, asking for technical and political solutions.

Acknowledgements

We would like to express our gratefulness to the Program Committee members of WEBKDD'99 who invested their time and mental effort to the reviewing process for the preparation of this volume: Peter Brusilovsky (Human-Computer Interaction Institute, Carnegie Mellon Univ., USA), Bamshad Mobasher (DePaul University, USA), Christos Papatheodorou (NCSR Demokritos, Greece), John Roddick (Univ. of South Australia), Ramakrishna Srikant (IBM, Almaden Research Center, CA, USA) and Alex Tuzhilin (Stern School of Business, New York University).

We would like to thank all people that contributed to the WEBKDD'99 workshop, including the original Program Committee that performed the first selection and reviewing of papers and the workshop panelists who brought forward their visions on the future of the WEBKDD community and motivated many thoughts that found expression in this volume. We are grateful to the KDD99 organizing committee, especially Rakesh Agrawal (workshops chair) and Usama Fayyad, for helping us in bringing the WEBKDD community together. We would also like to thank the many participants for their active involvement in the discussions, their comments and their ideas on the evolution of the WEBKDD research area. They motivated us to publish this volume on research in this domain and to engage on the further work and prospering of the new area.

Myra Spiliopoulou   Brij Masand

References

CMS99. Robert Cooley, Bamshad Mobasher, and Jaidep Srivastava. Data preparation for mining world wide web browsing patterns. *Journal of Knowledge and Information Systems*, 1(1), 1999. 1
Etz96.   Oren Etzioni.   The World-Wide Web: Quagmire or gold mine?   *CACM*, 39(11):65–68, Nov. 1996. 1
Hac99.   Richard D. Hackathorn. *Web Farming for the Data Warehouse*. Morgan Kaufmann Publishers, Inc., 1999. 1
MS00.   Brij Masand and Myra Spiliopoulou. Webkdd'99: Workshop on web usage analysis and user profiling. *SIGKDD Explorations*, 2, 2000. to appear. 2

Inferring Demographic Attributes of Anonymous Internet Users

Dan Murray and Kevan Durrell

SourceWorks Consulting
125 Wellington Street, Hull, Quebec, Canada, J8X 2J1
Tel: (819) 770-8800 x265, Fax: (819) 770-8890
{murray,kdurrell}@sourceworks.com

Abstract. Today it is quite common for web page content to include an advertisement. Since advertisers often want to target their message to people with certain demographic attributes, the anonymity of Internet users poses a special problem for them. The purpose of the present research is to find an effective way to infer demographic information (e.g. gender, age or income) about people who use the Internet but for whom demographic information is not otherwise available. Our hope is to build a high quality database of demographic profiles covering a large segment of the Internet population without having to survey each individual Internet user. Though Internet users are largely anonymous, they nonetheless provide a certain amount of *usage information*. Usage information includes, but is not limited to, (a) search terms entered by the Internet user and (b) web pages accessed by the Internet user. In this paper, we describe an application of the *Latent Semantic Analysis* (LSA) [1] information retrieval technique to construct a vector space in which we can represent the usage data associated with each Internet user of interest. Subsequently, we show how the LSA vector space enables us to produce demographic inferences by supplying the input to a three layer neural model trained using the scaled conjugate gradient (SCG) method.

1   Introduction

1.1   The Problem

The Internet attracts a large number of users and thus holds great potential as an advertising medium. Today it is quite common for web page content to include an advertisement. Since advertisers often want to target their message to people with certain demographic attributes, the anonymity of Internet users poses a special problem for them.

One way around this problem is simply to place the advertisement on a web page that is known to be of interest to the advertiser's target audience. For example, a circular-saw manufacturer might advertise on a web site that deals with building codes. Another way around this problem is to select an advertisement based on the Internet user's behavior. For example, if the Internet user enters the search terms

B. Masand and M. Spiliopoulou (Eds.): WEBKDD'99, LNAI 1836, pp. 7-20, 2000.
© Springer-Verlag Berlin Heidelberg 2000

"I want to buy a power tool", this clearly represents another opportunity for the circular-saw manufacturer.

Neither of the above solutions is entirely satisfactory. Consider an advertiser who wishes to target a message to Internet users who fall within a particular demographic group. For example, the message might be an advertisement for a sports car. The advertiser might know from experience that males aged 18-34 are very likely to be interested in this particular vehicle. Search terms and web site visits will not normally reveal the gender or age of the Internet user.

The traditional solution to this problem is simply to conduct a survey and subsequently target the message to those people whose survey responses match the desired demographic profile. Unfortunately, there are several problems with this approach. The most important issue is *non-response*. In general, people are reluctant to give away personal information over the Internet. A subtler issue is the fact that Internet users are typically recognizable only by transient identifiers (e.g. an IP address or a Netscape cookie) which must be linked to the survey data. Since the identifiers are transient, they must be refreshed on a regular basis.

The purpose of the present research is to find an effective way to infer demographic information about people who use the Internet but for whom demographic information is not otherwise available. Our hope is to build a high-quality database of demographic profiles covering a large segment of the Internet population without having to survey each individual Internet user.

The specific scientific and technological objectives of the research described in this paper are as follows:

- To establish the possibility of inferring up to six demographic facts (sex, age, income, marital status, level of education and presence of children in the home) with a minimum 60% confidence for a subset of the Internet population.
- To establish the possibility of making at least one demographic inference about a subset of web users who account for more than 50% of the Internet traffic observed at a popular web site.
- To establish the possibility of making demographic inferences in real-time, rather than building profiles of web users *a priori*. This would allow us to generate inferences as they are needed, using the most recent usage data.

The research effort was successful on the first two points while work on the final objective is ongoing.

1.2   The Solution

In this section, we propose an approach to address the stated scientific and technological objectives.

Before we can hope to produce demographic inferences, we need some input data. Fortunately, though Internet users are largely anonymous, they nonetheless provide a certain amount of *usage information*. Usage information includes, but is not limited to, (a) search terms entered by the Internet user and (b) web pages accessed by the Internet user.

Some advertisers already derive benefits directly from usage information. For example, if an Internet user visits the Excite search engine and enters the string "I want to buy a 1999 Porsche 944", it is fairly clear that a Porsche 944 advertisement would be a good choice for that user. Note that the advertiser in this example has no idea whether the Internet user matches the demographic profile normally associated with the purchase of a Porsche 944. In fact, if the user had entered the search string "I want to buy a car", the advertiser would probably benefit from a demographic profile on that user in order to select the most appropriate advertisement.

Once we have collected some usage information, the next step is to find a way to prepare it for the modeling activity. Our goal is to find a useful representation of the search terms entered and web pages accessed by Internet users. Our situation is very similar to the problem of representing terms and documents for the purpose of information retrieval. For this reason, we consider three different approaches from the field of information retrieval:

1.2.1   The Vector Space Model

In the vector space model [7], documents are represented as real-valued vectors in which each element corresponds to the frequency of occurrence of a particular term in the document. A document vector may thus be viewed as a histogram of its constituent terms. The main drawback of the vector space model is that since there are a large number of unique terms in any realistic document collection, the dimensionality of the resulting vector space is typically high. While this may not be a serious problem for information retrieval applications, it provides more of a challenge for statistical modeling.

1.2.2   Latent Semantic Analysis

Latent Semantic Analysis (LSA) [1] is an attempt to address some of the inherent difficulties with the vector space model, including the high dimensionality of document vectors. First, a matrix is formed in which each column is a document vector. The factors of the space spanned by the columns are then computed using the singular-value decomposition. Discarding all but the top 100-300 factors yields a much more reasonable vector space in which to conduct the modeling activity.

1.2.3   Randomly Projected Histograms

Randomly projected histograms [15] is another technique that may be used to reduce the dimensionality of the document vectors. The n-dimensional document vectors are simply pre-multiplied by a random $m \times n$ matrix, yielding a new set of m-dimensional document vectors. With m on the order of 100 or more, the similarity relations in the new vector space are good approximations to the corresponding relations between documents in the original vector space. This technique is particularly attractive since it does not entail the computational complexity associated with latent semantic analysis. It is thus a good choice in cases where the dimensionality of the original vector space is simply too high for the sensible application of latent semantic analysis.

Since we felt comfortable with our ability (and hardware) to perform the singular-value decomposition on the data sets associated with our experiments, we elected to represent our web usage data using LSA.

1.2.4   Neural Modeling

Once we have found a way to represent the usage data, the next step is to create a model that will enable us to produce demographic inferences. For this purpose we considered (a) linear regression, (b) a neural model trained using the standard backpropagation technique and (c) a neural model trained using the scaled conjugate gradient (SCG) [9] technique. Since we did not wish to ignore the possibility of a nonlinear relationship between the independent and dependent variables under consideration, we opted in favor of a neural model with non-linear elements. We selected the scaled conjugate gradient method after our initial experiments with standard backpropagation failed to converge reliably on a solution.

Note that since the SCG method requires known values of the dependent variables during training, it is important to be able to match survey responses with usage data for a subset of the Internet population. Hence, our approach requires a collection of survey responses keyed on an identifier that is also found in the usage data (in our experiments, we used the Netscape cookie identifier).

2   Latent Semantic Analysis

This section provides some background on LSA and the manner in which we have applied it in the present research.

2.1   Overview

LSA is an information retrieval technique that allows us to create a vector space from a collection of documents. The LSA vector space is of relatively low dimensionality (normally between 100 and 300) and, most importantly, similar documents are assigned similar vectors in the space. LSA has the added benefit of producing vectors for the individual terms found in the document collection as well. Term vectors can be combined to form document vectors using simple algebra [1]. LSA can be used to process a query by constructing a pseudo-document vector from the query terms and comparing it to all the document vectors in the LSA space.

LSA is a good choice for the present research since the usage data can be thought of as a collection of documents (the textual content of web pages accessed by the Internet user) and queries (the search terms entered by the Internet user). Using LSA, it is possible to create a single vector representing an Internet user by combining (a) vectors representing the web pages he or she has accessed with (b) a vector representing the pseudo-document of all the search terms he or she has entered.

The next section provides a brief introduction to vector space information retrieval, setting the stage for LSA.

2.2   Vector-Space Information Retrieval

Vector-space information retrieval techniques rely on the assumption that the meaning of a document can be derived from the document's constituent terms. Documents are represented as vectors of terms $d = (t_1, t_2, \ldots t_N)$ where t_i is a non-negative value denoting the number of occurrences of term i in document d. Hence, each unique term in the document collection corresponds to a dimension in the term-document vector space. Similarly, a query is represented as a vector $q = (t_1, t_2, \ldots t_N)$ where t_i is a non-negative value denoting the number of occurrences of term i in the query [5]. Both the document vectors and the query vector provide the locations of these objects in the term-document vector space. By computing the distance between the query and individual documents in the space, documents with similar semantic content to the query will be retrieved.

Document vectors are normally stored in a *term-by-document matrix* where the rows of the matrix represent individual terms and the columns represent individual documents in our collection.

In the simplest case, entry a_{ij} of the term-by-document matrix represents the number of occurrences of term i in document j. In the more general case, entry a_{ij} is some function of the number of occurrences of term i in document j. The function used to compute the term-by-document matrix entries is generally referred to as the *term-weighting scheme*.

While it is possible to construct a term-document vector space from a document collection by hand, there are tools that can be used to expedite this process. In particular, the authors have had some success with the SMART document retrieval system [7]. SMART is freely distributed and can be used to create a term-by-document matrix from a document collection. SMART has additional features that allow us to a) remove common words from consideration (e.g. "the", "and", etc.) and b) perform word stemming (e.g. "faster" and "fastest" have the common stem "fast").

Once we have created our term-document vector space, we could (in theory) proceed directly to the next step, i.e. create a neural model to make demographic inferences. Unfortunately, any realistic collection of documents will yield a term-document vector space of a dimensionality that renders the modeling task impractical (e.g. 60,000 documents by 100,000 terms is typical).

In the next section, we describe how LSA can help us to reduce the dimensionality of the term-document vector space.

2.3   The Singular Value Decomposition

The LSA paradigm views the terms in a document as somewhat unreliable indicators of the concepts contained therein. It assumes that the variability of word choice partially obscures the semantic structure of the document. By reducing the dimensionality of the term-document vector space, the underlying relationships between documents are revealed, and much of the noise (differences in word usage, terms that do not help distinguish documents, etc.) is eliminated.

In practical applications, the optimal dimensionality of the LSA vector space (i.e. the minimum number of dimensions that are required in order to represent the signal in the data while eliminating the noise) is in the range of 100-300 [1]. As we might expect, the modeling problem is much more tractable in a vector space of 100-300 dimensions than it is in a vector space of (typically) thousands of dimensions. LSA uses the *singular value decomposition* (SVD) [6] in order to reduce the dimensionality of the term-document vector space.

The SVD allows us to decompose the *txd* term-by-document matrix *A* into the product of a) a *txk* matrix *T* of term vectors, b) the transpose of a *dxk* matrix *D* of document vectors and c) a *kxk* diagonal matrix *S* of singular values…

$$A = TSD^t$$

(1)

…where the value of k is normally defined to be in the range 100-300.

While it is (faintly) possible to perform the SVD calculations on a term-by-document matrix by hand [8], there are tools that can be used to expedite this process. In particular, the authors have had some success with SVDPACKC [4]. SVDPACKC is freely distributed and can be used to perform the SVD on large sparse matrices.

3   Approach

In this section we describe each of the steps in our approach:

3.1   Collect Background Information

The first step is to gather a collection of documents consisting of popular web pages accessed by Internet users. Ideally, we would like to be able to construct LSA vectors for *all* the web pages on the Internet. This would ensure that we always have an LSA vector representing a web page accessed by a given Internet user. Since this is impractical, a sensible alternative is to create vectors for as many of the most popular web pages as possible. This will ensure that we have LSA vectors representing at least some of the web pages accessed by most Internet users.

Note that since pseudo-document vectors can be created from a collection of terms, it is possible to create LSA vectors for web pages that were accessed by Internet users but not represented by document vectors in our LSA space (we didn't bother).

For the purpose of the present research, documents were collected using a homegrown web-crawler and limited to roughly 4k bytes in size (larger documents were truncated).

3.2   Create a Term-by-Document Matrix

The next step is to create a term-by-document matrix from the document collection. The term-by-document matrix serves as input to the SVD calculation and can be created using the SMART document retrieval system (available from Cornell University).

For the purpose of the present research, we did not use any of the advanced features of SMART. We set the term-weighting option to "off" and used the default option settings otherwise.

3.3   Perform a Singular-Value Decomposition on the Term-by-Document Matrix

As per the theory of latent semantic analysis, the singular value decomposition not only reduces the dimensionality of the input space, it also yields a collection of term and document vectors that are located in the same low-dimensional output space.

For the purpose of the present research, we chose the *las2* utility of SVDPACKC in order to perform the singular value decomposition (as per the recommendation in [1]). We configured *las2* to produce a maximum of 300 singular values (it found 182) and used the default option settings otherwise.

3.4   Create Vectors for the Internet Users in our Modeling Data Set

In order to create LSA vectors for Internet users, we proceed as follows:

1. *Compute the sum of the vectors in the matrix* T *representing the search terms entered by the Internet user.* Some of the search terms may have vectors in T while others may not. Simply discard the search terms that do not have vectors in T.
2. *Scale the resulting vector by the inverse of the matrix* S. Vectors in the matrix D represent the documents in our collection while vectors in the matrix T represent the terms. Vectors in T must be scaled by the inverse of the matrix S before they can be compared to or combined with vectors in the matrix D [1].
3. *Add the document vectors representing the web pages accessed by the Internet user to the pseudo-document vector created in the previous step.* Some of the web pages may have vectors in D while others may not. Simply discard the web pages that do not have vectors in D.

The result of this process is an LSA vector representing all the usage data associated with each Internet user of interest.

3.5   Create a Neural Model

Once we have successfully created a vector space in which the usage data associated with the Internet users of interest can be represented, the next step is to proceed with the neural modeling activity.

For the present research, we used the freely distributed Stuttgart Neural Network Simulator (SNNS). We configured SNNS to train a 3-layer feed-forward neural model using the SCG method.

Like standard backpropagation, SCG is an iterative technique. While standard backpropagation proceeds down the gradient of the error function, SCG chooses the search direction by using information from a second order Taylor expansion of the error function. A nice feature of SCG is that the minimization performed in one step is not partially undone by the next, as is the case with standard backpropagation and other gradient descent methods.

The input layer consisted of 182 neurons representing each of the values in our LSA vectors. For the purpose of our experiments, the hidden layer was fixed at three neurons. The output layer consisted of a single neuron representing the (binary-valued) demographic variable of interest. We used the SNNS default settings otherwise.

3.6   The Modeling Data Set

The modeling data set was constructed by matching our usage data to a collection of Internet survey responses supplied by a participating web site. This process yielded a set of observations containing known values of the independent (search terms entered and web pages accessed) and dependent (demographic fields from survey responses) variables.

Initial experiments were conducted using the binary-valued demographic variable "gender" (male = 0, female = 1), then repeated with the remaining demographic variables. In each experiment, 40000 observations were used for training the SCG neural model and 20000 (different) observations were reserved for validation. The following table contains all the demographic variables under consideration and their possible values (note that they are all binary-valued):

Variable	Possible Values
Gender	male, female
Age Under 18	true, false
Age 18-34	true, false
Age 35-54	true, false
Age 55+	true, false
Income Under $50000	true, false
Marital Status	single, married
Some College Education	true, false
Children in the Home	true, false

Training data was balanced to contain equal proportions of the values of the dependent variable under consideration. For example, the 40000 training observations used to model the demographic variable "gender" contained 20000 female observations and 20000 male observations.

Validation data was balanced to contain true proportions of the values of the dependent variable under consideration (true proportions were supplied by Harris-Black Inc.).   For example, the 20000 validation observations used to model the demographic variable "gender" contained 9200 female observations and 10800 male observations (Harris-Black informed us that the true male/female breakdown of Internet users in July, 1998 was 54/46).

3.7   Assessing Model Performance

Once the trained model was applied to the validation data set, the resulting output values were sorted in descending order and divided into ten groups of equal size (this is the usual 10% *gains* distribution). The lift we observed in the top gains bucket was used as our measure of model performance. For example, if we found that 59% of the observations in the top gains bucket belonged to female Internet users, while random chance should only yield 46%, then the lift due to the model was reported to be the difference between the two values (i.e. 13%).

The neural scores corresponding to the boundaries of the gains buckets were used to assign inferences and associated confidence values to anonymous Internet users. For example, if we observed that 750 out of 1000 observations in the top gains bucket belonged to female Internet users, we assigned an inference of *female* with an associated confidence value of 75% to anonymous Internet users whose neural score placed them in the top gains bucket.   For reporting purposes, we allowed the boundaries of the gains distribution to float in order to produce confidence values in integer multiples of ten.

4   Experiments

In this section, we describe the experiments conducted in support of the stated scientific and technological objectives.

- *Experiment #1: Create a baseline model.* We gathered an initial collection of 38833 popular web pages and processed them using SMART. The singular-value decomposition was performed using the *las2* utility of SVDPACKC. The 182-valued term and document vectors produced by SVDPACKC were then used to create LSA vectors for a modeling data set based on 20 days of Internet usage data. The resulting neural model showed an 8% lift over random chance in the top 10% gains bucket when modeling with the demographic variable *gender*.
- *Experiment #2: Assess effect of using different document collections.* The size of the document collection was increased to 83196 documents. The resulting model showed a 12% lift over random chance in the top 10% gains bucket when modeling with the demographic variable *gender*.   We switched to the larger document collection for the remaining experiments.
- *Experiment #3: Assess effect of varying the data collection period.* The modeling period was decreased from 20 days to 10 days. No appreciable difference in model performance was detected.

- *Experiment #4: Assess the effect of various term-weighting schemes.* The SMART output was post-processed in order to implement the log term-weighting scheme. This experiment did not produce conclusive results. We conducted the experiment a second time using the log-entropy term-weighting scheme. A small decrease in model performance was observed.
- *Experiment #5: Assess the effect of varying the number of derived singular values.* We decreased the number of singular values from 182 to 100. A small decrease in model performance was observed.
- *Experiment #6: Assess the effect of normalizing term and document vectors to unit length.* The resulting model showed an 18% lift over random chance in the top 10% gains bucket when modeling with the demographic variable gender. This model allowed us to make gender inferences for 20% of the Internet users represented in our validation data set with an associated confidence level of 64% for the "female" inferences and 72% for the "male" inferences, meeting the first objective of the present research.
- *Experiment #7: Assess the effect of combining web page vectors into web site vectors.* In previous experiments, each document vector represented an individual web page. In this experiment, we combined all the document vectors associated with the same web site into a single *site vector.* Using document vectors representing web sites rather than individual web pages yielded a 26% lift over random chance in the top 10% gains bucket when modeling with the demographic variable gender. This model allowed us to make gender inferences for 20% of the Internet users represented in our validation data set with an associated confidence level of 72% for the "female" inferences and 80% for the "male" inferences.

- **Table 1.** Inferences derived from the best demographic models were merged (by Netscape cookie identifier) in order to create complete profiles. A sample Internet user profile follows:

Profile ID	Model	Confidence	Neural Score	Inference
61638	Age 18-34	60	0.714091	True
61638	Income Over $50k	60	0.344723	False
61638	Children at Home	60	0.435043	True
61638	Gender	80	0.870309	Female
61638	College Education	60	0.406918	True

The following diagram summarizes the results of our most promising experiments:

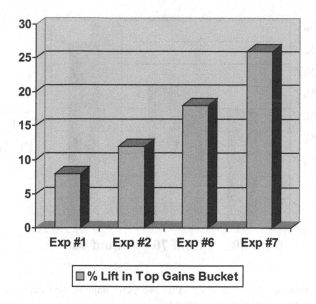

Fig. 1. Percent lift over random chance in the top 10% gains bucket for Experiments #1, 2, 6 and 7

5   Conclusions

The most important conclusion that we were able to draw from the present research is that it is in fact possible to make demographic inferences about Internet users for whom demographic information is not otherwise available.

Although we experienced poor results with some demographic categories (e.g. Age 55+), we have nonetheless established the possibility of inferring demographic facts with a minimum 60% confidence for a subset of the Internet population. Inferences are based on usage data (e.g. search terms entered, web pages accessed, etc.) collected over a period of (up to) ninety days at participating web sites.

We discovered that if the true proportion of a particular value of a demographic variable is low (e.g. less than 30%), the resulting models are unable to make inferences for that value with greater than 60% confidence. This is due to the fact that the calibration step is performed using a sample that is balanced to reflect the true proportion of the values of the dependent variable under consideration (our models rarely yield a 30% lift).

The following diagram shows the breakdown of gender inferences by confidence value as a percentage of the total number of records in the validation set associated with Experiment #7. For example, we were able to assign a male inference with 80% confidence to 10% of the records in the validation set. Note that the boundaries of the gains distribution were allowed to vary so that confidence values could be reported in integer multiples of ten.

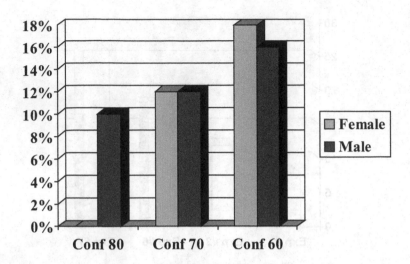

Fig. 2. Gender inferences by confidence value as a percentage of the total number of records in the validation set associated with Experiment #7

After applying our best models to the remaining usage data, we discovered that we could produce calibrated demographic inferences for a subset of web users who account for more than 68% of the Internet traffic observed at a popular web site (on a transaction-weighted basis, representing over 42 million Internet users). This meets our second stated objective.

Table 2. Some of our Internet user profiles turned out to be much richer than others. While we were able to make at least one demographic inference for each of roughly 42 million Internet users, we were able to make a full set of six demographic inferences for only 6,894,786 Internet users. The complete breakdown of inferences by Internet user is as follows:

Number of profiles with at least one inference:	42,639,375
Number of profiles with at least two inferences:	39,987,205
Number of profiles with at least three inferences:	35,808,547
Number of profiles with at least four inferences:	28,099,348
Number of profiles with at least five inferences:	17,337,169
Number of profiles with all six demographic inferences:	6,894,786

6   Future Work

With respect to the possibility of making demographic inferences in real-time, the key is to ensure that an Internet user's most recent activity is available to the scoring process. Further work is required in this area.

While our experiments were limited to search terms entered and web pages accessed by Internet users, it is important to note that there are other types of Internet usage data. Hence, our goal is to define ways in which other forms of Internet usage data might be used in future experiments.

According to Dumais [11], it is possible to improve the performance of LSA-based information retrieval by selecting an appropriate term-weighting scheme. In particular, log-entropy term weighting appears to be a good choice. Much to our surprise, we discovered that log-entropy term weighting did not improve our models. One explanation might be that term-weighting schemes are typically designed to increase the relative importance of terms that occur infrequently in the corpus, while we probably want to increase the relative importance of terms that are widely used. In any event, we plan to experiment with additional term-weighting schemes.

We made no attempt to vary the architecture of the SCG neural network during the course of our experiments. For example, it may be that a different number of hidden neurons might produce better models.

In our experiments, we simply ignored web pages that were accessed by Internet users but not represented by document vectors in our LSA space. Since it is possible to construct a pseudo-document vector for virtually any web page by combining the LSA vectors of its constituent terms [1], our hope is to incorporate this feature in future experiments.

Acknowledgements

The authors would like to thank Kathryn MacGeraghty for her assistance with the modeling and scoring activities. The authors would also like to thank Michael W. Berry for his assistance with SVDPACKC [4].

References

1. Deerwester, S., Dumais, S. T., Furnas, G. W., Landauer, T. K., & Harshman, R. Indexing by latent semantic analysis. Journal of the American Society For Information Science, 41(6), 1990.
2. Landauer, T. K., & Dumais, S. T., How come you know so much? From practical problem to theory. In D. Hermann, C. McEvoy, M. Johnson, & P. Hertel (Eds.), Basic and applied memory: Memory in context. Mahwah, NJ: Erlbaum, 105-126, 1996.
3. Landauer, T. K., & Dumais, S. T., A solution to Plato's problem: The Latent Semantic Analysis theory of the acquisition, induction, and representation of knowledge. Psychological Review, 104, 211-240, 1997.

4. M. W. Berry et al., SVDPACKC: Version 1.0 User's Guide, Tech. Rep. CS-93-194, University of Tennessee, Knoxville, TN, October 1993.
5. N. Belkin and W. Croft. Retrieval techniques. In M. Williams, editor, Annual Review of Information Science and Technology (ARIST), volume 22, chapter 4, pages 109--145. Elsevier Science Publishers B.V., 1987.
6. G. Golub and C. Van Loan. Matrix Computations. Johns-Hopkins, Baltimore, Maryland, second edition, 1989.
7. Salton, G. (ed), The SMART Retrieval System - Experiments in Automatic Document Processing, Englewood Cliffs, New Jersey: Prentice-Hall, 1971.
8. William H. Press, Saul A. Teukolsky, William T. Vetterling, and Brian P. Flannery. Numerical Recipes in C: The Art of Scientific Computing. Cambridge University Press, Cambridge, 2nd edition, 1992.
9. A. Zell et al., Stuttgart Neural Network Simulator: User Manual Version 4.1, University of Stuttgart, 1995.
10. Dumais, S. T. (1995), Using LSI for information filtering: TREC-3 experiments. In: D. Harman (Ed.), The Third Text REtrieval Conference (TREC3) National Institute of Standards and Technology Special Publication , in press 1995.
11. Dumais, S. T., Improving the retrieval of information from external sources. Behavior Research Methods, Instruments and Computers, 23(2), 229-236, 1991.
12. Dumais, S. T., Furnas, G. W., Landauer, T. K. and Deerwester, S., Using latent semantic analysis to improve information retrieval. In Proceedings of CHI'88: Conference on Human Factors in Computing, New York: ACM, 281-285, 1988.
13. Dumais, S. T., "Latent Semantic Indexing (LSI) and TREC-2." In: D. Harman (Ed.), The Second Text REtrieval Conference (TREC2), National Institute of Standards and Technology Special Publication 500-215 , pp. 105-116, 1994.
14. Dumais, S. T., "LSI meets TREC: A status report." In: D. Harman (Ed.), The First Text REtrieval Conference (TREC1), National Institute of Standards and Technology Special Publication 500-207, pp. 137-152, 1993.
15. Kaski, S., "Dimensionality reduction by random mapping: Fast similarity computation for clustering." In Proceedings of IJCNN'98, International Joint Conference on Neural Networks, volume 1, pages 413-418. IEEE Service Center, Piscataway, NJ. , 1998.

A Generalization-Based Approach to Clustering of Web Usage Sessions

Yongjian Fu, Kanwalpreet Sandhu, and Ming-Yi Shih

Computer Science Department
University of Missouri-Rolla
{yongjian,ksandhu,mingyi}@umr.edu

Abstract. The clustering of Web usage sessions based on the access patterns is studied. Access patterns of Web users are extracted from Web server log files, and then organized into sessions which represent episodes of interaction between the Web users and the Web server. Using attribute-oriented induction, the sessions are then generalized according to a page hierarchy which organizes pages based on their contents. These generalized sessions are finally clustered using a hierarchical clustering method. Our experiments on a large real data set show that the approach is efficient and practical for Web mining applications.

1 Introduction

With the rapid development of the World Wide Web, or the Web, many organizations now put their information on the Web and provide Web-based services such as on-line shopping, user feedback, technical support, etc. Web mining, the discovery of knowledge on the Web, has become an interesting research area [8]. Research in Web mining has been broadly classified into Web content mining and Web usage mining [7], where the former finds patterns in Web pages and links, and the later finds patterns in the usage of the Web.

An important topic in Web usage mining is the clustering of Web usage sessions. A *Web usage session*, or simply a *session*, is an episode of interaction between a Web user and the Web server. A session consists of the pages the user visited in the episode and the time spent on each page. Because of the number and diversity of Web users, it is obviously unrealistic to study individual sessions. Therefore, an important step in Web usage mining is to cluster the sessions based on their common properties. By analyzing the characteristics of these clusters, webmasters may understand Web usage better and may provide more suitable, customized services to users. The clustering of sessions can provide a very useful tool for many applications in education and e-commerce.

In this paper, the clustering of sessions based on browsing activities or access patterns on the Web is studied. Sessions that exhibit similar browsing activities are grouped together. For example, if a number of customers spend quite a lot time on browsing pages about "baby furniture", "baby toys", and "maternity wear", their sessions may be clustered into a group which could later be analyzed

B. Masand and M. Spiliopoulou (Eds.): WEBKDD'99, LNAI 1836, pp. 21–38, 2000.

by webmasters or domain experts as "expecting parents". The webmaster then may arrange the Web pages so that the above pages are linked together and proper advertizements may be inserted. Additionally, when a user has browsed the "baby furniture" and the "baby toys" pages, a link to "maternity wear" pages can be dynamically created and inserted in the current page.

In our approach, the server log data is first processed to identify the sessions. Sessions are then generalized using attribute-oriented induction [9] which will greatly reduce the dimensionality of data. The generalized data is finally clustered using an efficient hierarchical clustering algorithm, BIRCH [24]. The approach is tested on a large, real world data set. Our experiments show that the approach is efficient and we have found several interesting clusters within the data set.

The paper is organized as follows. In Section 2, the background and related work in Web usage clustering are introduced. In Section 3, the process to identify sessions from a Web server log is discussed. We propose a generalization-based clustering method in Section 4, along with its application in the clustering of sessions. In Section 5, results from the experiments of the proposed approach on a large data set are presented. Issues related to session identification and generalization are discussed in Section 6. The study is concluded in Section 7.

2   Background

Earlier studies on Web usage, such as access statistics, lack the in-depth understanding of user browsing patterns, such as pages traversed and times spent on those pages. These user browsing patterns provide accurate, active, and objective information about Web usage. Moreover, most Web servers, e.g., NCSA's HTTPD and Microsoft's IIS, contain such information in their logs of page requests.

A lot of studies have been conducted in Web usage mining. Some focus on the mining of association rules and navigation patterns in the user access paths [3,7,5]. Others build data cubes from Web server logs for OLAP and data mining [22,4]. There is also research on data preparation [6] and query language [19] for Web usage mining.

Let us first explain the Web server log since it is the source for almost all Web usage mining. A Web server log contains records of user accesses. Each record represents a page request from a Web user (called client). A typical record contains the client's IP address, the date and time the request is received, the URL of the page requested, the protocol of the request, the return code of the server indicating the status of the request handling, and the size of the page if the request is successful. Several examples are given below which are excerpted from the log of the University of Missouri-Rolla's (UMR) Web server, which runs HTTPD 1.0. The IP addresses are modified for privacy reasons. The URLs of the pages are relative to the UMR's home page address, http://www.umr.edu.

```
john.cs.umr.edu - - [01/Apr/1997:01:20:01 -0600]
  "GET /~regwww/ssfs97/fs97.html HTTP/1.0" 200 1094
john.cs.umr.edu - - [01/Apr/1997:01:20:01 -0600]
  "GET /~regwww/ssfs97/rdball.gif HTTP/1.0" 200 967
john.cs.umr.edu - - [01/Apr/1997:01:20:17 -0600]
  "GET /~regwww/ssfs97/depf97.html HTTP/1.0" 200 5072
john.cs.umr.edu - - [01/Apr/1997:01:21:08 -0600]
  "GET /~regwww/ssfs97/ecf97.html HTTP/1.0" 200 12146
```

In Web usage clustering, sessions are extracted from the Web server log and clustered by a clustering algorithm.

The data preparation process to identify the sessions in our approach is similar to that in many other studies, such as [15,21,18,19]. It produces reasonable results with a simple and fast algorithm. More sophisticated approaches are possible, such as those discussed in [6].

Clustering has been studied extensively in statistics, machine learning, pattern recognition, and database systems, with a large number of algorithms developed [12,13,14,2,24]. Recently, an algorithm, Balanced Iterative Reducing and Clustering using Hierarchies (BIRCH) [24], was proposed in the database area. It represents clusters in a Clustering Feature (CF) tree and uses a similar insertion algorithm to the B+ tree insertion algorithm. BIRCH has several features which are desirable for our purpose.

- It usually creates a good clustering in just one scan of the data set. The complexity of the algorithm is $O(n \log(n))$, so it scales up well for very large data sets.
- It builds clusters hierarchically such that a high-level cluster is further divided into subclusters and so on. A high-level cluster may represent the sessions which reflect general common interests and their subgroups represent more specific common interests.
- It is an incremental algorithm such that when new data arrives the clustering can be updated incrementally, not starting from scratch. This is important because new data continues to be added as long as users continue browsing the Web pages.

However, the direct application of BIRCH on the primitive user access data as described above is very inefficient and may not find many interesting clusters as explained below.

- A Web server usually contains thousands, even millions of pages. It is obviously impractical to represent each session as a high dimensional vector in which each dimension represents a page. A sparse representation will cause the dimensionality of the clusters to change dynamically, i.e, the non-sparse items in the centroid of a cluster may grow when new vectors are added. This imposes a lot of overhead on memory and storage management as well as on data structure handling.

– Our goal is to cluster the sessions with similar access patterns. However, it is not easy to find many sessions with common pages because of the diversity of the Web users. This will lead to either small clusters or clusters with little similarity. It is more likely to find groups who share the common interests in the themes of pages. For example, we may not find a large number of users who visit pages on "Okla Homer Smith Mavado crib - white finish", "Kids II Bright Starts musical mobile", and "Dividends Maternity Pullover Tunic", but we can probably find lots of users who browse pages on "baby furniture", "baby toys", and "maternity wear".

Based on the above observations, we propose a *generalization-based clustering method* which combines attribute-oriented induction [9] and BIRCH to generate a hierarchical clustering of the sessions. In this method, the sessions are first generalized in attribute-oriented induction according to a data structure, called page hierarchy, which organizes the Web pages into a hierarchical structure based on their topics. The generalized sessions are then clustered by BIRCH.

The clustering of sessions based on access patterns has been studied in [21] and [18]. In [21], a page space is constructed by treating each page as a dimension and a browsing session of a user is mapped into a point (vector) in the space, represented by the time the user spent on each page. However, the clustering algorithm used, the *leader algorithm*, is simple and the quality of the final clusters is unpredictable.

An applet-based user profiler is proposed in [18] which can more accurately record the times users spend on pages. Using the k-means method, sessions are clustered based on their navigation paths, i.e., the pages as well as the order they are requested and the links the users follow. However, the advantages of using paths are not convincing and the computation is much more complex. Besides, the k-means method works in a batch mode whereas the data are generated intermittently.

Unlike previous approaches to Web usage clustering in [21] and [18], our approach employs an efficient, incremental, and hierarchical clustering algorithm, BIRCH. More significantly, we introduce attribute-oriented induction to generalize sessions before they are clustered. Our approach has the following advantages over the previous approaches.

– The generalization of sessions allows us to find clusters which cannot be found in the original sessions. These additional clusters represent similarities at higher levels of abstraction. It should be pointed out that the clustering of generalized sessions will still find clusters in the original sessions, since the generalization is performed according to the page hierarchy which tries to preserve the original structure of the pages.
– The dimensionality of sessions is greatly reduced because of the generalization. This not only reduces the computational complexity, but also relaxes the memory requirement. In fact, the dimensionality of our data set is so large that BIRCH cannot run or does not give a meaningful clustering (it generates a single cluster) in many cases without generalization.

- As we mentioned earlier, BIRCH is more appropriate for the clustering of sessions than the leader algorithm in [21] and the k-means algorithm in [18]. It should be noted, though, that the generalization is independent of the clustering algorithm. Our approach can be easily adapted to use other clustering algorithms.

Our contributions can be summarized as follows.

- A generalization-based clustering method for clustering sessions is introduced.
- A simple and intuitive method to construct the page hierarchy is developed.
- Experiments have been conducted to understand the effectiveness of the generalization-based clustering method.

The use of attribute-oriented induction for conceptual clustering which has been mentioned in [11], deals with nominal data. To the best of our knowledge, attribute-oriented induction has not been used for clustering numerical data or sessions. In our approach, it is employed to deal with sessions which contain numerical data, the elapsed times on the pages.

3   Session Identification

A Web user may visit a Web site from time to time and spend an arbitrary amount of time between consecutive visits. To deal with the unpredictable nature of Web browsing and make the problem tractable, a concept, *session*, is introduced to represent an episode of interaction between a user and a Web server. We cluster the sessions instead of the users' entire history. This can be justified because our goal is to understand the usage of the Web and different sessions of a user may correspond to the visits of the user with different purposes on mind. Concepts similar to session have been proposed in other studies [6,19,16,15,18].

A session consists of the pages accessed and the times spent on these pages by a user in the episode. The boundary of a session is determined by a threshold, *max_idle_time*. If a user stays inactive (not requesting any page) for a period longer than *max_idle_time*, subsequent page requests are considered to be in another episode, thus another session. The threshold *max_idle_time* may be updated according to some statistics, such as the ratio of time over page size, to reflect individual's differences in browsing habits. The use of *max_idle_time* could avoid extremely long sessions and non-stop sessions. For example, a user may leave for lunch in the middle of browsing and totally forget about it. When the person comes back hours or days later, a new session will be generated.

Sessions are identified by grouping consecutive pages requested by the same user together. The data in a Web server log is transformed into a set of sessions in the form of $(session\text{-}id, \{\langle page\text{-}id, time \rangle\})$, where *session-id* and *page-id* are unique IDs assigned to sessions and pages. For example, a session $(sid_0, p_0, 10, p_1, 30, p_2, 20)$ indicates a user spent 10 seconds on page p_0, 30 seconds on page p_1, and 20 seconds on page p_2.

The Web server log is scanned to identify sessions. A session is created when a new IP address is met in the log. Subsequent requests from the same IP address are added to the same session as long as the elapse of time between two consecutive requests does not exceed *max_idle_time*. Otherwise, the current session is closed and a new session is created.

Two other thresholds, *min_time* and *min_page*, are used to exclude noises in the data. If the time spent on a page is less than *min_time*, the page is assumed to be uninteresting to the user or an index page [6] and is discarded. If a particular session contains less than *min_page* pages, the session is assumed to be noise and is removed.

The time spent on a page is estimated to be the difference between the page's request date/time and the date/time of the next request from the same client. The time spent on the last page of each session is approximated by the average time of all other pages in the session.

The algorithm for identifying sessions is outlined as follows.

1. While there are more records in the Web server log file, do the following steps.
2. Read the next record in the Web server log file.
3. Parse the record to get IP address, URL of the page, and time and date of the request.
4. If the page is a background image file, it is discarded. The image files can be detected by looking at their file name extensions, e.g, .gif, .jpeg, etc. [20]
5. Decide the session according to the IP address.
6. If the elapsed time from last request is within *max_idle_time*, the page is appended into the session.
7. Otherwise, the session is closed and a new session is created for the IP address. The closed session is filtered using *min_time* and *min_page*, and output.

In addition, two tables, an IP table which maps session-ids to IP addresses and a URL table which maps page-ids to URLs, are generated. Moreover, statistics, such as the mean and variance of the time over page size ratio, can be collected as basis for tuning *max_idle_time*.

4 Generalization-Based Clustering of Sessions

The sessions obtained as described in Section 3 will be generalized, which is explained in Section 4.1, and then clustered, which is discussed in Section 4.2.

4.1 Generalization of Sessions

As described in Section 3, a session consists of a set of (page-id, time) pairs. Such a sparse representation would give a lot of problems for clustering algorithms, especially for BIRCH whose core data structures are of a fixed size. A straightforward solution is to represent the sessions on all pages, padding zeros for pages not in a session. However, this works poorly when the total number of pages is large.

Moreover, the objective of clustering is to finds groups with similar access patterns, which do not necessary correspond to page level. Groups that are not obvious at page-level may emerge when considered at a higher level, as explained in Section 2.

By analyzing the pages, we realize that they are not randomly scattered, but are organized into a hierarchical structure, called a page hierarchy. A *page hierarchy* is a partial ordering of the Web pages, in which a leaf node represents a Web page corresponding to a file in the server. A non-leaf node in a page hierarchy represents a Web page corresponding to a directory in the server. A link from a parent node to a child node represents the consisting-of relationship between the corresponding pages. A page hierarchy for some pages in the UMR Web server is shown in Fig. 1. For example, a graduate electrical engineering course page is in the graduate course page which in turn is in the registrar office's page.

To distinguish the two kinds of pages, a page represented by a leaf node is called a *simple page*; and a page represented by a non-leaf node is called a *general page*. For example, the page hierarchy in Fig. 1 has four simple pages and three general pages.

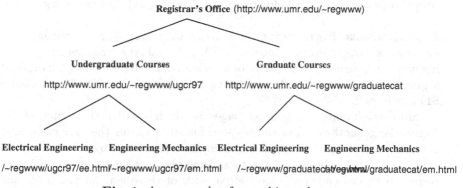

Fig. 1. An example of page hierarchy

The page hierarchy can be created automatically based on the URLs of the pages. For example, the page hierarchy in Fig. 1 can be constructed from the four simple pages below (the mnemonic names of the general pages are optional). The root of the hierarchy which is the home page of UMR is not shown in Fig. 1 for simplicity.

```
http://www.umr.edu/~regwww/ugcr97/ee.html
http://www.umr.edu/~regwww/ugcr97/em.html
http://www.umr.edu/~regwww/graduatecat/ee.html
http://www.umr.edu/~regwww/graduatecat/em.html
```

The steps to construct the page hierarchy are outlined as follows.

1. The page hierarchy is initialized with only the root which represents the home page of the Web server.
2. For each URL in the URL table generated as described in Section 3, if it does not already exist in the page hierarchy:
   (a) A node for the page is created. Next, the URL is parsed and for each prefix which is a legal URL, a node for the general page is created if it does not exist in the page hierarchy.
   (b) For every pair of nodes in which one's URL is the longest prefix of the other's, a link is added if it is not already in the page hierarchy.

For example, for a URL `http://www.umr.edu/~regwww/ugcr97/ee.html`, nodes for itself, its first prefix `http://www.umr.edu/~regwww/ugcr97/`, and its second prefix `http://www.umr.edu/~regwww/` will be created, if they are not already in the page hierarchy. A link is added between itself and its first prefix, between its first prefix and its second prefix, and between its second prefix and the root.

The sessions are generalized using attribute-oriented induction [9]. In attribute-oriented induction, the simple page in each session is replaced by its corresponding general page in the page hierarchy. Duplicate pages are then removed with their times added together. The session is said to be generalized and a session so obtained is called a generalized session. For example, for a session of simple pages in Fig. 1, ((Undergraduate Electrical Engineering Courses, 25),
(Undergraduate Engineering Mechanics Courses, 48), (Graduate Electrical Engineering Courses, 32), (Graduate Engineering Mechanics Courses, 19)), attribute-oriented induction will generalize it to a generalized session ((Undergraduate Courses, 73), (Graduate Courses, 51)) at level 2.

Since the number of general pages is much smaller than that of simple pages, the generalization of the sessions greatly reduces the dimensionality. As a result, a generalized session can then be represented by a vector, ($session$-$id, t_1, t_2, \cdots, t_n$), where t_i is the total time the user spent on the i-th general page and its descendents. Note the page-ids of these general pages are not included in the vector because all sessions are based on the same set of general pages.

Another advantage of the generalization of sessions using the page hierarchy is that the resulting data representation can accommodate updates on the Web site, such as addition and deletion of pages, as long as the higher level structure is stable.

4.2 Clustering of Generalized Sessions

The generalized sessions are clustered using BIRCH [24] which can be summarized as follows.

BIRCH builds a Clustering Feature (CF) tree as the result of clustering by incrementally inserting objects (represented by vectors) into the CF tree. A CF tree is a multidimensional structure, like a B+ tree, in which a nonleaf node stores B (called branching factor) entries of $(CF_i, pointer\_to\_child\_i)$, and a leaf node stores B entries of (CF_i), where CF_i is a CF vector. A CF vector is a triple containing the number, the linear sum, and the square sum, of the vectors in the subtree rooted at a child.

When a new vector is inserted into the CF tree, it goes down from the root to a leaf node by choosing the closest child according to a distance measure, such as Euclidean distance. If any entry of the leaf node can incorporate the new object within a diameter threshold T, that entry's CF vector is updated. Otherwise, the object is put into an empty entry in the leaf node. In the later case, if there is no empty entry left in the leaf node, it is split into two. In case there is a split, an empty entry in the parent node is used to record the new leaf node. The parent node is split in a similar way if there is no empty entry and if this goes up to the root, the tree is one level deeper. When the tree grows too large to be held in memory, the threshold T is enlarged and the current tree is converted into a new tree by inserting all leaf node entries of the current tree into the new tree, which is guaranteed to be smaller.

The generalized sessions are read by BIRCH and inserted into an initially empty CF tree one by one. The resulting tree is a hierarchical clustering of the generalized sessions. The general pages in the clusters can be interpreted by referring to the page hierarchy. A minor change is made in BIRCH to increase its node size so that it can accommodate high dimensional data.

5   Experiments

The algorithms have been implemented and tested on a data set collected from UMR's Web server log (http://www.umr.edu). It contains more than 2.5 million records with a total size of 270MB. The experiments are carried out on a Sun SparcStation Ultra 1 with 64MB of memory running Solaris 2.5.

Several test sets are used in our experiments, which are subsets of the data set, as summarized in Table 1. The thresholds max_idle_time, min_time, and min_page are set to 30 minutes, 1 second, and 2 pages, respectively. The max_idle_time is set according to common practices[6]. The min_time and min_page are set to include as many pages and sessions as possible. Our experiments show similar results for other settings. The branching factor B in BIRCH is set to 3. The threshold T in BIRCH is initialized to 0 such that each entry holds one vector (generalized session).

5.1   Effectiveness of Generalization

The effects of generalization on dimensionality and cluster quality are examined. We have tested our approach on subsets of the Web site. A subset of the Web site is specified by restricting pages in a session to be in a sub-hierarchy of the

Table 1. Test sets

test set	no_of_records	no_of_distinct_pages	no_of_distinct_hosts
50k	50,000	5,731	3,694
100k	100,000	8,168	6,304
200k	200,000	12,191	11,473
300k	300,000	15,201	16,498
400k	400,000	17,574	21,153
500k	500,000	21,308	26,107

page hierarchy. Pages that are not in the sub-hierarchy are ignored. This reduces the dimensionality and cardinality of the generalized sessions, thus enabling us to examine the clusters in detail and to cluster sessions without generalization.

Three sub-hierarchies are selected in various domains. The root of the RO sub-hierarchy is the home page of the Registrar's Office (˜regwww). The root of the MAEM sub-hierarchy is the home page of the Department of Mechanical Engineering, Aerospace Engineering, and Engineering Mechanics (˜maem). The root of the HELP sub-hierarchy is the home page of the Help Desk of Computing Services (helpdesk). The sub-hierarchies are summarized in Table 2. The 500k test set is used and the number of sessions for each sub-hierarchy is reported in Table 2. The sessions are generalized to level 2 which is the level just below the root.

Table 2. Sub-hierarchies of the page hierarchy

sub-hierarchy	total_nodes	leaf nodes	no_levels	no_sessions
RO	137	134	3	663
MAEM	102	92	4	132
HELP	101	43	5	243

The dimensionality of the sessions before and after the generalization is shown in Fig. 2. It is obvious from the figure that the generalization significantly reduces the dimensionality. In the MAEM case, it is reduced by an order of magnitude.

To examine the effects of generalization on clustering quality, the leaf clusters (leaf nodes in the resulting CF tree) are examined, as they are good representatives of the final clustering.

The number of leaf clusters with generalization are compared with that without generalization in Fig. 3. In the HELP and the RO cases, we get fewer leaf clusters as expected, since clusters are merged after generalization. In the MAEM case, we get more leaf clusters, probably because the data is more diverse and BIRCH mislabels some clusters. In all three cases, the differences are within 10%. This is because the number of leaf clusters is dominated by the number of sessions, which is the same with or without generalization.

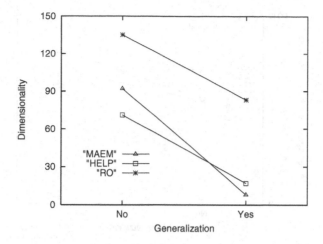

Fig. 2. Dimensionality of the sessions

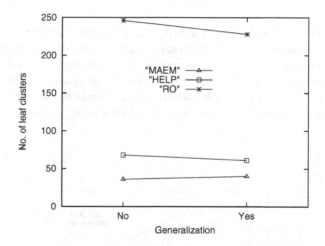

Fig. 3. Number of leaf clusters

It is more interesting to look at the number of nontrivial leaf clusters. A nontrivial leaf cluster is a leaf cluster that contains more than one session and has at least one common page among the sessions in the cluster. Fig. 4 shows the percentage of total leaf clusters that are nontrivial. In all three cases, the generalization increases the percentages by more than 10. In the HELP case, the generalization increases the percentage of nontrivial leaf clusters by almost 20. This clearly demonstrates that generalization improves the quality of clustering.

To study the effects of different generalization levels, the HELP sub-hierarchy is used because it has the largest number of levels. Experiments are performed at

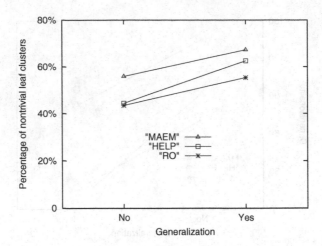

Fig. 4. Number of nontrivial leaf clusters

all levels except the level 1 (root) which is meaningless. The number of leaf clusters, number of nontrivial leaf clusters, and dimensionality, are shown in Fig. 5. The higher we generalize, the more nontrivial leaf clusters we find. However, it is possible some of them are false clusters created by generalization. In general, the generalization level should be selected to the highest level which still keeps the logic of page hierarchy. It is also a good idea to try several generalization levels.

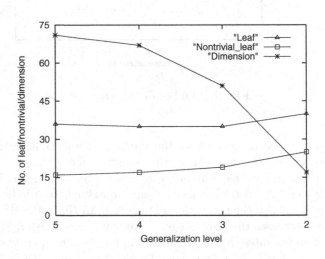

Fig. 5. Effects of generalization levels

5.2 Scale Up of the Method

The execution times in session identification/generalization and clustering for the test sets are shown in Fig. 6. All the sessions are generalized to level 2. The page hierarchy is the same for all the test sets. The generalized sessions have a dimensionality of 1,628 except for the 50k test set which is 1,194. Basically, all general pages at level 2, or their descendents, are accessed except in the case of 50k. The time in session identification/generalization is linear to the number of records in the test sets. This is not surprising as the session generalization is linear to the number of sessions which is found to be linear to the number of records in the test sets. The time in clustering is almost linear to the number of records in the test sets except for the 50k test set which is much less when compared with the others. This is because the 50k test set has a smaller dimensionality which makes the distance computation in BIRCH less expensive.

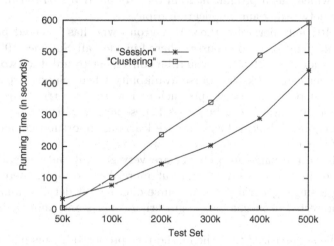

Fig. 6. Execution time

This demonstrates that our approach scales up well for large data sets. The results also confirm the analysis on BIRCH [24] and attribute-oriented induction [11].

5.3 Cluster Analysis

A preliminary analysis of the clustering has been performed to verify that the clusters make sense. The resulting clusters are analyzed by examining the general pages in them. Most clusters in the hierarchical clustering contain only a few general pages which are considered as the general interest of the group. However, because of the complexity of the task and our limited manpower, we have not done sophisticated analysis. The clustering will be passed on to the webmasters of the University for more thorough analysis, who are more familiar with the Web pages.

In each of the three sub-hierarchies we tested, we find some interesting clusters that are not in the original sessions. For example, in the MAEM sub-hierarchy, there are three groups who spent 5-8, 15-25, and 30+ minutes, respectively, on the personal home pages of the faculty and staff in the Department. This is not found in the original sessions because the sessions consist mostly of different home pages. The general page that represents them is actually the most visited general page. Most of the users are internal, that is, from UMR. Based on the finding, the department may, for example, provide help to the faculty and staff for developing their home pages.

In the HELP sub-hierarchy, generalization leads to the finding of a large group who look for help about the Web, instead of small groups who are interested in specific topics about the Web. This justifies the arrangement of the helpdesk Web page which has a prominent item on *help on WWW/Internet*, separating from other networking and application topics.

In the RO sub-hierarchy, there is a group who has browsed pages on the course catalog and pages on courses offered in the Fall/Summer 1997 semesters (the log was for April 1997). It would be convenient to link the two together so that a student can check the course availability when making a plan. Another group looks at pages on transcripts such as how to get a transcript in addition to the course offerings. It can be guessed these users are students who are going to apply for jobs. A link to long-distance learning opportunities may be helpful to some of them.

Sometimes, the pages in a cluster are very general and we can look at the simple pages in the data set to find out more. For example, there is a cluster containing a single general page on course offerings. A detailed analysis reveals a group interested in mechanical engineering courses and another in economics courses.

It can be summarized that the method we proposed in this paper is effective in finding interesting clusters and that it scales up well for large data sets. In particular, the generalization not only greatly reduces the dimensionality of the sessions, but also improves the quality of the clustering. A few meaningful clusters which are not in the original sessions have been found in our data set.

6   Discussion

The related issues in session identification and generalization are addressed in this section.

6.1   Session Identification

Although a lot of progress has been made in session identification, it is still a difficult problem. The difficulties in session identification are discussed below.

1. It is sometimes hard to identify unique users based just on server logs. One problem is that many Web servers only record the IP address of clients, which can be shared by more than one user. This does not pose a serious threat if the session boundary can be clearly decided since each session is usually contributed by a single user.

   A more serious problem arises when some Internet routers, proxy servers, and ISPs hide the actual IP address of clients by a random or anonymous IP address. The solutions proposed so far include cookies, user registration, and heuristics based on the clients' browser type and links among pages [6]. However, none of these provides a fail-proof solution.

   A somewhat related issue is to identify concurrent sessions from the same user. This can happen, for example, when a user opens multiple windows of a browser. The activities from all windows will be represented as one session in our approach. This could cause a problem if each window corresponds to a task in the user's mind, and thus needs to be represented as a session. Heuristics such as referal pages [6] may help if the windows follow different paths.

2. In our approach, the time spent on a page is estimated by subtracting the times of two consecutive requests. The time spent on the last page is estimated using the average time of all other pages. However, the actual time spent on each page is almost always different from the estimation because of network traffic, server load, user reading speed, etc. A user profiler is proposed in [18] which uses a client side JAVA applet and can capture more accurately the time spent. However, this requires the deployment of a client side program and modification of Web pages on the server. Besides, it is still impossible to measure the user's actual viewing time because the person may be distracted after the page is loaded.

   A possible sidewalk solution is to discard the time information all together. The sessions can be simply represented by the pages in them. Each page now becomes a binary variable. Our preliminary analysis is that the clusters found will be similar to those found with time information. More experiments need to be conducted to make a conclusive claim.

3. A lot of Web browsers have caching functions so that the server log may not reflect the actual history of browsing. If a cached page has been accessed in the session, the page will be in the session, but its time may be inaccurate. Some proxy servers also cache pages for different users, thus the cached pages are not present in many sessions. One way to deal with it is to disable caching by expiring a page right after it is fetched. This, however, defeats the purpose of caching. Some heuristics used to detect unique users can also be used to identify the missing pages [6].

6.2 Generalization

Two important factors in generalization are the generalization level and the page hierarchy, which are discussed below.

1. In the generalization of sessions, a level is given or implied from a threshold to determine the general pages which are going to replace the simple pages. This level plays an important role in forming the generalized sessions as well as the final clustering, as demonstrated in our experiments. If the level is set too high, over-generalization may occur in which too many details are lost and the validity of the clusters may be in question. On the other hand, if the level is set too low, the clustering algorithm may not find the clusters existing only at higher levels. Besides, the dimensionality may be too large. We report an initial experience in our data set, but experiments on other data sets are needed to gain more insights on the issue.
2. The construction of the page hierarchy based on the URLs of pages implies that the underlying page organization reflects the semantics of the pages. In case this cannot be assumed, the page hierarchy should be constructed according to the semantics of the pages, e.g., by using a document clustering [17,23] or categorization method [16]. A semi-automatic approach with the help of the webmaster is another alternative. Our approach can be easily extended to use page hierarchies so constructed.

In all, the generalization of the sessions reveals clusters which are more general and broad. The goal is to find high-level patterns without losing important details. However, the generalization will lose some information and may group sessions which do not belong to the same cluster. In some extreme cases where clustering on the original sessions is needed, the generalization level should be set to positive infinity so the sessions are not generalized.

7   Conclusion

The clustering of the Web usage sessions based on access patterns has been studied. A generalization-based clustering method is proposed which employs attribute-oriented induction in clustering to deal with the high-dimensional data in Web usage mining. Our experiments on a large real data set show that the method is efficient and practical for Web mining applications.

It is found that even after attribute-oriented induction, the dimensionality of generalized sessions may still be very large. One possible solution is to use a subspace clustering algorithm which partitions the vector space for clustering [1]. Another is to dynamically adjust the page hierarchy [10] to further reduce the dimensionality at higher levels.

The clustering algorithm used in our experiments, BIRCH, seems to degrade when the dimensionality increases. There are lots of singleton leaf clusters in the final clustering for almost all the test sets. Currently several alternative clustering algorithms are under consideration. We are also working on the improvement of the BIRCH algorithm.

A natural extension of our method is to combine user registration information, such as age, income level, address, etc, with their access patterns in clustering. It would be interesting to see how each can contribute to the quality of clustering.

An important topic for future research is the use of clustering in applications such as education and e-commerce. A possible direction could be how to design Web pages that are attractive to targeted groups.

Acknowledgments

This work is supported by University of Missouri Research Board Grant R-3-42434. We thank Dr. Tian Zhang for the source code of BIRCH and Meg Brady and Dan Uetrecht for the data set. Mario Creado's help during the experiments is greatly appreciated.

References

1. R. Agrawal, J. Gehrke, D. Gunopulos, and P. Raghavan. Automatic subspace clustering of high dimensional data for data mining applications. In *Proc. ACM SIGMOD Int. Conf. on Management of Data*, Seattle, Washington, 1998. 36
2. J. C. Bezdek and S. K. Pal. *Fuzzy Models for Pattern Recognition*. IEEE Press, 1992. 23
3. J. Borges and M. Levene. Mining association rules in hypertext databases. In *Proc. 1998 Int'l Conf. on Data Mining and Knowledge Discovery (KDD'98)*, pages 149–153, August 1998. 22
4. A. Büchner and M. Mulvenna. Discovering internet marketing intelligence through online analytical web usage mining. *SIGMOD Record*, 27, 1998. 22
5. M. S. Chen, J. S. Park, and P.S. Yu. Efficient data mining for path traversal patterns in distributed systems. *Proc. 1996 Int'l Conf. on Distributed Computing Systems*, 385, May 1996. 22
6. R. Cooley, B. Mobasher, and J. Srivastava. Data preparation for mining world wide web browsing patterns. *Journal of Knowledge and Information Systems*, 1, 1999. 22, 23, 25, 26, 29, 35
7. R. Cooley, B. Mobasher, and J. Srivastava. Web mining: Information and pattern discovery on the world wide web. In *Proc. Int. Conf. on Tools with Artificial Intelligence*, pages 558–567, Newport Beach, CA, 1999. 21, 22
8. O. Etzioni. The world-wide web: Quangmire or gold mine? *Communications of ACM*, 39:65–68, 1996. 21
9. J. Han, Y. Cai, and N. Cercone. Knowledge discovery in databases: An attribute-oriented approach. In *Proc. 18th Int. Conf. Very Large Data Bases*, pages 547–559, Vancouver, Canada, August 1992. 22, 24, 28
10. J. Han and Y. Fu. Dynamic generation and refinement of concept hierarchies for knowledge discovery in databases. In *Proc. AAAI'94 Workshop on Knowledge Discovery in Databases (KDD'94)*, pages 157–168, Seattle, WA, July 1994. 36
11. J. Han and Y. Fu. Exploration of the power of attribute-oriented induction in data mining. In U.M. Fayyad, G. Piatetsky-Shapiro, P. Smyth, and R. Uthurusamy, editors, *Advances in Knowledge Discovery and Data Mining*, pages 399–421. AAAI/MIT Press, 1996. 25, 33
12. A. K. Jain and R. C. Dubes. *Algorithms for Clustering Data*. Printice Hall, 1988. 23
13. L. Kaufman and P. J. Rousseeuw. *Finding Groups in Data: an Introduction to Cluster Analysis*. John Wiley & Sons, 1990. 23

14. R. S. Michalski and R. Stepp. Automated construction of classifications: Conceptual clustering versus numerical taxonomy. *IEEE Trans. Pattern Analysis and Machine Intelligence*, 5:396–410, 1983. 23

15. B. Mobasher, N. Jain, S. Han, and J. Srivastava. *Web Mining: Pattern Discovery from World Wide Web Transcations*. Technical Report, University of Minnesota, avialable at ftp://ftp.cs.umn.edu/users/kumar/webmining.ps., 1996. 23, 25

16. J. Moore, S. Han, D. Boley, M. Gini, R. Gross, K. Hastings, G. Karypis, V. Kumar, and B. Mobasher. *Web Page Categorization and Feature Selection Using Association Rule and Principal Component Clustering*. Workshop on Information Technologies and Systems, avialable at ftp://ftp.cs.umn.edu/users/kumar/webwits.ps., 1997. 25, 36

17. M. Perkowitz and O. Etzioni. Adaptive web pages: Automatically synthesizing web pages. In *Proc. 15th National Conf. on Artificial Intelligence (AAAI/IAAI'98)*, pages 727–732, Madison, Wisconsin, July, 1998. 36

18. C. Shahabi, A. Z. Zarkesh, J. Adibi, and V. Shah. Knowledge discovery from users web-page navigation. In *Proc. of 1997 Int. Workshop on Research Issues on Data Engineering (RIDE'97)*, Birmingham, England, April 1997. 23, 24, 25, 35

19. M. Spiliopoulou and L. Faulstich. Wum: A web utilization miner. In *Proc. EDBT Workshop WebDB'98*, Valencia, Spain, 1998. 22, 23, 25

20. A. Woodruff, P. M. Aoki, E. Brewer, P. Gauthier, and L. A. Rowe. *An Investigation of Documents from the World Wide Web*. 5th Int. World Wide Web Conference, Paris, France, May, 1996. 26

21. T. W. Yan, M. Jacobsen, H. Garcia-Molina, and U. Dayal. *From User Access Patterns to Dynamic Hypertext Linking*. 5th Int. World Wide Web Conference, Paris, France, May, 1996. 23, 24, 25

22. O. R. Zaïane, X. Xin, and J. Han. Discovering web access patterns and trends by applying olap and data mining technology on web logs. In *Proc. Advances in Digital Libraries*, pages 19–29, 1998. 22

23. O. Zamir, O. Etzioni, O. Madani, and R. Karp. Fast and intuitive clustering of web documents. In *Proc. 1997 Int'l Conf. on Data Mining and Knowledge Discovery (KDD'97)*, pages 287–290, Newport Beach, CA, August 1997. 36

24. T. Zhang, R. Ramakrishnan, and M. Livny. BIRCH: an efficient data clustering method for very large databases. In *Proc. 1996 ACM-SIGMOD Int. Conf. Management of Data*, pages 103–114, Montreal, Canada, June 1996. 22, 23, 28, 33

Constructing Web User Profiles: A Non-invasive Learning Approach

Philip K. Chan

Computer Science, Florida Institute of Technology
Melbourne, FL 32901
pkc@cs.fit.edu
http://www.cs.fit.edu/~pkc/

Abstract. Our web user profiles consist of Page Interest Estimators (PIE's) and Web Access Graphs (WAG's). We discuss a non-invasive approach to estimating the user's interest of a web page without directly asking the user. A time and space efficient method is proposed for locating multi-word phrases to enrich the common bag-of-words representation for text documents. PIE's are then learned to predict the user's interest on any web page. A WAG summarizes the web page access patterns of a user. We describe how a user profile can be utilized to analyze search results and recommend new and interesting pages. Our empirical results on PIE's are encouraging.

1 Introduction

Recently researchers have started to make web browsers more *adaptive* and *personalized*. A *personalized* web browser caters to the user's interests and an *adaptive* one learns from the users' (potentially changing) access behavior. The goal is to help the user navigate the web. Lieberman's Letizia [23] monitors the user's browsing behavior, develops a user profile, and searches for potentially interesting pages for recommendations. The user profile is developed without intervention from the user (but the details of how that is performed is not clear in [23]). While the user is reading a page, Letizia searches, in a breadth-first manner, from that location, pages that could be of interest to the user. Pazzani et al.'s Syskill & Webert [28,29] asks the user to rank pages in a specific topic. Based on the content and ratings of pages, the system learns a user profile that predicts if pages are of interest to the user. They investigated a number of topics and a different user profile is learned for each topic. Pages are recommended from preselected web sites. Similar to Syskill & Webert, Balabanovic's Fab [2] requires the user to rank pages and learns a user profile based on the rankings and content of pages. However, Fab considers recommendations based on profiles of all the other users on the system (though Fab does not identify users of similar interests). Fab's collection agent performs an off-line best-first search of the web for interesting pages.

Our approach toward an adaptive personalized web browser does not require the user to explicitly provide information to the browser. Instead, it monitors the

B. Masand and M. Spiliopoulou (Eds.): WEBKDD'99, LNAI 1836, pp. 39–55, 2000.

user's access behavior and captures his/her interests in a user profile. We developed a metric for estimating interestingness of each visited page. A user profile consists of two components: a *Page Interest Estimator* (PIE) and a *Web Access Graph* (WAG). Based on the content of web pages, a page interest estimator, learned from the user's access behavior, characterizes the interests of a user. A web access graph summarizes the web page access patterns of a user. To provide personalized on-line search, our search engine consults multiple existing search engines ([38,39]), collates the returned records, and ranks them according to the user profile. Using similar search techniques, recommendation and prefetching of interesting pages are performed off-line at night.

In this article we focus on PIE's (Section 2), and investigate how a user's interest of a page can be approximated without asking the user (Section 2.1) and how phrases can be identified to enrich the common bag-of-words representation for documents (Section 2.2). We then describe WAG's in Section 3. In Section 4 we discuss on how user profiles can be utilized in analyzing search results and recommending novel pages. We evaluate PIE learning on data from our web site in Section 5. Finally, we conclude in Section 6 with some remarks on the challenging issues that PIE learning exhibits.

2   Page Interest Estimator (PIE)

We can identify patterns in pages that constitute the user's interest. For example, certain words or phases, are of interest to the user. Given a set of labeled (interesting or not interesting) pages, we can apply learning algorithms (for example, C4.5 [32]) to induce classifiers that predict if a page is of interest to the user. These classifiers are called *Page Interest Estimators* (PIE's). More concretely,

$$Interest \leftarrow PIE_{user}(Page)$$

and PIE can be learned:

$$PIE_{user} \leftarrow MachineLearningAlgorithm(Page, Interest).$$

In addition, PIE's are learned, stored, and used at the individual users' sites, hence privacy is maintained.

Related work in this area usually takes an *invasive* approach that requires user involvement in providing ranking (for example, [2,29]). However, as we will discuss our *non-invasive* approach in the next section (Section 2.1), the user interest of each visited page can be approximated without any user involvement. Also, how can a page be represented so that machine learning algorithms can be applied? We discuss page representation in Section 2.2.

2.1   User Interest of a Page

How do we find out if a user is interested in a page? One way is to ask the user directly (e.g., [29]). This is the common approach, but it is *invasive* and, in most cases, requires the user to provide some ad hoc ranking score (e.g., 0 to 10 or bad to good). Furthermore, the user may provide inconsistent rankings across pages and the process is time consuming. Another way is to monitor the user's behavior and evaluate the user's interest. This approach is *non-invasive* and the user is not subject to ad hoc ranking.

Throughout the course of web browsing, a user leaves behind a trail of information that can be used to model his or her interests. Four general sources of information are available: *history*, *bookmarks*, content of pages, and *access logs*.

1. A web browser usually maintains a *history* of the user's requests in the current session and in the past. The history of the current session allows the user to go back and forth between the pages he/she has visited. In addition, a global history maintains the timestamp of the last time each page is visited (this allows links to expire after a specified amount of time and be displayed as if they have not been visited). In Netscape's Navigator [27], the title, URL, first visit timestamp, last visit timestamp, expiration timestamp, and visit count of each visited URL is stored in the global history. We conjecture that a higher frequency and more recent visits of an URL indicate stronger user interest of that URL.

2. *Bookmarks* serve as a quick access point for interesting URL's chosen by the user. With a few mouse clicks, a user can easily jump to URL's in his/her bookmarks. It seems natural to assume that pages that are bookmarked are of strong interest to the user.

3. Each page usually contains links to other pages. If the page is interesting to the user, he/she is likely to visit the links referenced by the page (Lieberman [23] made a similar observation). Hence, a higher percentage of links visited from a page indicates a stronger user interest in that page. This is particularly important for index pages, which contain a lot of related links and on which the users spend less time than pages with real content.

4. Each entry in an *access log* corresponds to an HTTP request, which typically contains the client IP address, timestamp, access method, URL, protocol, status, and file size. A sample entry is:

   maelstrom.cs.fit.edu - - [19/Jun/1998:19:02:15 -0400] "GET /toc.html HTTP/1.0" 200 2540

   From these entries, time spent on each page can be calculated. The longer a user spent on a page, the likelier the user is interested in the page. If a page is not interesting, a user usually jumps to another page quickly. Experimental studies in [25,19] confirm this observation. However, a quick jump might be caused by the short length of the page, hence the user's interest might be more appropriately approximated by the time spent on a page normalized by the page's length. We note that activities other than surfing the web (e.g., answering a phone call) can inadvertently be included in the time spent on a page. We cannot avoid this problem without a more complicated way of obtaining time statistics (e.g., tracking the gaze of user's eyes [42,43]). However, to reduce the problem, we impose an upper limit on time (e.g.,

15 minutes) spent on a page and time intervals of more than the upper limit are considered as separate sessions. Unfortunately, browsers usually have a *history*, but not an *access log* (which is essentially a more detailed history) since a history is sufficient for traversing pages in a session and maintaining timestamps for link expiration. Access logs are usually found in HTTP servers. In order to maintain an access log for the browser client, one can modify the source code of the browser (e.g., [26]). However, this requires changes to a complex piece of software and is browser-dependent. A simpler approach is to use a web proxy server that logs HTTP requests (e.g., [41]). A proxy serves as a relay between the browser client and the Web—it is usually used for security (clients behind firewalls), performance (system-wide caching of external pages), and/or filtering (blocking out undesirable sites).

User Interest Approximation. Given the above four sources of information, we can devise a measure for approximating the interest of a page to a user. One simple measure is:

$$Interest(Page) = Frequency(Page), \qquad (1)$$

where $Frequency(Page)$ is the frequency of $Page$ visited by the user. We consider the number of visits a primary indicator of interest. A more sophisticated measure uses $Frequency(Page)$ as a base and incorporates all the factors discussed above:

$$Interest(Page) = Frequency(Page) \times (1 + IsBookmark(Page) +$$
$$Duration(Page) + Recency(Page) + LinkVisitPercent(Page)), \qquad (2)$$

where
$$IsBookmark(Page) = \begin{cases} 1 \text{ if } page \text{ is a bookmark} \\ 0 \text{ otherwise} \end{cases},$$

$$Duration(Page) = \frac{TotalDuration(Page)/Size(Page)}{\max_{Page \in VisitedPages}(TotalDuration(Page)/Size(Page))},$$

$$Recency(Page) = \frac{Time(LastVisit) - Time(StartLog)}{Time(Now) - Time(StartLog)}, and$$

$$LinkVisitPercent(Page) = \frac{NumberOfLinksVisited(Page)}{NumberOfLinks(Page)}.$$

The maximum value of $Interest(Page)$ is $Frequency(Page) \times 5$.

All the visited pages can be considered interesting to various degrees since the user accessed them. However, how do we find pages that are not interesting to the user? It is easier if the user is required to rank pages, but the user is not actively involved in our case. Furthermore, we cannot assume any page not visited on the web is of no interest to the user because he or she might not know of its existence (not to mention the staggering number of pages on the web). Since pages usually contain links to other pages and, in most cases, not all of them are followed by the user, one approach to identifying pages not interesting to the user is to consider links in visited pages that are not followed by the user. Related work is in text categorization, where documents are mapped into categories using learned models [1,22,47]. Usually, the documents are grouped into many categories and all the documents are known in advance. Our task, however, is to group the pages into two categories (interesting or not interesting) and cannot assume that all the pages on the web are known in advance.

Evaluation of User Interest Approximation. Based on the frequency of visits, in Equation 2, we value each factor equally. Some weighted scheme will likely be more appropriate after we perform some experiments to validate this model. Such experiments will involve surveying the user's actual degree of interest and measuring the square errors. Regression techniques can be used to tune the weights in our model.

2.2   Page Representation

Various representations of a web page have been widely studied. Most researchers use the vector-space model pioneered by Salton [36]. In this model each document is represented by a vector of weights, each of which corresponds to a feature, a word in most cases. The word ordering information in the document is usually not retained and hence the name "bag-of-words."

However, much research focuses on single words (unigrams) as features. This is partly due to the large combination of possible multi-word phrases. Another reason is that earlier results from "syntactic" and "statistical" phrases were mixed [11]. We suspect that the ad hoc way of constructing statistical phrases might have been a problem [13]. Much of the statistical work in building multi-word features focuses on co-occurrence (e.g., [9]), that is, if two words appear frequently together, they probably form a phrase. One co-occurrence metric is *mutual information*. Consider a and b are two words within a window of some size, the mutual information:

$$MI(a,b) = \log \frac{P(a,b)}{P(a)P(b)} \qquad (3)$$

measures the reduction of uncertainty in knowing b's presence in the window if a's presence is known (or vice versa, the metric symmetric). However, this metric does not consider the effect of the absence of either or both words in the window. Note that if two words always appear together or not at all, they are more likely to be a phrase than other situations. *Expected (or average) mutual information* [34,35] (or *information gain* [32]) captures the effects of word absences.

$$EMI(A,B) = \sum_{a,\bar{a} \in A} \sum_{b,\bar{b} \in B} P(A,B) \log \frac{P(A,B)}{P(A)P(B)} \qquad (4)$$

measures the expected mutual information of the four combinations of the presence and absence of a and b. Although larger $MI(a,b)$ and $MI(\bar{a},\bar{b})$ provide

PALO ALTO, Calif. – The ink on the first draft of the history of the Internet stock boom isn't yet dry, and the revisionists are already having their say. Even as Internet shares were tumbling from their highs, three of the companies backed by Accel Partners, a venture capital firm, went public last month. Though their net losses total $56 million, the three now have a combined market capitalization of $10 billion. "Astounding," James W. Breyer, the firm's managing partner, calls that performance, echoing the giddiness common in Silicon Valley when people talk about the Internet.

Fig. 1. First Paragraph of "Feeding a Frenzy: Why Internet Investors Are Still Ravenous[18]"

Table 1. Top twelve bigrams selected by MI, EMI, and $AEMI$

Metric	Top twelve bigrams (in ranked order)
MI	schwab dlj, ruth porat, research report, fiercest competitor, dlj direct, charl schwab, wit group, san francisco, p o, net loss, menlo park, equal stand
EMI	ventur capitalist, silicon vallei, new york, wall street, m whitman, go public, morgan stanlei, invest banker, doesn t, san francisco, p o, menlo park
$AEMI$	ventur capitalist, silicon vallei, invest banker, new york, go public, m whitman, morgan stanlei, wall street, invest bank, internet stock, doesn t, york time

more evidence for "ab" to be a phrase, larger $MI(a,\overline{b})$ and $MI(\overline{a},b)$ supply more counter evidence. Therefore, we introduce *augmented expected mutual information* (AEMI) which appropriately incorporates the counter-evidence:

$$AEMI(A,B) = \sum_{(A=a,B=b),(A=\overline{a},B=\overline{b})} P(A,B) \log \frac{P(A,B)}{P(A)P(B)} -$$

$$\sum_{(A=a,B=\overline{b}),(A=\overline{a},B=b)} P(A,B) \log \frac{P(A,B)}{P(A)P(B)} \quad (5)$$

In essence supporting evidence is summed, while damaging evidence is subtracted. Furthermore, we define A as the event of the first word, and B as the event in the words (of some window size W) following the first word. That is, a higher value of $AEMI$ indicates a is likely followed by b and one is less likely to be present when the other is absent. Moreover, window size W allows flexibility in the number of gaps between words in a phrase.

Evaluating the Variants of Mutual Information. We tested MI, EMI, and $AEMI$ on a New York Times article on the recent frenzy of internet companies going public in the stock market [18]. Table 1 lists the top twelve bigrams (two-word phrases) selected by the three metrics (words were stemmed by Porter's algorithm [31,14] beforehand). We observed that the bigrams selected by MI are not as relevant to the article as EMI and $AEMI$, which are quite similar for the top twelve bigrams. However, while "internet stock," a key phrase, was ranked 10th by $AEMI$, it was ranked 37th by EMI. Another relevant bigram, "internet compani" was ranked 33rd by $AEMI$, but lower than 65th by EMI. This provides some empirical evidence for $AEMI$'s ability to find more relevant phrases than the other two metrics.

Efficient Identification of n-Grams. Using $AEMI$ with a threshold, we can find highly probable two-word phrases (bigrams) from a training corpus. n-word phrases (n-grams) can be found using the same method—event A is the first $n - 1$ words and event B is a word in the following W (window size) words. However, the memory requirement of storing the necessary statistics to find n-grams is $O(s^n)$, where s is the number of unique words in the corpus; this could be prohibitive even for locating trigrams. Consider that s is 1,000 (a relatively small number) and each counter takes 1 byte, one gigabytes are needed to find trigrams! However, to reduce the combinatorial explosion, one can safely consider only a small number of bigrams with high $AEMI$ values as event A. Though this scheme is memory efficient, it requires a second pass of the corpus, which incurs disk I/O time, since the $AEMI$ values can only be calculated at the end of one pass. This scheme requires $n - 1$ passes for identifying n-grams.

We propose an approximate approach to finding n-grams without requiring a lot of storage and multiple passes on the disk-resident corpus. For each bigram with $AEMI$ above some threshold T, a directed edge is inserted into a graph, whose vertices are the words. A trigram, "abc," is identified if the edges $a \rightarrow b$, $b \rightarrow c$, and $a \rightarrow c$ exist. Similarly, a quadgram, "$abcd$," is located if, in addition to the three edges for trigram "abc," the edges $a \rightarrow d$, $b \rightarrow d$, and $c \rightarrow d$ also exist. Our scheme needs $O(s^2)$ storage ($O(s^2)$ for the counters plus $O(s^2)$ for the graph, which is sparse and requires much less than s^2 storage) and a single pass on the corpus. Formally, $ngram$ is defined as:

$$ngram(w_1, w_2, ..., w_n) =$$
$$\begin{cases} edge(w_1, w_2) & \text{if } n = 2 \\ ngram(w_1, w_2, ..., w_{n-1}) \wedge \bigwedge_{i=1}^{n-1} edge(w_i, w_n) & \text{if } n > 2, \end{cases} \quad (6)$$

where

$$edge(w_i, w_j) = \begin{cases} true & \text{if } AEMI(w_i, w_j) > T \\ false & \text{otherwise} \end{cases}$$

Window size W plays a role in our method of building n-grams. Given a W, our scheme allows larger gaps in shorter phrases and smaller gaps in longer phrases. This notion stems from the observation that shorter phrases might have additional intervening words but longer phrases usually do not. For instance, when W is set to 2 for building n-grams upto trigrams, we allow an additional word between the words in bigrams but none in trigrams.

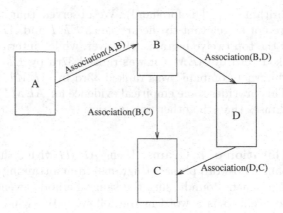

Fig. 2. A sample Web Access Graph (WAG)

3   Web Access Graph (WAG)

In addition to the Page Interest Estimator (PIE), our user profile contains a *Web Access Graph* (WAG). A WAG is a weighted directed graph that represents a user's access behavior (a similar but simpler graph is described in [45]). Each vertex in the graph represents a web page and stores the access frequency of that page. If the user visited $Page_A$ followed by $Page_B$, a directed edge exists from $Page_A$ to $Page_B$. For example, Figure 2 shows that the user traversed two sequences of web pages: $A \rightarrow B \rightarrow C$ and $A \rightarrow B \rightarrow D \rightarrow C$. The weight on each edge represents the degree of association between the two pages or the likelihood of accessing $Page_B$ from $Page_A$. One measure for association is the frequency of visits from one page to the other. That is,

$$Association(Page_A \rightarrow Page_B) = Frequency(Page_A \rightarrow Page_B), \qquad (7)$$

where $Frequency(Page_A \rightarrow Page_B)$ is the number of visits from $Page_A$ to $Page_B$. A user's web access graph can be displayed graphically to help the user locate related interesting pages that the user has visited [45]. It enhances the bookmark facility, which merely records what the user wants to store. Graphically displaying the web access graph provides a more user friendly and informative interface.

For instance, the intensity of a vertex indicates the interest level of the corresponding page and the thickness of an edge depicts the degree of association. Since a user can visit many pages, a web access graph can be quite complex to display. One approach to solve this problem is to partition the graph by clustering vertices/pages and display each subgraph separately.

3.1   Clustering

Clustering techniques can be used to find pages that are closely associated with each other and are likely to be accessed by the user consecutively. Before clus-

tering algorithms can be applied, we need an undirected graph and a distance
metric. The weighted directed web access graph can be converted into a weighted
undirected graph. For each pair of vertices, the two directed edges (if one or both
exist) are replaced by an undirected edge. The association of the undirected edge
is the sum of the association of the directed edges:

$$Association(Page_A, Page_B) = Association(Page_A \rightarrow Page_B) +$$
$$Association(Page_B \rightarrow Page_A). \qquad (8)$$

The distance metric is the reciprocal of association.

Given a certain k, k-means clustering [16] yields k clusters. Since a user cannot effectively visualize a cluster that is too large, cluster size should be limited
to some reasonable number (e.g., 30). Consequently, we have a way to determine k. Moreover, we can use the k most interesting pages, instead of random
pages, to seed the centroids of the initial clusters. Another clustering method
can be utilized if the user's bookmarks are organized into folders. Each folder
corresponds to a cluster and the bookmarked pages are not moved from the clusters. Pages that are not bookmarked are assigned to the closest cluster measured
by the average distance to each bookmarked page in the cluster. A maximum
cluster size is maintained and only the closest pages are kept in the cluster.
Pages that are not in any clusters go through the k-means clustering process.
Besides k-means clustering, we plan to investigate hierarchical agglomeration
clustering algorithms and the connected-component method used in [30].

The generated clusters can be ranked according to the average interest, average pair-wise distance, or a combination of the two in each cluster. This ranking
provides a way of ordering the clusters to be indexed and displayed. Besides
rendering a cluster graphically, we can also display it textually in the form of a
hierarchical list. Starting from the page with the highest interest as the root, we
can apply a minimal spanning tree algorithm to generate the hierarchical list.

Evaluating Clusters. How do we know the generated clusters are indeed useful
to help the user navigate? One evaluation metric is to measure how likely it is
that when a page in a cluster is referenced, then another page (or other pages)
in the same cluster is also accessed in the same session [30]. An alternative
measure is the number of pages visited by the user in a cluster during a session.
Furthermore, in order to evaluate the predictiveness of the clusters, we evaluate
on sessions that are disjoint from sessions used in clustering. This evaluation
metric can also be used to rank clusters for display purposes.

3.2 Alternatives for Association

As discussed above, $Association(Page_A \rightarrow Page_B)$ can be simply approximated
by the frequency of access from $Page_A$ to $Page_B$. However, we observe that a
user would have a stronger desire to visit $Page_B$ if it is more interesting. Hence,

a more sophisticated association metric considers the interest (Section 2.1) of the destination page and is defined as:

$$Association(Page_A \rightarrow Page_B) = P(Page_A|Page_B) \times Interest(Page_B), \quad (9)$$

where $P(Page_A|Page_B)$ is the probability of $Page_A$ being the source page given $Page_B$ is the destination page and is approximated from the user's access frequencies. In other words, the interest at a destination vertex (page) is spread backward to the incoming edges. This way, an edge leading to a more interesting vertex has a larger weight and hence a stronger directed association between the two pages. (Note that if $Interest(Page)$ is simply $Frequency(Page)$, $Association(Page_A \rightarrow Page_B)$ degenerates back to $Frequency(Page_A \rightarrow Page_B)$.) We next discuss how a user profile can be utilized.

4   Utilization of a User Profile

A user profile contains a Web Access Graph (WAG) and a Page Interest Estimator (PIE). The profile provides a personalized context for analyzing results from search engines (Section 4.1) and recommending interesting pages (Section 4.2).

4.1   Analysis of Search Results

In order to provide a high success rate of returning relevant pages from search engines, we propose to use the user profile as a personalized filtering and ranking mechanism. Given a search query from the user, our search engine forwards the query to multiple search engines (similar to MetaCrawler [39]) and collates the returned records by removing duplicates. The PIE then determines if the pages are pertinent to the user preferences; i.e., $Ranking(Page) = PIE(Page)$. If the PIE is a classifier and provides confidence values of its classification, the pages are ranked accordingly. If the PIE is a regressor, the pages are sorted according to the estimated interest values.

Since the user does not want to wait too long for a search engine to return results, we need to consider the speed performance of various classifiers and regressors. Typically, 30 seconds should be the maximum amount of time to wait. We plan to employ multiple processors to collect, collate, and analyze the returned records in parallel. Each processor collects results from a different search engine. The results are collated using a "tournament-like" algorithm in a binary-tree manner—results from different search engines are at the leaves and pairs of results are merged recursively until the root is reached. In the process, we marked the pages that are purged on each processor. We then use the PIE to rank the collated pages in parallel. Using a "merge-sort-like' algorithm, ranked pages on each processor are recursively merged into the final sorted list of ranked pages.

Using different learning algorithms and combining the learned models has been demonstrated to be effective in improving performance [3,4,8,37,46]. We plan to investigate using multiple estimators to analyze and combine the results in parallel. Meta-learning [6] is one combining approach and we intend to examine other voting-based methods [7].

Properly evaluating how the user responds to the results returned by our search engine is important. In information retrieval, the common metrics are *precision* and *recall*. From all pages returned by the search engine, *precision* measures the percentage of pages that are relevant. From all possible relevant pages, *recall* calculates the percentage of relevant pages returned by the search engine. There is usually a trade-off between precision and recall. By varying the parameters of the search engine, different pairs of precision and recall can be obtained. Graphs can then be plotted to compare the different methods. Alternatively, some researchers use the *break-even* point [1] as a single value for comparison. The break-even point occurs when precision is the same as recall. The *F*-measure [21] allows weighting precision and recall differently. In our task, since we do not know all the relevant web pages that are of interest to the user, measuring recall is quite impossible. Furthermore, our search engine provides a ranking of pages, hence it considers some pages are more relevant than the others to the user. Another issue is which pages are considered relevant and of interest to the user. To measure the performance of our search engine, we propose to use $Interest(Page)$ (Section 2.1) to measure the relevance and calculate the sum of the interest values weighted by the ranking of pages. We then normalize the sum by the summation of rankings. (Note that if a page is not visited by the user, $Interest(Page)$ is zero.) Formally, the performance of our search engine is defined as:

$$\frac{\sum_{Page \in ReturnedPages} (Interest(Page) \times Ranking(Page))}{\sum_{Page \in ReturnedPages} Ranking(Page)}, \tag{10}$$

where $Ranking(Page)$ is the rank assigned by our search engine to $Page$ and is larger if it is more relevant to the user. Hence, the metric imposes larger reward/penalty to higher ranked pages and higher reward to pages that are more interesting to the user.

The user's behavior on the results returned by the search engine provides a feedback for the system to improve the user profile. Accordingly, the visited pages update the web access graph and become positive examples. On the other hand, the ignored (not visited) pages become negative examples. An updated PIE is then learned.

4.2   Recommendation of New and Interesting Pages

Recommending new and potentially interesting pages is a challenging problem mainly due to the large number of available pages. One approach is to perform a systematic search starting from terms that are of interest to the user or from pages visited by the user recently and recursively visit the referenced links [2,23]. Potential interest of each page is estimated by PIE's. This approach necessitates large amounts of communication and computation in retrieving pages and analyzing them using PIE's. Alternatively, we propose to use a *collaborative* [15,19] (or *social* [40]) approach. This approach assumes that users with comparable interests behave similarly. Hence, recommendations are based on unseen items seen by different but similar users. Related work compares users of how they rank music [40] and movies [17]. However, our non-invasive goal precludes asking the user to rank pages. We have already identified, in Section 2.1, how to estimate an user's interest of a page. Moreover, related work mainly investigates techniques in a relative small collection of items. Here, we try to examines techniques for arbitrary web sites. For efficiency reasons, we propose to analyze access behavior of web sites (domain names) instead of web pages. Here, we address how to find users with similar interests efficiently and which pages to recommend.

From a user's WAG, we can obtain the access frequency of visited sites. To identify users with similar behavior efficiently, we divide the process into two phases: the first provides a coarse filter and the second examines the degree of similarity. Phase one ignores the frequency information and calculates the degree of overlap between two users' visited sites and the top overlapping users are passed to the second phase. Phase two uses the frequency information to measure the similarity between two users. One metric is the Pearson r correlation coefficient [44]:

$$r = \frac{\sum xy - \sum x \sum y/n}{\sqrt{[\sum x^2 - (\sum x^2/n)][\sum y^2 - (\sum y^2/n)]}}, \tag{11}$$

where x and y are the paired values and n is the number of pairs. This calculates the degree of correlation between the site access frequency of two users. Moreover, instead of using all the users [33,40], we select users that are correlated with high confidence according to:

$$t = \frac{r}{\sqrt{(1 - r^2)/(n - 2)}}, \tag{12}$$

which is t-distributed with $n - 2$ degrees of freedom [44]. Among the selected similar users (S), we weight each page's interest by the correlation coefficient:

$$Recommendation(Page) = \sum_{s \in S} r(CurrentUser, s) \times Interest_s(Page). \tag{13}$$

Furthermore, we propose to convert the frequencies into probabilities and use Kullback divergence [20]:

$$\sum_x P(x) \log \frac{P(x)}{P_a(x)}, \tag{14}$$

to measure the degree of similarity. P is the original probability distribution (current user) and P_a is the approximate one (one of the other users). Pearson correlation has an underlying assumption of a linear relationship between the paired values if they are correlated; however, Kullback divergence does not have this assumption and hence might provide a closer estimate of similarity in our task.

5   Preliminary Experiments on PIE's

To evaluate the performance of Page Interest Estimators (Section 2), we conducted experiments on data obtained from our departmental web server. We analyze how accurate PIE's are in predicting if a web page is interesting to a user. By analyzing the server access log from January to April 1999, we identified hosts that accessed our site at least 50 times in the first two months and also in the second two months. We use data from the first two months for training and the last two months for testing. We filtered out proxy, crawler, and our computer lab hosts, and identified "single-user" hosts, which are at dormitory rooms and a local company.

For each text web document (.html or .txt), we first extracted words, then applied a stop list to remove common articles, prepositions, and verbs, and finally stemmed the words according to Porter's stemming algorithm [31,14]. Bigrams and trigrams were identified using our scheme described in Section 2.2. The threshold T was .0025 and the window size W was 2 (i.e., the words in a bigram might not be next to each other, but those in a trigram must be adjacent to each other in the text). Two hundred and fifty Boolean features of the presence and absence of words/phrases were selected based on *expected mutual information* (Equation 4) [48] and ties were broken with preference to features with higher document frequency in interesting documents and features from longer phrases. Moreover, accessed pages were considered interesting to the user and pages not accessed were not interesting. For simplicity, we randomly picked unaccessed pages to be included in training and testing. The number of unaccessed pages is the same as accessed pages, hence the class ratio is 1:1 in the training and test sets.

We ran C4.5 [32], CART [5], naive BAYES [12], and RIPPER [10] on the data set. Table 2 has two groups of columns on the right: one for results from features with words and phrases and the other for features with words only. The two groups are for comparing the utility of adding phrases into the feature sets (in both groups, only 250 selected features were used in training and testing). For all four algorithms, based on the paired t-test with 95% confidence, the difference in accuracy is significant—adding phrases led to higher accuracy in CART, BAYES, and RIPPER, but lower accuracy in C4.5. For User 12, phrases improved the performance of CART and RIPPER by more than 10%. This provides empirical evidence that phrases can improve the accuracy performance of learned PIE's. Among the algorithms, RIPPER achieved significantly higher accuracy in the first group and C4.5 in the second group (paired t-test with 95% confidence), while BAYES was consistently less accurate than the other algorithms. The overall top performer was C4.5 with word-only features. On average, except for BAYES, 70% (significantly higher than the default 50%) accuracy can be obtained. Finally, we would like to point out that the success of our approach largely depends on the user's behavior pattern. For instance, although User 13 has one of the smallest training sets and the largest test set, many of the algorithms achieved the highest accuracy on this user. Inspection

Table 2. Accuracy performance of PIE's learned from four algorithms and fifteen users

User	Train size	Test size	Words and Phrases				Words Only			
			C4.5	CART	BAYES	RIPPER	C4.5	CART	BAYES	RIPPER
1	102	114	67.5	73.7	58.8	73.7	69.3	73.7	57.0	73.7
2	148	162	77.2	74.7	67.3	74.7	80.2	71.6	72.8	74.1
3	106	76	80.3	77.6	54.0	78.9	82.9	84.2	57.9	78.9
4	68	96	67.7	58.3	57.3	64.6	70.8	61.5	58.3	66.7
5	52	64	60.9	64.1	59.4	67.2	60.9	59.4	54.7	65.6
6	80	62	58.1	58.1	59.7	58.1	74.2	67.7	59.7	58.1
7	86	150	54.7	65.3	54.0	65.3	60.0	65.3	53.3	65.3
8	42	70	58.6	48.6	54.3	64.3	55.7	48.6	54.3	64.3
9	44	46	65.2	69.6	65.2	69.6	71.7	69.6	54.3	69.6
10	128	80	82.5	76.2	60.0	77.5	76.2	77.5	66.2	70.0
11	38	36	75.0	80.6	72.2	69.4	83.3	75.0	58.3	69.4
12	64	116	69.0	67.2	53.5	70.7	65.5	56.0	51.7	52.6
13	46	196	83.7	84.2	54.1	84.2	82.7	84.2	55.1	84.2
14	44	112	59.8	66.1	65.2	67.0	61.6	60.7	58.0	67.0
15	76	76	80.3	80.3	64.5	80.3	80.3	80.3	63.2	80.3
Avg.	74.9	97.1	69.4	69.6	60.0	71.0	71.7	69.0	58.3	69.3

of the generated trees and rules reveals that the user has a consistent appetite in pages that contain the word "java."

6   Concluding Remarks

We discussed a non-invasive learning approach to constructing web user profiles. Each user profile has a Page Interest Estimator (PIE) and a Web Access Graph (WAG). The construction of PIE's and WAG's are based on machine learning techniques. Various techniques were proposed to address the different research issues. We also describe how analyzing search results, recommending novel pages, and presenting information can benefit from user profiles.

We demonstrated that our proposed technique for locating multi-word phrases is time and space efficient and the reported preliminary empirical results indicate that our phrase-finding metric compares favorably to existing ones. Our results also show that PIE's can predict, with an average accuracy of 70% (significantly higher than the default 50%), whether a page will be visited by a user. Furthermore, including phrases as features to enrich the common bag-of-words representation of text documents can improve predictive accuracy.

More investigation will be conducted to evaluate and validate our proposed techniques; additional research issues will also be studied. Most machine learning tasks (including text categorization) assume all the features are known beforehand and are applicable to both the training and test sets. However, in PIE learning, words in the documents change over time, and so do the user's preferences. A monolithic classifier/regressor with a fixed set of features will not be able to adapt to these changes. We plan to investigate a multi-classifier approach with a different feature set for each classifier that is learned in a particular time period. The ensemble can then be combined via meta-learning [7].

Besides identifying phrases, other feature construction techniques can be used to enrich the bag-of-words representation. For instance, lexical knowledge from WordNet [24] can be used to group words semantically into synonym sets. Also, we can pay more attention to words in html tags like $< title >, < b >, < i >$...

In our experiments a page that is visited multiple times has only one record in the training or test sets. Removing duplicate instances from the training set is common in machine learning, mainly for efficiency reasons. However, in PIE learning, weighting pages proportional to the number of visits during training, in an effort to emphasize the relevant features in repeatedly visited pages, could enhance performance. Similarly, during testing, pages that are visited multiple times can be weighted accordingly to closely approximate the performance of PIE's.

Due to the high dimensionality of PIE learning (and related text retrieval tasks), feature selection is necessary for many learning algorithms. Besides using expected mutual information for feature selection, domain-specific heuristics like document frequency of features corresponding to interesting pages is beneficial since features identifying interesting pages are more valuable than those associated with uninteresting pages—the first kind is much rarer than the second and we want to find interesting pages, not the uninteresting ones. Also, multi-word phrases are intuitively more valuable than individual words.

Furthermore, our user profiles can be used on the server side as well. They can guide the customization of web pages displayed to the user (e.g., putting frequently accessed links at the top) and recommendation of pages that are of interest to similar users (collaborative filtering).

References

1. C. Apte, F. Damerau, and S. Weiss. Towards language independent automated learning of text categorization models. In *Proc. ACM SIGIR-94*, pages 23–30, 1994. 43, 49
2. M. Balabanovic. An adaptive web page recommendation service. In *Proc. 1st Intl. Conf. Autonomous Agents*, pages 378–385, 1997. 39, 40, 49
3. L. Breiman. Bagging predictors. *Machine Learning*, 24:123–140, 1996. 48
4. L. Breiman. Stacked regressions. *Machine Learning*, 24:41–48, 1996. 48
5. L. Breiman, J. H. Friedman, R. A. Olshen, and C. J. Stone. *Classification and Regression Trees*. Wadsworth, Belmont, CA, 1984. 51
6. P. Chan and S. Stolfo. Meta-learning for multistrategy and parallel learning. In *Proc. Second Intl. Work. Multistrategy Learning*, pages 150–165, 1993. 49
7. P. Chan and S. Stolfo. A comparative evaluation of voting and meta-learning on partitioned data. In *Proc. Twelfth Intl. Conf. Machine Learning*, pages 90–98, 1995. 49, 53

8. P. Chan, S. Stolfo, and D. Wolpert, editors. *Working Notes for the AAAI-96 Workshop on Integrating Multiple Learned Models for Improving and Scaling Machine Learning Algorithms*, Portland, OR, 1996. AAAI. 48

9. L. Chen and K. Sycara. Webmate: A personal agent for browsing and searching. In *Proc. 2nd Intl. Conf. Autonomous Agents*, pages 132–139, 1998. 43

10. W. Cohen. Fast effective rule induction. In *Proc. 12th Intl. Conf. Machine Learning*, pages 115–123, 1995. 51

11. B. Croft, H. Turtle, and D. Lewis. The use of phrases and structure queries in information retrieval. In *Proc. SIGIR-91*, pages 32–45, 1991. 43

12. R. Duda and P. Hart. *Pattern classification and scene analysis*. Wiley, New York, NY, 1973. 51

13. J. Fagan. *Experiments in Automatic Phrase Indexing for Document Retrieval*. PhD thesis, Linguistics, Cornell Univ., Ithaca, NY, 1987. 43

14. W. Frakes and R. Baeza-Yates, editors. *Information retrieval: data structures and algorithms*. Prentice Hall, Englewood Cliffs, NJ, 1992. 45, 51

15. D. Goldberg, D. Nichols, B. Oki, and D. Terry. Using collaborative filtering to weave an information tapestry. *Comm. ACM*, 35(12):61–70, 1992. 49

16. J. Hartigan. *Clustering algorithms*. Wiley, New York, NY, 1975. 47

17. W. Hill, L. Stead, M. Rosenstein, and G. Furnas. Recommending and evaluating choices in a virtual community of use. In *Proc. ACM CHI-95*, pages 194–201, 1995. 50

18. L. Holson. Feeding a frenzy: Why internet investors are still ravenous. New York Times, June 6 1999. 44

19. J. Konstan, B. Miller, D. Maltz, J. Herlocker, L. Gordon, and J. Riedl. GroupLens: Applying collaborative filtering to usenet news. *Comm. ACM*, 40(3):77–87, 1997. 41, 49

20. S. Kullback. *Information Theory and Statistics*. Dover, New York, NY, 1968. 50

21. D. Lewis and W. Gale. A sequential algorithm for training text classifiers. In *Proc. ACM SIGIR-94*, pages 3–12, 1994. 49

22. D. Lewis, R. Schapire, J. Callan, and R. Papka. Training algorithms for linear text classifiers. In *Proc. ACM SIGIR-96*, pages 298–306, 1996. 43

23. H. Lieberman. Letizia: An agent that assits web browsing. In *Proc. IJCAI-95*, 1995. 39, 41, 49

24. G. Miller. WordNet: A lexical database for English. *Comm. ACM*, 38(11):39–41, 1995. 53

25. M. Morita and Y. Shinoda. Information filtering based on user behavior analysis and best match text retrieval. In *Proc. SIGIR-94*, pages 272–281, 1994. 41

26. Netscape. Netscape Mozilla. http://www.mozilla.org/. 42

27. Netscape. Netscape Navigator. http://www.netscape.org/. 41

28. M. Pazzani and D. Billsus. Learning and revising user profiles: The identification of interesting web sites. *Machine Learning*, 27:313–331, 1997. 39

29. M. Pazzani, J. Muramatsu, and D. Billsus. Syskill & Webert: Identifying interesting web sites. In *Proc. AAAI-96*, 1996. 39, 40

30. M. Perkowitz and O. Etzioni. Adaptive web sites: Automatically synthesizing web pages. In *Proc. AAAI-98*, 1998. 47

31. M. Porter. An algorithm for suffix stripping. *Program*, 14(3):130–137, 1980. 45, 51

32. J. R. Quinlan. *C4.5: programs for machine learning*. Morgan Kaufmann, San Mateo, CA, 1993. 40, 43, 51

33. P. Resnick, N. Iacovou, M. Sushak, P. Bergstrom, and J. Riedl. GroupLens: An open architecture for collaborative filtering of netnews. In *Proc. CSCW-94*, 1994. 50

34. C. Van Rijsbergen. *Information Retrieval.* Butterworths, London, 1979. 43

35. R. Rosenfeld. A maximum entropy approach to adaptive statistical language modeling. *Computer, Speech, and Language*, 10, 1996. 43

36. G. Salton. *Automatic Text Processing.* Addison-Wesley, Reading, MA, 1988. 43

37. R. Schapire. The strength of weak learnability. *Machine Learning*, 5:197–226, 1990. 48

38. E. Selberg and O. Etzioni. Multi-service search and comparison using the metacrawler. In *Proc. WWW4*, 1995. 40

39. E. Selberg and O. Etzioni. The metacrawler architecture for resource aggregration on the web. *IEEE Expert*, 12(1):8–14, 1997. 40, 48

40. U. Shardanand and P. Maes. Social information filtering: Algorithms for automating "word of mouth". In *Proc. ACM CHI-95*, pages 210–217, 1995. 50

41. Squid. Squid internet object cache. http://squid.nlanr.net/Squid/. 42

42. R. Stiefelhagen, M. Finke, J. Yang, and A. Waibel. From gaze to focus of attention. In *Proc. Work. Perceptual User Interfaces*, pages 25–30, 1998. 41

43. R. Stiefelhagen, J. Yang, and A. Waibel. Tracking eyes and monitoring eye gaze. In *Proc. Work. Perceptual User Interfaces*, pages 98–100, 1997. 41

44. F. Wall. *Statistical Data Analysis Handbook.* McGraw-Hill, New York, NY, 1986. 50

45. A. Wexelblat and P. Maes. Footprints: Visualizing histories for web browsing.   http://wex.www.media.mit.edu/people/wex/Footprints/footprints1.html, 1997. 46

46. D. Wolpert. Stacked generalization. *Neural Networks*, 5:241–259, 1992. 48

47. Y. Yang. An evaluation of statistical approaches to text categorization. Technical Report CMU-CS-97-127, CMU, Pittsburgh, PA, 1997. 43

48. Y. Yang and J. Pedersen. A comparative study on feature selection in text categorization. In *Proc. Intl. Conf. Machine Learning*, 1997. 51

Data Mining, the Internet, and Privacy

Alan J. Broder

White Oak Technologies, Inc.
Silver Spring, MD 20901 USA
ajb@woti.com

Abstract. This paper addresses the inherent technological conflict between the desire for privacy by World Wide Web users, and the need of Web content providers and advertisers to more fully collect and utilize data about users. As the other papers in this volume illustrate, the Data Mining community has now turned its collective attention towards the Web as a fertile venue for research and development. In doing so, Data Miners have found themselves at the nexus of this conflict.

We present the technical issues regarding privacy from two perspectives. First, from the perspective of the Web user who may be unaware of the degree to which identifying information can be inadvertently disclosed. And second, from the perspective of a Data Miner we consider the extent to which privacy enhancing technologies could substantially invalidate data mining results.

1   Introduction

Recently, there has been increased attention given to the application of traditional Data Mining techniques to the analysis of World Wide Web usage data. Such data is typically obtained from Web server usage logs that provide time-stamped details of a user's retrieval of a site's content. Concurrently, there has been greater public awareness of privacy issues, resulting in several technical solutions intended to protect surfers' privacy.

¿From the Data Miner's perspective, the two most notable impediments to successful application of data mining algorithms have been the growing prevalence of caching proxies and the increasing popularity of anonymizing services. These technologies effectively mask the identity or continuity of Web surfing sessions.

Users, on the other hand, are confronted with a dizzying escalation in the number and variety of techniques that are used to collect ever more detailed profiles of their Internet usage. The impetus behind this flurry of Web mining innovation is clearly commercial - a recent report [1] indicates that the Internet is now regularly used by 40% of Americans and Canadians over the age of 16.

At every level of technical sophistication, Internet users are unable to properly assess the impact that Web technologies will have on their privacy. One recent survey [2] of "heavy Internet users" revealed "considerable confusion" regarding the privacy impact of the often-maligned browser cookies. Some users

B. Masand and M. Spiliopoulou (Eds.): WEBKDD'99, LNAI 1836, pp. 56–73, 2000.
© Springer-Verlag Berlin Heidelberg 2000

appeared to believe (incorrectly) that cookies could be used to automatically transmit personal information about them from their PCs to Web sites. In sharp contrast, others were not aware that cookies could be used to track their online behavior. Indeed, even technically sophisticated users are sharply divided [3] on the extent of the threat posed by cookies.

This paper summarizes the major technologies being used to track Internet users and to mine their behaviors. In Section 2, we describe the basic elements that identify Web users to servers that they visit. In doing so, we consider various types of IP numbering schemes currently and soon to be available, as well as the system used to associate domain names with IP numbers. Next, in Section 3 we briefly examine the types of usage data that are commonly collected by Web servers, as well as the so-called "cookies", or persistent identifiers that are deposited on users' computers in order to maintain state between Web transactions. Then, in Section 4, we review how usage data is typically processed by data mining algorithms.

Section 5 describes the various technologies that can obfuscate the identity or continuity of a Web surfing session. Some of these occur transparently to the end-user, and their privacy-enhancing effect is a mere consequence of desired Web performance enhancements. Other technologies may be employed by users with the explicit intention of increasing their anonymity.

In Section 6, we consider the rise of new Web usage collection techniques that we dub as "Omniscient Observers". Unique in their impact on users' privacy, Omniscient Observers employ instrumented browsers or multi-site cookies to track users' behavior, and sometimes correlate users with separately obtained personal data. Finally, in Section 7, we summarize issues for future Web usage mining research, vis-a-vis increasing demands for consumer privacy protection.

2   Identifying Web Users

2.1   Data Mining Context

Before considering *how* Web users can be identified, it is important to understand *why* Data Miners and marketers wish to obtain identifying data. Traditional Data Miners view the "click-stream" of activity generated by a Web user as just another form of transactions to be mined. Thus, Data Miners focus on identifying the trail of an individual user's web browsing within and across sites so that behavioral patterns can be analyzed and predicted. For these Data Miners, the identity of a particular user may not be particularly relevant. Many of the techniques described in this paper, particularly those in this section, are useful for this purpose of reconstructing a user's behavior, without regard to identity.

At the other extreme, marketers are interested in learning not just *what* a Web user does, but *who* the user is. In other words, marketers aim to develop an increasingly detailed profile of individual users which includes not only their Web surfing habits, but personal details such as name, address, income, and other demographic and psychographic elements. This combination can enable marketers to target online advertising with astonishing accuracy, and to coordinate online messages with messages delivered to users through other one-to-one media such as personalized postal service mail. To accomplish these objectives, Data Miners working on marketing applications also employ the techniques described in this paper. Persistent and global identifiers such as "super cookies" and other Omniscient Observing techniques (see Section 6) allow marketers to capture and profile the browsing habits of users across vast numbers of unrelated web sites. Then, if a user can be persuaded to reveal any element of personally identifying information at a single participating site, her profile can be combined with other personally identifying elements obtained from other sites as well as with her global browsing patterns. This data can then be shared with all cooperating sites. [1]

Finally, a hybrid of the two approaches is also proving to be useful [15]. Reconstructed web browsing sessions can be combined with anonymous demographic attributes such as gender or geographical region. The result is more powerful and accurate predictions of user behavior, and the ability to infer the anonymous demographics of users by examining their web usage patterns.

2.2   Internet Protocol Numbers

The Internet Protocol (IP) number is the fundamental element that identifies a computer on the Internet or on a private Intranet. An IP number is simply a 32-bit number, which is commonly rendered as a group of four "octets" or numbers (corresponding to groups of eight bits) separated by periods. For example, "204.133.231.3", "208.255.151.33", and "63.76.92.81". An IP number effectively constitutes a computer's "address" on the Internet. All transactions, whether they are requests to view a web page, email messages, or remote logins to systems are stamped with the originating and destination IP numbers.

Several worldwide authorities control the allocation of IP numbers to businesses and other organizations. For North and South America, this function is served by ARIN, the American Registry for Internet Numbers [2]. ARIN maintains a searchable database that can be used to convert IP numbers back into an identification of the owning organization. For example, if one observed that IP number 204.133.231.3 was browsing at a Web site, the ARIN database could be consulted to determine that the number is part of a block assigned to Microsoft - Denver.

From a privacy perspective, it is significant to note that IP numbers alone do not identify people, nor do they necessarily identify the organization that requested the allocation of addresses from the IP number authority. At best, IP numbers can identify the computer with which they are associated. But, since IP numbers could be sub-let to other organizations without the authority's

---

[1] In a recent development, it has been alleged by privacy activists that such usage profiling, compiling of personal data, and information sharing is already taking place [31].

[2] See http://www.arin.net/

knowledge, an IP number could be associated with a computer from an entirely unknown organization.

Frequently, there is not even a constant association between IP numbers and specific computers. Rather, an organization controlling a range of IP numbers can assign them dynamically to computers each time a connection is made to the Internet. This is known as dynamic IP numbering, and is necessarily used by Internet Service Providers (ISPs) since the number of subscribers far exceeds the number of IP numbers allocated to each ISP. For an ISP user, this offers an increased degree of anonymity since each time the user connects to the Internet she presents a different IP number persona. Conversely, data miners must contend with the fact that the vast majority of Internet users are currently connected via ISPs that employ dynamic IP numbers. As we discuss in Section 6, much effort is being applied to develop techniques that can tie together the activity of a user at a single computer across many dynamic IP incarnations.

For ease of maintenance, organizations with multiple computers will typically assign a permanent IP number to each computer. Such a scheme is known as static IP numbering, and results in a computer presenting a consistent IP number across all of its Internet activity sessions. When static IP numbering is used for desktop computers, users can be exposed to a greater degree of data mining scrutiny. Section 2.3 illustrates how this problem can be magnified by organizations that publish person-identifying host names associated with their static IP numbers.

Static IP numbering is also currently enjoying a significant surge in prevalence in the consumer ISP market. This is due to the growing popularity and availability of broadband ISP services via cable modem and DSL, many of which distribute static IP numbers to their subscribers. While some broadband ISPs do use dynamic IP, the network connection tends to be "always on", effectively presenting the Internet with a constant IP number over a long period of time. Thus, like corporate users, these early adopters of broadband services may also be at increased risk of privacy compromise.

2.3   Privacy and the Future of IP - IPv6

The rapid growth of the Internet has virtually depleted the available inventory of 32-bit IP numbers. Accordingly, the Internet Engineering Task Force (IETF) has developed a specification (IPv6) for a new generation of 128-bit IP numbers. Privacy advocates were quick to note [4] that the new standard introduced an ominous alternative to dynamically assigned IP numbers employed under the previous IP numbering standard. Using "stateless address autoconfiguration", an Internet user's computer would automatically generate its own 128-bit IP number. Embedded within the IP number is a unique identifier extracted from the computer's network interface card. The threat to privacy of this new standard, so the advocates claimed, would be as significant as the controversial introduction by Intel of unique, software accessible serial numbers in the Pentium III family of processor chips.

IETF's response [5] addresses these concerns, and provides a clear framework for the protection of users' privacy. The IPv6 privacy extensions introduce randomization into the address autoconfiguration process, so that the resulting address can not be directly associated with the originating hardware. In addition, the extension specifies that at least once a day a new IPv6 number is randomly generated, and in a manner that the new number can not be correlated with previous numbers.

In the aftermath of IPv6, it is likely that the challenges for data miners will be more formidable than the current ones posed by widespread use of dynamic IP numbering. From day to day, users will appear in their Internet transactions as associated with uncorrelated, anonymous IP numbers. And, for users of "always on" connections, privacy will be enhanced and data miners thwarted by IP numbers that are guaranteed to change at least once per day.

2.4   The Domain Name System

The Domain Name System (DNS) provides computers and users with a more convenient way to refer to other computers and devices on the Internet. Instead of using IP numbers, users can specify any computer on the Internet with a multi-part hostname, e.g. "ws1.woti.com". Individual top-level domains (such as "woti.com") maintain their own part of the worldwide DNS, providing names for all computers within their purview. When a user specifies an Internet hostname, the DNS software on their computer attempts to locally resolve the name into an IP address. If local DNS servers are unable to resolve the request, the request is passed to servers with successively broader coverage of the Internet, until the appropriate DNS server can be identified.

The DNS also offers a reverse-lookup functionality, which takes an IP number as input and translates it into the corresponding complete hostname. This function is of great interest to data miners, and a potentially significant privacy threat to Internet users. Of course, the worst threat to privacy is if the local system administrators have chosen to name desktop computers after the human user of the system. Our experience with the DNS indicates that while not common, some sites do implement such a policy. As an example, consider the sample names in Table 1. These are some of the people's names that appear as the leftmost component of hostnames found in the publicly accessible access log data from a popular University web site [6]. While some of the names may represent fictional or historical characters, at first glance it appears that many of them may be at least the partial names of actual computer users, and, in combination with the entire hostname, could allow a data miner to identify an actual person in an organization.

Of course, data miners who attempt to use hostnames to identify actual users must remain mindful of the fact that a hostname only identifies a computer. Even if a real person's name is embedded in the hostname, there is no way to know who was actually using the computer when the IP number was observed.

Even when not containing personal identifying information, hostnames provide the data miner with coarse information regarding the hierarchy of organiza-

Table 1. Sample of user names disclosed by DNS

adam-sherwood	andrew-henry	andrew-small	atwood_ken
brian-moores	cbailey	david_pendleton	dgiovanni
djones	hampton_alan	jacki_kratz	john-dibattista
jparker2	jwmorgan	kcook	lauralee-dubois
lcwilson	lmatthews2	morrison	mparker
phall	phillip-platt	rcmatthews	richard-perry
robert-arritt	rramirez	samuel-winchenbach	sathompson
sgreenberg	shirley_essam	wshanney	vanwieren_jack

tions that visit a Web site. This opens the possibility of construction of profiles of topical Web interest at the multinational, corporate, and departmental level.

Finally, analysis of hostnames for a single organization may provide clues as to whether hosts have been assigned dynamic or static IP numbers. As a simple example, hostnames employing mnemonics as the leftmost part of the name are likely to be associated with static IP numbers. Conversely, hostnames containing the words "pop" or "dialin" are likely to be associated with dynamic IP numbers. Clearly, data miners could use more sophisticated analyses of the hostname structure and cardinality to reliably associate successive Internet sessions originating from the same (static) host.

3   Web Access Logs

By now, most are familiar with the use of Web browsing clients such as Netscape or Internet Explorer. A user starts a web browsing session by typing into the browser the Uniform Resource Locator (URL) of the site that he wishes to visit. The browser software connects to the specified web site host computer and requests the specified page, which when returned is displayed on the user's computer screen.

Today, it is rare to find a text-only web page, where all of the displayed content is contained in the single returned page. Rather, most pages are embellished with graphical images, fancy text rendered as imagery, and even sound or music clips. The browser is responsible for retrieving and rendering all of these additional elements. It accomplishes this by parsing the web page source code (usually presented in the Hypertext Markup Language, or HTML), extracting the URLs of embedded elements, retrieving the elements from the host computer, and rendering the elements in the appropriate places on the screen. Some URLs in a web page represent hyperlinks to other pages, served by either the same host or an entirely unrelated host. The browser renders those URLs as highlighted textual or graphical fields where a user may click with a mouse to indicate the next page to be retrieved and viewed.

At the other end of this exchange is the web server software, which receives separate requests for specific textual or graphical page elements and returns them back to the requesting browser client. The web server is not only stateless, it may also be entirely ignorant of the structure of the pages that it serves. Instead, the server relies on the browser client to correctly identify the sequence of URL's that are needed to render a complete page.

```
ip-27.net-242.firstam.com - - [01/Jun/1998:09:41:51 -0700]
"GET / qtl/mountain/yosemite/ HTTP/1.0" 200 16334

ip-27.net-242.firstam.com - - [01/Jun/1998:09:41:51 -0700]
"GET / qtl/gallery/shield5.s.gif HTTP/1.0" 200 22394

ip-27.net-242.firstam.com - - [01/Jun/1998:09:41:51 -0700]
"GET / qtl/gallery/nose1.s.gif HTTP/1.0" 200 17093

ip-27.net-242.firstam.com - - [01/Jun/1998:09:41:51 -0700]
"GET / qtl/Icons/new.gif HTTP/1.0" 200 144

ip-27.net-242.firstam.com - - [01/Jun/1998:09:41:51 -0700]
"GET / qtl/Icons/cr.gif HTTP/1.0" 200 76

ip-27.net-242.firstam.com - - [01/Jun/1998:09:41:51 -0700]
"GET / qtl/Icons/mountain.gif HTTP/1.0" 200 231

ip-27.net-242.firstam.com - - [01/Jun/1998:09:41:51 -0700]
"GET / qtl/Icons/french.gif HTTP/1.0" 200 316
```

Fig. 1. Sample log entries for the display of a single web page

Each time a web server delivers a requested piece of content, a record is made of the transaction. In the default format commonly used by most web servers, a log entry includes the IP number or hostname of the requester, the local date, time, and timezone of the server, the HTTP command that was issued by the client (i.e. browser) to request the content, a status code indicating whether the transfer was successful, and the number of bytes transmitted to the client. Figure 1 illustrates a sequence of log entries from a public web server [6] corresponding to the display of all the elements on a single web page.

3.1   The Referer Field

Other elements may also appear in web server log entries, and may be quite useful to a data miner. One such element is the "referer" (the incorrect spelling of which is acknowledged in the HTTP standard [8]), which indicates the prior web page that the browser was viewing before requesting the current page. By convention, almost all browsers transmit the referer data to the server, which would otherwise be unable to determine that information.

Originally, the referer field was intended to assist web maintainers in identifying web pages that had links to non-existent pages - hardly a privacy concern. Today, however, the referer field is critical to the data mining process. As we describe in the next section, the referer field enables a data miner to reconstruct the path that a user takes through a web site.

```
doegate.doe.gov - - [04/Oct/1999:12:17:12 -0400]
"GET dcrest.html HTTP/1.0" 200 6854
"http://www.askjeeves.com/main/askJeeves.asp?
ask=Lobster+Restaurants+in+DC+Area"

excelsior-716.fuse.net - - [05/Oct/1999:15:29:48 -0400]
"GET history.html HTTP/1.1" 200 8533
"http://ink.yahoo.com/bin/query?p=queen+isabella+of+castille"

cc3b098.navsea.navy.mil - - [07/Oct/1999:11:55:41 -0400]
"GET north.978 HTTP/1.0" 200 10113
"http://ink.yahoo.com/bin/query?p=sympathy+for+lost+of+father+poems"

tcnet11-041.sat.texas.net - - [01/Sep/1999:22:24:04 -0400]
"GET inst.html HTTP/1.1" 200 3546
"http://search.excite.com/search.gw?search=how+electric+ranges+work"
```

Fig. 2. Sample log entries with referrer queries

The referer field can also indicate *why* the user has come to a web site. The web server log extracts in Figure 2 illustrate this point. In each of these examples, the user was previously at a search engine web site, and entered a query searching for pages containing specific key words. When the user selected a choice from the search engine's query result, her browser transmitted to the selected site the entire query string which had become embedded in the referring site's URL.

The privacy implications of the referer data are clear. Indeed, the accepted standard for the HTTP protocol makes special mention of such privacy issues [8]:

> "Note: Because the source of a link may be private information or may reveal an otherwise private information source, it is strongly recommended that the user be able to select whether or not the Referer field is sent. For example, a browser client could have a toggle switch for browsing openly/anonymously, which would respectively enable/disable the sending of Referer and From information."

Yet, of three major browsers currently in use, only the Opera browser [9] implements the RFC's recommendation to allow a user to disable referer transmission. The vendors of other browsers [10,11] do not offer such a feature, though it is interesting to note that the same companies also operate commercial Web portals.

3.2 Cookies

The Hypertext Transfer Protocol (HTTP) defines the standard mechanism for exchanging data between clients (i.e. browsers) and Web servers. HTTP is stateless, meaning that each successive retrieval of a Web page is unconnected to all previous requests. Thus, from the perspective of a Web site operator (and a data miner attempting to mine the site's transactions), it can be difficult to weave together all the transactions for a user into a single session. Commercial sites, in particular, require some form of state so that, for example, the content of a user's shopping cart or the identity of a subscriber may be maintained between transactions.

Cookies [7] were introduced as one solution to this problem of statelessness. When a Web server receives a request for a page of content, it can embed in the header of the returned page a hidden directive instructing the client computer to store the attached identifying data (known as a "cookie") on its local disk, and associate that data with the specified Web page. The next time the user's browser visits the same Web page, or another page within the originating site, the user's browser sends the stored cookie data back to the server along with the request for the page. Unless a user explicitly deletes the cookies from her computer's disk drive, cookies will continue to be re-transmitted to the originating host, even after multiple re-boots of the user's computer.

4   Log Mining Paradigms

The other papers in this volume should be consulted for more detail on how data mining algorithms are applied to mine web access log data. For the purpose of this discussion, it is sufficient to note the common features of many of these techniques:

4.1   Simple Usage Statistics

Web access log data is tabulated to present simple statistics about access patterns. For example, most frequently visited pages, number of accesses by domain and country, traffic by time of day, day of week, etc...

4.2   Reconstruction of Browsing Sessions

The individual page accesses recorded in the site's log are woven together to create a session that details the path a user took through the site. If cookies are collected at the site, then a user's session can be trivially reconstructed by associating all the page accesses requested by a particular user.

In the absence of cookies, but if referer data is available, then the reconstruction can still be accomplished - each web page access is chained to the next one by linking the requested page in one log entry to the referer page in a subsequent entry. In the absence of referer data, it is possible to achieve the same effect by analyzing the topology of the links embedded in the site's HTML content. In both non-cookie approaches, ambiguities can arise when multiple users from a single host computer are simultaneously traversing a web site. In that case, other clues can be employed to untangle the sessions (see [12,13] for a comprehensive treatment).

4.3   Pattern Discovery

User sessions are analyzed to discover deeper knowledge embedded within the logs. Sequential associations predict the most likely link that a user will click on given his prior browsing history. Association rules indicate which parts of a web site are frequently viewed together during a session.

Merging the log data with demographic data can further refine such behavioral predictions. One commercial site [14] reports an accuracy of between 70% - 90% in predicting users' behavior. Sites that require registration obtain personal and demographic data as part of the registration process. Even if some users provide obviously bogus registration data, their demographics can be inferred from existing data by comparing their browsing habits with the habits of users with known demographics [15].

5   Degrees of Anonymity

We have so far presented the interaction of a web browser and server in an idealized form - browser client software makes a request for content, and the web server delivers the content to the requester. In fact, in a typical web content transaction there may be intermediate mechanisms that could obscure the origin or continuity of a web browsing session. Some of these mechanisms are passive, natural side effects of the normal operation of ISPs and the Internet. Other mechanisms are deliberately employed by web users in an attempt to hide their identities while browsing. In either case, this has the effect of increasing the anonymity of web users while frustrating attempts by data miners to analyze and predict their behavior.

This section identifies the most common mechanisms that enhance web user anonymity. Section 6 provides an overview of techniques being deployed by web data miners to defeat attempts at anonymity.

5.1   Caching

Local Caching. In a typical web browsing session, a user may return to the same page several times. For example, a user may frequently return to a favorite home page, or repeatedly press the "back" button to retrace his steps through a site. Instead of incurring the bandwidth to re-request a page that has recently been viewed, modern browser software employs a local cache to store recently viewed content.

Browser clients differ in their implementation of caching policy, though most provide the user with the ability to enable or disable caching, and to force a reload of the content from the target web server. Depending on the aggressiveness of the selected caching policy (i.e. how long the browser retains the cached page), a user can experience a marked improvement in anonymity - once a site's pages have been retrieved and viewed, they may be very infrequently requested for re-transmission from the server. Consequently, data miners may be unable to construct a coherent view of the user's session, since the server is oblivious to much reading and browsing of its content [16].

Similarly, most browsers provide an offline browsing capability, whereby a user specifies web sites to be completely and autonomously downloaded for later viewing while offline. When the complete download is activated, the user's browser leaves a trail of web access log entries that traverses the entire target server. For data mining purposes, such log entries are relatively useless, other than to indicate the downloading client has an interest in some unknown part of the site's content. Later, when the user browses selected parts of the downloaded content offline, no access log entries result at all, forever depriving the data miner of knowledge regarding the user's specific interests.

Caching Proxies. Another level of caching occurs at the corporate or ISP level. Typically, the HTTP requests of users are passed through a proxy server that provides a caching service. ISPs with large user bases enjoy significant bandwidth cost savings by radically reducing the number of retransmission requests for pages from popular web sites. A recent study has determined that as many as 17% of all web users access the Internet through caching proxies [17].

Users of caching proxies obtain a two-fold improvement in anonymity. First, when a proxy receives a URL request that is not currently cached, it initiates an HTTP request for the content using its own IP number, instead of the IP number of the original requester. Thus, to the web server, all users from a proxy-cached ISP appear in access logs to be aliased to the few IP numbers of the ISP's proxy servers. Second, popular sites are highly likely to have their content already cached by ISP's proxies, resulting in most subsequent requests occurring with the server oblivious to the requests.

As AOL is arguably the largest ISP in the world, data miners may find it instructive to examine their stated caching policy [18], which is based on RFC 2068 [8]. Most notable is the complete caching flexibility extended to web servers. Servers can specify on an object-by-object basis whether the content may be cached, and if cached, by what date and time the content must expire. In addition, AOL does not cache dynamically generated web content such as ASP and CGI generated pages. Finally, in the absence of stricter caching guidance from servers, AOL currently guarantees that cached content will be retained for no more than 24 hours.

5.2 Proxies

In addition to the caching service offered by caching proxies, a variety of other proxies are currently in use, each offering its own challenge to the data miner, while offering varying degrees of anonymity enhancement. This section provides an overview of the most popular types of proxies, with references included for more in-depth study.

Firewalls and Routers. Corporations and other institutions frequently employ dedicated systems known as firewalls and routers, commonly combined in a single device. A router serves as the interface between a corporation's internal network (or intranet) and the external Internet, and may provide firewall functions to screen incoming and outgoing IP traffic. Routers can also provide a proxy-like function, by translating IP numbers in outgoing IP requests to the IP number of the router itself. Thus, similar to a caching proxy, all web users behind a corporate router appear in a web server's access logs as originating from a small number of routers' IP numbers. While individual users enjoy improved privacy, data miners can still associate web transactions with the originating organization.

Anonymizing Proxies. An increased level of privacy can be obtained through the use of commercially operated anonymizing proxies such as anonymizer.com. Individuals or corporations establish an account with the proxy operator, and configure their browser to pass all HTTP requests through the proxy. In this configuration, the user is still accessing the Internet through their own ISP. For even greater privacy, anonymous dial-in accounts are available that allow the user to directly access the anonymizing service as their primary ISP.

Commercial anonymizers offer several important privacy benefits over corporate proxies [19]:

Suppression of corporate origin - web access logs and data miners can only observe that web requests originate at the anonymizer. Thus, corporate profiling is not possible.

Interception of cookies and intrusive code - transmission of cookies, in either direction, is prevented, without further action on the part of the user. Invasive Javascript code is automatically eliminated.

Referer elimination - the anonymizer intercepts and deletes referer data from HTTP requests - even if the user's browser doesn't support referer disabling.

Elimination of personal connection - establishment of accounts and payment for services can be done entirely via cash transaction. Even the anonymizer service is thus unable to identify the user of an account.

Randomizing Proxies. The Crowds [20] system offers its participants mathematically provable privacy. Crowds is, in essence, a large pool of cooperating proxy servers. When a user of a member of a Crowd issues an HTTP request through her browser, the request is forwarded to the proxy of a random member of the Crowd. The HTTP request is repeatedly relayed through random proxies within the Crowd until a random choice is made to route the HTTP request directly to the specified web server. When the requested content is returned to the Crowd exit point, the data is relayed back along the original randomized path until it reaches the originator.

The privacy property of a Crowd derives from the use of random selection to decide whether to forward a request to another member of the Crowd, or to send the request on to the specified web server. Clearly, at any point in the Crowd relay path a Crowd member computer can not determine whether the incoming request originated from the predecessor in the path, or whether the predecessor was just relaying a request from another Crowd member.[3]

Crowds can be quite confusing to the data miner who may even be completely unaware that Crowds proxies are being employed. Indeed, the HTTP requests logged at the server may appear as if they are originating from a single computer; and, there is provably no way to determine who is the actual originator of the browsing session.

Crowds does not currently enjoy widespread acceptance, possibly due to the need for stable high bandwidth connections for Crowds members. As broadband technology continues to gain mass-market penetration, we expect that Crowds and similar technologies [21] will enjoy a concomitant growth in availability. Due to the mathematically robust nature of Crowds' privacy, this development will bode well for Internet users, and ill for web data miners.

6   Omniscient Observers

As the previous sections demonstrate, data miners are continually stymied by the myriad of ways in which users' web identities and activities are accidentally or intentionally hidden:

- IP numbers and cookies are too volatile;
- Caching and proxies obscure session continuity;
- Access logs provide at best a myopic view of a user's activity at just a single web site.

This section examines several new approaches that have been developed that appear to address these shortcomings. This class of new techniques, which we have dubbed "Omniscient Observers", is indeed powerful, and in many cases could theoretically provide to the data miner a comprehensive record of all or most of a user's web browsing, even across many unrelated web sites.

In examining these technologies, it is crucial to distinguish between what is theoretically possible and what the wielders of the technology have pledged to the public regarding how the collected data will be used. Understanding the theoretical capability of Omniscient Observer technologies exposes the potential risk to web users' privacy if the technologies were misused, and clarifies the need for explicit disclosure and strict enforcement of Omniscient Observers' privacy policies.

---

[3] Subsequent URLs requested by the user are passed through the Crowd via the same random path that was originally selected. Because of this, web access logs will record a session of requests coming from the exit-point member of the crowd. Superficially, this might seem to offer less anonymity then a path that is randomly constructed for each HTTP request. In fact, it can be demonstrated to the contrary that completely re-randomizing the Crowds path for each request can actually subject the originator to a "triangulation" attack whereby the origin of the requests may ultimately be discerned.

6.1   Cookies and Banner Advertising

Section 2.4 describes how cookies are used by web sites to maintain continuity of a user's browsing session within the site. Early in the definition of standards for cookies under HTTP, it was understood that a major threat to user's privacy would be created if cookies could be set and read back across many different sites. Thus, RFC 2109 [7] states:

> "To prevent possible security or privacy violations, a user agent rejects a cookie (shall not store its information) if any of the following is true: ... The value for the request-host does not domain-match the Domain attribute."

In other words, RFC 2109 specifies that web browser software will only accept cookies that originate from the same host as the domain specified within the cookie. Similarly, when a user's browser later requests content from the same site, the browser software will only transmit the cookie to the server if the domain of the server matches the domain of the original transmitter of the cookie.

Subsequent developments in web content delivery technology have heightened the specter of a cookie privacy threat by exploiting a loophole in the RFC 2109 specification. Specifically, RFC 2109 requires that the domain of a cookie must match the domain of the server delivering the cookie. It does not, however, require that the domain of all sub-elements displayed on a page, such as GIF images and their cookies, must match the domain of the server that delivered the base HTML page.

The first line of advertising on the web currently appears as a hyperlink associated with a small, standard-sized GIF image, known in the trade as a "banner advertisement". Today, a few large companies (e.g. DoubleClick.net [22]) manage and deliver most banner advertising on the web from centralized servers. When a user visits a web site, the site returns the HTML web page to the browser along with any site-specific cookies. Along with the usual links to GIF images, the HTML page can also contain a link to request a GIF image from the centralized advertising service's banner ad server. The ad server returns a selected advertisement GIF, along with its own cookie, which happens to be legitimately associated with the domain of the ad server.

Advertising servers' cookies thus transcend the domains of all the servers that carry their advertising (i.e. they are Omniscient Observers). When a web user subsequently visits any site carrying a banner ad, the stored cookie is returned to the advertising server, along with the URL of the site at which the ad was displayed. In this way, advertising servers are able to collect, and data miners could mine, a very comprehensive list of all URLs visited by a browser.

6.2   Super Cookies

Omniscient Observers that augment their cookies with Java or JavaScript ("Super Cookies") code can obtain even more detailed data. As of this writing, one of many such systems, the HitBox system (www.hitbox.com), was claiming to have instrumented over 353,000 web sites and was logging usage data across all those sites for over 55 million visitors per day. It is instructive to examine the JavaScript-augmented HTML source code of sample health-oriented [23] and career-oriented [24] web sites subscribing to HitBox, revealing the following advantages of Super Cookies above and beyond traditional cookies:

Guaranteed referrer transmittal - The referrer is transmitted as part of the generated banner URL, even if the browser or server is not configured to record the referrer.

Local time transmittal - The local time in hours is transmitted, presumably to allow the Hitbox server to derive the time zone in which the user is located. In theory, this information could be combined with minimal additional identifying information to further refine the user's location or identity.

Defeat of caching - The access of every page is recorded by the HitBox server (but not necessarily the site's own web server) even if the page is cached by a caching proxy or by a browser cache. This is accomplished by forming the HitBox banner request URL in the form of a CGI request for dynamic content - almost all known caching systems will pass CGI requests directly to the HTTP server instead of attempting to transparently serve the request from cache.

Banner invisibility - Hitbox subscribers who pay an additional fee are licensed to use the Hitbox super cookie technology but receive ad banners that are but one pixel by one pixel - effectively invisible. Even the most technically savvy users may thus be unaware that a third party is setting and receiving cookies across the many sites that they browse.

6.3 Instrumented Browsers

Several firms offer popular browser add-ons that augment the functionality and appearance of conventional browsers. As part of their enhanced functionality, the add-ons instrument the underlying browsers to transmit certain web usage data back to a central database. Working together, the add-on and the database qualify for the Omniscient Observer label, since they theoretically enable the system operator to observe a user's web usage habits across many web sites. Nonetheless, virtually every system also offers an explicit privacy policy that precludes collection and/or analysis of individual's activities, stating that the data is processed only in the "aggregate".

For example, the NeoPlanet (www.neoplanet.com) browser functions as an add-on to Internet Explorer, adding easy-to-use "channels" that organize web content and that can be customized and shared among users. NeoPlanet's privacy policy acknowledges the ability to track both channel usage as well as the use of pre-determined URL's, but asserts that "NeoPlanet does not track individual user's surfing activities" [25].

The Alexa system (www.alexa.com) is available as an add-on to Internet Explorer, and is also available as the built-in "What's Related" feature of Netscape

Navigator. One feature of Alexa continuously displays suggested web sites that contain material related to the URL currently being viewed in the browser. Presumably, this is implemented by the Alexa add-in transmitting each URL back to the central server, so that the server can return a list of related URLs. Clearly, as a side-effect of this process, the Alexa system receives a comprehensive stream of all the URLs visited by a particular browser. However, Alexa also asserts that

> "When using the service, we collect information on Web usage which remains anonymous. This information is used in the aggregate to cluster related Web sites together." [26]

These are but two examples of many such browser instrumentation add-ons (see also [27,28] for a recent interesting controversy). By capturing the URL stream at the browser and transmitting it to a central server, a powerfully Omniscient Observer results. The pledge that the data will only be analyzed in the aggregate is of some solace to those desiring Internet privacy. Yet, because the captured data is actually of higher quality and comprehensiveness than single-site web logs, some critics have asserted that future changes in privacy policies could facilitate a rather straightforward correlation with personally identifying information.

6.4   ISPs and Online Services

The revenue streams of traditional ISPs and Online Service providers (such as AOL) depend on the confidence that the public places in their ability and commitment to protect users' privacy. Yet, by their very nature, ISPs are the carrier through which all of a user's web interaction passes. Recognizing this, new ISPs are being formed which employ a new business model - trading a loss of some web privacy in exchange for free Internet access. For example, the NetZero [29] service openly acknowledges that it will exploit its Omniscient Observer status:

> "NetZero also tracks subscribers' traffic patterns throughout their online session, including which Web sites a subscriber visits. NetZero uses the information it collects to display advertisements and content that may be of interest to subscribers."

NetZero also admits that it uses personal demographic and psychographic data provided at registration time "to tailor a subscriber's experience of our service, such as by displaying advertisements and content that might be of interest to the subscriber." Despite the obvious privacy implications, many Internet users appear willing to trade their privagcy for free access - as of this writing NetZero claims to have registered two million users [30].

7   Future Considerations

This paper has provided an overview of the privacy and free-market dynamics that are energizing the evolution of web mining capabilities. Marketers and Web data miners are striving to increase the quality, richness, and continuity of usage data via innovative uses of Web standards and technologies. Consequently, users are provided with a compelling range of cost-benefit choices: cookies allow web sites to provide customized experiences, but at the cost of anonymity; browser add-ons add essential functionality, yet transmit the URL stream to a central third party; free ISPs can save hundreds of dollars - but at the cost of an overbearing degree of custom-targeted advertising.

Users who are provided with a clear advance explanation of the potential risks of these technologies can make an informed decision as to the cost-benefit tradeoff. Unfortunately, what little research exists tends to indicate that users are in fact not making informed choices. Internet users are still divided as to the true privacy impact of the simplest of all techniques: site-specific cookies. What then of the many other more sophisticated user-tracking techniques that we have illustrated herein?

How commonly do users actually read privacy policies of the sites and services that they use? When users do read the privacy disclosures, do they fully understand the privacy exposure that they are accepting? And, for covert techniques such as Super Cookies, and multi-site ad banners, how can a user even be aware that a privacy threat actually exists?

As Data Miners continue to develop new techniques for Web session tracking, reconstruction, and mining, they will inevitably be faced with the conflicting needs for data accuracy and user privacy. Increasingly sophisticated Web users may make growing use of anonymizing technologies for which Data Miners will have to compensate. Marketers who drive much of the need for detailed personal data will continue to leverage the products of Data Mining research to produce ever more accurate profiles and behavioral predictions. Yet, the practices of these very marketers will come under increasing scrutiny by consumers and regulatory bodies. Future Data Mining techniques that can accurately model user behavior while protecting user privacy may be one solution to this dilemma.

References

1. The Industry Standard: http://www.thestandard.com/powerpoint/ 062899webstats.ppt (1999) 56
2. Cranor , L., Reagle, J., Ackerman, M.: Beyond Concern: Understanding Net Users' Attitudes About Online Privacy. AT&T Labs-Research Technical Report TR 99.4.3 http://www.research.att.com/library/trs/TRs/99/99.4/99.4.3/report. htm (1999) 56
3. Slashdot: Cookies, Ad Banners, and Privacy. http://slashdot.org/article.pl?sid=99/10/22/0249212&mode=thread 57
4. Frezza, B.: Where's All The Outrage About The IPv6 Privacy Threat? Internet Week, Issue 783 http://www.techweb.com/se/directlink.cgi?INW19991004S0052 (1999) 59
5. Narten, T., Draves, R.: Privacy Extensions for Stateless Address Autoconfiguration in IPv6. ftp://ftp.isi.edu/internet-drafts/draft-ietf-ipngwg-addrconf- privacy-01.txt (1999) 60

6. Department of Electrical Engineering and Computer Sciences University of California, Berkeley : CS Access Log Files. http://www.cs.berkeley.edu/logs/   60, 62
7. Kristol, D., Montulli, L.: RFC 2109 - HTTP State Management Mechanism. http://www.cis.ohio-state.edu/htbin/rfc/rfc2109.html (1999) 64, 69
8. Fielding, R., Gettys, J., Mogul, J., Frystyk, H., Berners- Lee, T. RFC 2068 - Hypertext Transfer Protocol - HTTP/1.1. http://www.cis.ohio-state.edu/htbin/rfc/rfc2068.html (1997) 62, 63, 66
9. Opera Software Features. http://www.opera.com/features.html 63
10. Netscape Navigator browser software. http://home.netscape.com/ 63
11. Internet Explorer 5.0 Home Page. http://www.microsoft.com/windows/ie /default.htm 63
12. Wu, K., Yu, P., Ballman, A.: SpeedTracer: A Web usage mining and analysis tool. IBM Systems Journal, Vol 37, No. 1 (1997) 64
13. Cooley, R., Mobasher, B., Srivastava, J.: Data Preparation for Mining World Wide Web Browsing Patterns. Journal of Knowledge and Information Systems, Vol. 1, No. 1 (1999) 64
14. CMP Tech Web: Web Data - Tapping The Pipeline. http://www.planetit.com/techcenters/docs/Storage/News/PIT19990319S 0023/3 (1999) 65
15. Murray, D., Durrell, K: Inferring Demographic Attributes of Anonymous Internet Users. (in this volume) 58, 65
16. Pitkow, J.: In Search of Reliable Usage Data on the WWW. Proceedings of the Sixth International WWW Conference (1997) 66
17. Thompson, M: Making 10 Million Surfers Look Like 8 Million: Proxy servers undercount Web traffic. http://www.thestandard.com/metrics /display/0,2149,992,00.html 66
18. AOL Webmaster Info. http://webmaster.info.aol.com/ 66
19. Anonymizer FAQ. https://www.anonymizer.com/3.0/help/faq.cgi 67
20. Reiter, M., Rubin, A.: Anonymous Web Transactions with Crowds. Communications of the ACM, Vol 42. No 2., Page 32 67
21. Goldschlag, D., Reed, M., Syverson, P.: Onion Routing for Anonymous and Private Internet Connections. Communications of the ACM, Vol 42. No 2., Page 39 68
22. Double Click Network Privacy Policy. http://www.doubleclick.net/privacy_policy/ 69
23. http://www.healingwell.com/ HealingWell.com - Guide to Diseases, Disorders and Chronic Illness 70
24. Headhunter.Net - This is the way to work. http://www.headhunter.net/ 70
25. NeoPlanet Privacy Statement. http://www.neoplanet.com/user_central/ privacy/index.html 70
26. Alexa Privacy Policy. http://www.alexa.com/whatisalexa/privacy_policy.html 71
27. Comet Systems - The Cursor Changing People. http://www.cometsystems.com/ 71
28. Bridis, T: Cursor Software Monitors Customers. Associated Press, http://dailynews.yahoo.com/h/ap/19991129/tc/internet_privacy_1.html l 71
29. Privacy Statement for the NetZero Service. http://www.netzero.com/join /service_privacy.html 71
30. NetZero Reports First-Quarter Results. http://www.netzero.net/company /19991025quarter.html 71
31. Rodger, W.: Activists charge DoubleClick double cross. http://www.usatoday.com/life/cyber/tech/cth211.htm 58

User-Driven Navigation Pattern Discovery from Internet Data*

Matthias Baumgarten[1], Alex G. Büchner[1], Sarabjot S. Anand[2],
Maurice D. Mulvenna[3], and John G. Hughes[1]

[1] Northern Ireland Knowledge Engineering Laboratory, University of Ulster
{m.baumgarten,ag.buchner,jg.hughes}@ulst.ac.uk
[2] School of Information and Software Engineering, University of Ulster
ss.anand@ulst.ac.uk
[3] MINEit Software Ltd, Faculty of Informatics, University of Ulster
maurice@mineit.com

Abstract. Managers of electronic commerce sites need to learn as much as possible about their customers and those browsing their virtual premises, in order to maximise the return on marketing expenditure. The discovery of marketing related navigation patterns requires the development of data mining algorithms capable of the discovery of sequential access patterns from web logs. This paper introduces a new algorithm called M*i*DAS that extends traditional sequence discovery with a wide range of web-specific features. Domain knowledge is described as flexible navigation templates that can specify generic navigational behaviour of interest, network structures for the capture of web site topologies, concept hierarchies and syntactic constraints. Unlike existing approaches M*i*DAS supports sequence discovery from multidimensional data, which allows the detection of sequences across monitored attributes, such as URLs and http referrers. Three methods for pruning the sequences, resulting in three different types of navigational behaviour are presented. The experimental evaluation has shown promising results in terms of functionality as well as scalability.

1 Introduction

Direct marketing is the process of identifying likely buyers of products or services and promoting them accordingly [12]. The difference between traditional and electronic commerce marketing is the availability of more detailed data, the necessity for the incorporation of web marketing-specific domain knowledge, the potential application of more sophisticated direct marketing strategies, and, thus, the

---

* This research has partly been funded by the ESPRIT project N° 26749 (MIMIC — Mining the Internet for Marketing IntelligenCe).

B. Masand and M. Spiliopoulou (Eds.): WEBKDD'99, LNAI 1836, pp. 74-91, 2000.

requirement for more assorted data mining goals [16]. A key to discovering marketing intelligence in electronic businesses is that of finding navigational patterns, which can be used for online promotion and personalisation activities. The objective of this paper is to describe a novel method for discovering marketing-driven navigation patterns from Internet log files.

The outline of the paper is as follows. In Section 2, the structure and content of web log files is described, which is accomplished by web-specific domain knowledge, namely navigation templates, topology networks, concept hierarchies and syntactic constraints. In Section 3, the algorithmic navigation pattern discovery, which has been termed M*i*DAS (Mining Internet Data for Associative Sequences) is described. In Section 4, a case study is presented, which demonstrates the application of the proposed research. In Section 5, the experimental evaluation of M*i*DAS is presented, which includes complexity measurements, as well as performance results. In Section 6, related work is evaluated, before Section 7 concludes with a summary of contributions and the outline of further work.

2   Web Data and Domain Knowledge

This section describes the structure and content of web log files as well as different types of supported web-specific domain knowledge, which include syntactic constraints, navigation templates, network topologies and concept hierarchies.

2.1   Web Log Files

The data available in web environments is three-fold and includes server data in the form of log files, web meta data representing the structure of a web site, and marketing transaction information, which depends on the products and services provided. For the purpose of this paper it is assumed that goal-orientated materialised views have been created *a priori*, for instance, as part of a web log data warehouse [6]. Thus, this paper concentrates on the core activity of discovering navigational patterns in the form of web-specific sequences from pre-processed Internet log files.

The data input for M*i*DAS is a set of navigations sorted by primary and secondary key. The structure of a log file consists of a primary key (for instance, session id, customer id, cookie id, etc.), a secondary key (date and time related information, such as login time), and a sequence of hits, which holds the actual data values (for example, URLs or http referrers). Web meta data is treated as domain knowledge by M*i*DAS rather than input data (see Section 2.2.3).

Definition 1. A log file L is defined as a sequence of navigations $L = <N_1, N_2, N_3, ...>$. Each N_i is of the form (a, b, H), a representing the primary key, b the secondary key, and H a non-empty sequence $H_i = <h_1, h_2, h_3, ...>$, where each h_i is a hit which represents a single web page access.

Table 1 below shows five records of an example log file that is used throughout the paper for demonstration purposes.

Table 1 Example Log Data

Host	Date / Time	Referrer	Hit	Hit	Hit
1	01/06/99 16:48:27	Ecom.infm.ulst.ac.uk/	/	/products	/products-emw
1	12/06/99 14:08:43	Kdnuggets.com/sift/t-textweb.html	/products-emw	/products	/products-capri
2	24/05/99 06:34:24	Kdnuggets.com/solutions/internet-mining.html	/	/company	
3	03/06/99 12:14:20	Kdnuggets.com/sift/t-textweb.html	/products-emw	/products	/products-capri
3	03/06/99 15:47:03	Kdnuggets.com/solutions/internet-mining.html	/	/company	

In Table 1, the primary key is the host identifier and the secondary key is the navigation session, which is identified by the Date/Time field. The host identifier may be an IP address, cookie, login name or any other key that identifies an individual as the browser of the web site.

2.2   Domain Knowledge Specification

In order to discover web-specific sequential patterns, domain knowledge may be incorporated with the objective to constrain the search space of the algorithm, reduce the quantity of patterns discovered and increase the quality of the discovered patterns [2]. For the purpose of discovering marketing intelligence from Internet log files, four web-specific types of domain knowledge are supported, namely syntactic constraints, navigation templates, topology networks, and concept hierarchies.

2.2.1   Syntactic Constraints

Syntactic constraints for M*i*DAS are expressed as the threshold sextuple $\tau = (\sigma, \delta, \lambda^-, \lambda^+, \gamma^-, \gamma^+)$. $\sigma \in [0,1]$ represents the minimum support and $\delta \in [0,1]$ the minimum confidence, which are identical to their counterparts in traditional association and sequence discovery algorithms. λ^- and λ^+ specify the minimum and maximum length of a sequence, respectively. Through this mechanism, it is possible to eliminate shallow navigational patterns of non-active users, as well as their opposite. γ^- and γ^+ represent the minimum and maximum time gap between two hits, which facilitates the extirpation of search robots (with a very small gap) and also enables a limit to be set for the time a browser spends on one page.

2.2.2   Navigation Templates

In order to perform goal-driven navigation pattern discovery it is expected that a virtual shopper has passed through a particular page or a set of pages. This can include start, end, as well as middle pages. A typical start locator is the home page; a typical middle page of a site is a URL providing information about a special marketing campaign; and a regularly specified end page, where a purchase can be finalised. For simplification, all three constructs are accumulated to *navigation templates*, where a template consists of constants, wildcards, and predicates restricting the permissible values of the wildcards.

Definition 2. A navigation template T is a generalised navigation of a web site, defined as $T = \{t_1, t_2, t_3, ...\}$. Each t_i is a non-empty sequence of hits h_i, where each item h_k is either a page or a placeholder taken from $\{*, ?\}$. The placeholders * and ? have the same semantics as in classic string matching.

An example here illustrates the specified additions to standard sequences, in order to specify regular expression constraints in the form of navigation templates. Imagine the analysis of a marketing campaign within an online bookstore, introducing reduced gifts (line 1, item 3). Only those customers who have navigated through the site's home page (line 1, item 1) are of interest, and only transactions that have led to purchases are to be considered (line1, item 5) at the same or at a different visit. Furthermore, the standard special offers are to be excluded from the analysis (lines 2-4). This navigation template is shown in Fig. 1.

<table>
<tr><td colspan="2">[

(1) <index.htm | * | /offers/gifts.htm ; * , purchase.htm | ?>
(2) ^<* ; offers/reduced.htm ; *>
(3) ^<* ; offers/junk.htm ; *>

(4) ^<? ; offers/2ndhand.htm ; *>

]</td></tr>
</table>

		same visit	, across visits	; either same or across visit
	* wildcard	? place holder	
		^ negation	

Fig. 1. Example Navigation Template

Consider the following extract from a log file:

Host	Date / Time	Hit	Hit	Hit
1	01/06/99 16:48:27	/index.htm	offers/gifts.htm	
1	12/06/99 14:08:43	purchase.htm	offers/gifts.htm	
2	24/05/99 06:34:24	/index.htm	offers/gifts.htm	purchase.htm
3	03/06/99 12:14:20	/index.htm	offers/junk.htm	
3	03/06/99 15:47:03	purchase.htm		

Given the navigation template in Figure 1, only the navigation by Host 1 will satisfy this template. Host 2 also carries out a similar navigation, however, as the purchase is undertaken on the same visit as the hit on 'offers/gifts.htm' this navigation violates the template that specifically specifies that the purchase must be in a separate visit by using the comma. The use of the semi-colon in (1), before the asterisk, implies that the browser may navigate the web site on a number of separate visits between the visit in which he/she visits the 'offers/gifts.htm' page and the visit to purchase. Additionally he/she may carry on viewing pages on the site in the same visit as the one in which he/she visited the 'offers/gifts.htm' page. Host 3 satisfies the negation term, (3), in the template and therefore his/her navigation does not match the template.

The given example makes use of the URL document name only, and thus the field name does not have to be specified. However, it is also possible to handle more than one field in navigation templates. For instance, when tracking visitors who have come from a specific site, say a popular search engine at which a banner ad has been placed, the template and the discovery algorithm must distinguish between URL names and http referrers. MiDAS supports both mechanisms: the formal specification of navigation templates, which include field names, is omitted for simplicity.

2.2.3   Network Topologies

The second type of taxonomical domain knowledge is that of *network* structures, which is useful when the topology of web site or only a sub-network of a large site has to be used for the discovery of knowledge. Within MiDAS it is used to include or exclude certain parts of a web site, as shown in Fig. 2.

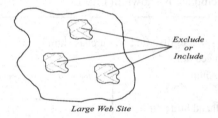

Large Web Site

Fig. 2. Usage of Network Domain Knowledge

Definition 3. A network $w(N, E)$ is a directed, connected, cyclic graph, which is defined by a set of nodes $N = \{n_1, n_2, n_3, ...\}$ and connecting edges $E = \{e_1, e_2, e_3, ...\}$. Each node n_i represents a web page and $e_{ij} = <n_i, n_j>$ represents the existence of a hyperlink from page n_i to n_j.

In general, a network can be represented as a set of navigational patterns. The reason for distinguishing these two types of domain knowledge is that navigational templates are goal dependent and may change with each run of MiDAS. A network on the other hand is based on the structure of the web site and so is less likely to change with the same frequency. An example network of a bookstore is shown graphically in Fig. 3(a), where words in small caps describe pages that can be reached from any other page on the site. The textual counterpart is depicted in Fig. 3(b), where an asterisk denotes the set of all pages.

In addition to creating network topologies manually, which is only feasible in relatively small sites, two methods exists for creating the structure automatically. The first uses spider technology, which allows the discovery of all pages in an entire site, while the second derives the topology from log files themselves, based on all site internal http referrers – URL document name links [6]. The drawback of this approach is that only those links and pages are found which have been navigated through by at least a user-specified number of visitors.

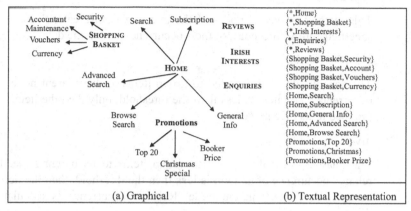

| (a) Graphical | (b) Textual Representation |

Fig. 3. Example Network Topology

The advantage of this mechanism is that high hit pages, links and areas, as well as strong intra-topology connections can be found, which allows the discovery of sub-networks, as depicted in Fig. 2. Thus, we favour the log file based approach, which has proven sufficient in data mining exercises (see also case study in Section 4).

2.2.4   Concept Hierarchies

The third type of taxonomical domain knowledge that is supported is *concept hierarchies* [11].

Definition 4. A concept hierarchy is a tree with each level of non-leaf nodes, l_i, representing a generalised concept of the previous level, l_{i-1}. The leaf nodes, represented in level l_0 represent individual values of the attribute appearing within the log file. Nodes in level l_i are referred to as the parents of the nodes that they are connected to in level l_{i-1}.

In addition to marketing-related hierarchies, such as product categorisations or customer locations, a typical application is the topological organisation of Internet domain levels [6]. An example concept hierarchy is depicted in Fig. 4.

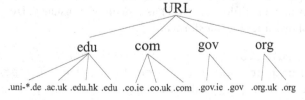

Fig. 4. Example Concept Hierarchy

The usage of multi-level concept hierarchies within M*i*DAS is based on concept levels, absolute or relative threshold values. These methods are described below.

- Concept Levels

    This method groups all nodes of the tree to a level greater than the user-specified cut-off threshold for their occurrence within the data.

- Absolute Threshold

    The absolute threshold is used to group items to their parent node. If the occurrence of an item is less then the threshold, only then the item will be grouped to its parent node.

- Relative Threshold

    The relative threshold is used to group items to its parent node. If the relative occurrence of an item is less then the threshold, then the item will be grouped to their parent node. Relative occurrence is calculated as follows.

$$relative\ occurence = \frac{occurrence\ of\ the\ current\ item*100}{\sum occurrence\ of\ all\ items\ at\ the\ same\ level}$$

3   Navigation Pattern Discovery

This section describes the three stages of the M*i*DAS algorithm and defines the different navigation types that can be discovered, which are represented as contained in relationships.

3.1   Problem Statement and Notation

Given a log file that represents customer interactions on a web site, the objective is to discover navigation patterns in the form of sequences, using user-defined domain knowledge.

The log file L (as specified in Definition 1) is partitioned into $P_1, P_2, P_3,...$, where each partition can be uniquely identified by the primary key (Host, in example log file in Table 1). A partition is converted into a sequence S, using the secondary key (Date/Time, in example log file in Table 1) as a pivot. For instance, Host 1 in Table 1 would look as follows after the transformation:

```
<ecom.infm.ulst.ac.uk | / | /products | /products-
emw , kdnuggets.com/sift/t-textweb.html | /product-
emw | /products | /products-capri>
```

A navigational pattern is treated as a sequence and thus the two terms are used interchangeably. A sequence is defined as follows.

Definition 5. A sequence $S = \langle s_1, s_2, s_3, ... \rangle$, where each s_i represents a non-empty sub-sequence $\langle h_1\ h_2\ h_2, ... \rangle$, each h_i being an hit and each sub-sequence being a session/visit. A sequence of n sub sequences is called an *n-sequence*, while a sub-sequence consisting of m hits is called an *m-sub-sequence*.

	MiDAS ← Sorted log file L, thresholds $\tau(\sigma, \delta, \lambda^-, \lambda^+, \gamma^-, \gamma^+)$, domain knowledge $K(T, W, c)$	
A priori	$M = \{$all 1-sequences$\}$	// Input data preparation
	Map c onto M	// Concept Hierarchies
	$L_T = \{l_1, l_2, l_3 ...\}$	// Data transformation (log file)
Discovery	**Foreach** l_i **in** L_T **do** // Build pattern tree P for each 1-sequence	
	Foreach *1-sequence* **in** M **do**	
	$P_{1\text{-}sequence} := \text{Update}(l_i, P_{1\text{-}sequence})$ // Increase frequency counter if	
	hit $h \in l_i$ exists, add h to P	
	otherwise	
	End	
	End	
	Foreach P_i	
	Read all *n-sequences*, with σ from P_i and append them to answer set U	
	End	
A posteriori	Filter out all sequences in U where $u_i \in T$ and $u_i \in W$) // Navigation Templates & Network Topology	
	Delete all sequences in U which are not maximal and satisfy $\delta, \lambda^-, \lambda^+, \gamma^-, \gamma^+$ // Pruning	
	MiDAS → U	

Fig. 5. The MiDAS Algorithm

3.2   The MiDAS Algorithm

The MiDAS algorithm consists of three major phases, which are described in the following sub-sections. The algorithm itself is shown in Fig. 5.

3.2.1   A Priori Phase

The first step of the *a priori* phase is the input data preparation, which consists of data reduction and data type substitution. The former counts the number of all item occurrences (hits) in L for each of the individual web pages and excludes the hits, which have a support less than σ. The latter replaces all hits in L with a hit identifier h_i. Let M be the set of all hits. Each $h_i \in M$ represents a unique hit and its frequency. Each h_i is also the basis for the pattern tree construction phase, discussed later. Concept hierarchies defined on the web pages are used during data reduction using either concept level generalisation, absolute threshold or relative threshold generalisations. This further reduces the number of unique hits (see [11] for generation and refinement of concept hierarchies).

In the data transformation phase a new database L_T is created that includes only the hit identifiers for the values that are included in M. The database includes the primary and secondary key, as provided by the original log file. The transformed hits in L_T do not contain any field names, since this information is represented through hit identifiers, which is shown in the Table below.

Table 2 Example Log Data

Host	Date / Time	Referrer	Hit	Hit	Hit
1	01/06/99 16:48:27	1	4	6	5
1	12/06/99 14:08:43	2	5	6	8
2	24/05/99 06:34:24	3	4	7	
3	03/06/99 12:14:20	2	5	6	8
3	03/06/99 15:47:03	3	4	7	

3.2.2   Discovery Phase

The pattern tree is the core element of MiDAS used to discover sequences of hits. Simplified, the pattern tree is a directed, acyclic graph, where a node contains the properties of a hit and the arcs represent the relationship between two nodes. The depth d of a node also represents the position of a hit in an n-sequence. There exist two different link types for describing the relationships between two nodes. *Sequence arcs* connect two nodes that go across sub-sequences (multiple visits on a web site), and *tuple arcs*, which connect two nodes that are in the same sub-sequence (same visit). An example abstract pattern tree is shown in Fig. 6.

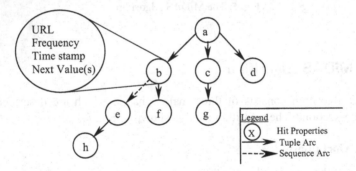

Fig. 6. Abstract Pattern Tree

As shown in Fig. 5 a pattern tree P is created for each 1-sequence $\in M$. Since the root node is always the first item in a sequence, which is stored in the current tree, it is used as anchor. For every hit $\in l_i$ that occurs after the anchor a hit node is created and then linked to their parent node or updated if already in existence. Due to the fact that MiDAS needs one pass over the database for creating each new tree level, the above process will loop until no new hit is found in each $l_i \in L$. Finally, a set of sequences U is created that satisfies the syntactic constraints defined in Section 2.2.

3.2.3   A Posteriori Phase

The first step in the *a posteriori* phase is to filter out all sequences that do not fulfil the criteria laid out in the specified navigation templates T and the topology network W.

The pruning phase is the last stage of the M*i*DAS algorithm. It removes all sequences that are not *maximal*.

Definition 6. In a set of sequences Q, a sequence Q_i is *maximal* if Q_i is not *contained* in any other sequence Q_j, that is $Q_i \not\prec Q_j$.

M*i*DAS provides three different methods to decide when a sequence Q_i is contained in another sequence Q_j. It produces different kinds of result sequences, which can be *associative, partial* or *full*.

To describe the different pruning methods, a set of input sequences $U = \{Q_1, Q_2, Q_3, \ldots\}$ is defined. Each Q_i is of the form $< H_1^i\ H_2^i\ H_3^i\ \ldots >$, where each H_j^i is a sub-sequence and declared as $H = < h_{j_1}^i\ h_{j_2}^i\ h_{j_3}^i\ \ldots >$, each element being a hit. If a sequence is contained in another sequence, then it is not maximal and will be removed.

Associative sequences represent patterns, which have maximal length, independent of their time ordering. These represent visited page sequences of customers during relatively long stays where the aim is to discover pages that are frequently hit in the same session. Clearly the time ordering of the hits is not important in this context. Similar methods have been applied in the context of web data in order to discover path traversal patterns [8].

Definition 7. A sequence Q_i is associatively contained in another sequence Q_j $(Q_i \prec_a Q_j)$ iff ⌣ ‥ ⌣ ‥ .

For example, $<(d)(a)> \prec_a <(a)(c\ d)(h\ f\ i)(b)>$, since $(d) \subseteq (c\ d)$ and $(a) \subseteq (a)$. However, $\langle(e)(d)\rangle \not\prec_a \langle(a)(c\ d)(h\ f\ i)(b)\rangle$ because $(e) \not\subset (a)$, $(e) \not\subset (c\ d)$, $(e) \not\subseteq (h\ f\ i)$, and $(e) \not\subseteq (b)$.

Partial sequences are similar to their associative counterparts, but take into account the time ordering of individual sessions attributed to a browser (user of the web site). The intuitive motivation for these types of sequences is that often we are interested in discovering as to how the browsers navigation behaviour is changing over time. Partial sequences provide us within this knowledge as they utilise the time ordering across sessions. The "partially contained in" relationship is identical to the "contained in" relationship proposed by [1].

Definition 8. A sequence Q_i is set to be partially contained in another sequence Q_j, $(Q_i \prec_p Q_j)$ iff $\forall k \exists H_v^j \ni H_k^i \subset H_v^j \wedge k < v \wedge H_l^i \not\subset H_v^j$ $(\forall l = 1, \ldots k - 1)$.

For instance, $<(a)(h\ i)(b)> \prec_p <(a)(c\ d)(h\ f\ i)(b)>$, since $(a) \subseteq (a)$, $(h\ i) \subseteq (h\ f\ i)$ and $(b) \subseteq (b)$. However, $<(a\ h)(i)(b)> \not\prec_p <(a)(c\ d)(h\ f\ i)(b)>$ because $(a\ h) \not\subseteq (a)$, $(a\ h) \not\subseteq (c\ d)$, $(a\ h) \not\subseteq (h\ f\ i)$ and $(a\ h) \not\subseteq (b)$. Generally, this means that the sequence $\langle(x)(y)\rangle$ $\not\prec_p \langle(x\ y)\rangle$ and vice versa.

The difference between partial and *full sequences* is that in the latter, the time-ordering of hits within a session is also considered and missing 'hits' (pages which have not been visited, hence skipped) are considered in the discovery of sequences.

Definition 9. A sequence Q_i is set to be fully contained in another sequence Q_j $(Q_i \prec_f Q_j)$ iff $\exists k, p \ni H_k^i \subset H_p^j \wedge \exists r, s \ni h_{(r+v)k}^i = h_{(s+v)p}^j \wedge H_{k+g}^i \approx H_{p+d}^j$.

The symbol $\approx$ denotes the notion of equivalent sub-sequences, which is a special case of the strict containment relationship. H_k^i is said to be strictly contained in H_l^j ($H_k^i \prec_s H_l^j$) iff $\forall r, s \ni h_{(r+v)k}^i = h_{(s+v)l}^j$. If $r = 1$ and $s = 1$ we say that H_k^i and H_l^j are equivalent sub-sequences ($H_k^i \approx H_l^j$) making it a special case of the strict containment relationship.

For example, $<(d)(h\ f\ i)(b)> \prec_f <(a)(c\ d)(h\ f\ i)(b)>$, since (d) $\subseteq$ (c d), (h f i) $\subseteq$ (h f i) and (b) $\subseteq$ (b). However, $<(c)(h\ f\ i)(b)> \nprec_f <(a)(c\ d)(h\ f\ i)(b)>$ because d follows c in (c d).

4   Case Study

In this section a case study is presented, which exemplifies the usage of the MiDAS algorithm in one particular type of web mining goal.

4.1   Objective of Study

The overall objective of the study carried out was to discover interesting navigational behaviour from the log file of the MINEit Software Ltd web site (*www.MINEit.com*).

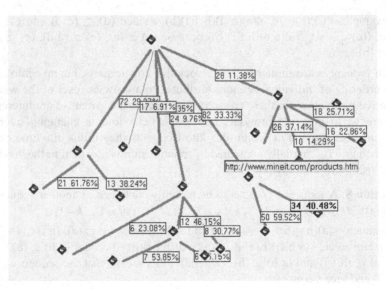

Fig. 7. Topology of analysed web site

More specifically, the goal of the web mining was to discover the behaviour of visitors coming from the *www.kdnuggets.com* site (where two new product entries and an entry on MINEit were placed prior to the analysis) against visitors from elsewhere. The site topology is shown in Fig. 7, where each node represents a page on the web site, and each is allotted the number of visitors as well as its percentage of all hits.

Using M*i*DAS (as any other traditional sequential pattern discoverer) without domain knowledge resulted in non-actionable results. Either the sequences were very specific (very high support), or a multitude of navigational patterns was returned (very low support). Thus, it was decided to incorporate domain knowledge that is tailored towards the topology seen above and the sub-tree for products in particular.

4.2   Domain Knowledge Incorporation

In order to get meaningful results a concept hierarchy shown in Fig. 8 is introduced. The hierarchy consists of two main branches; first representing the visitors who have come from www.kdnuggets.com, second representing all other users. The branches are used to discover different behaviour from targeted users versus non-targeted users.

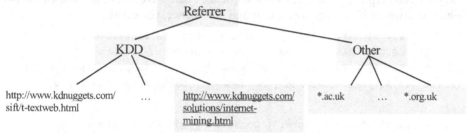

Fig. 8. Referrer Concept Hierarchy

In order to filter out all other unwanted visitors, the following navigation templates have been specified, which are depicted in Fig. 9 and Fig. 10, respectively.

```
^[<Referrer = kdd>;<*>; < Referrer = mineit>;<*>]
^[< Referrer = kdd>;<*>; < Referrer = kdd>;<*>]
[<Referrer = kdd>;<*>;<DocName = /products-emw.htm>]
[<Referrer = kdd>;<*>;<DocName = /products-capri.htm>]
[<Referrer = kdd>;<DocName = /products.htm>;<DocName = /products-emw.htm>]
[<Referrer = kdd>;<DocName = /products.htm>;<DocName = /products-capri.htm>]
```

Fig. 9. Targeted Visitors

> ^[< Referrer = other>;<*>; < Referrer = mineit>;<*>]
> ^[< Referrer = other>;<*>; < Referrer = other>;<*>]
> [<Referrer = other>;<*>;<DocName = /products-emw.htm>]
> [<Referrer = other>;<*>;<DocName = /products-capri.htm>]
> [<Referrer = other>;<DocName = /products.htm>;<DocName = /products-emw.htm>]
> [<Referrer = other>;<DocName = /products.htm>;<DocName = /products-capri.htm>]

Fig. 10. Un-targeted Visitors

Based on the above specified domain knowledge, as well as task-specific syntactic constraints in the form of M*i*DAS parameters, it is now possible to discover more user-driven navigation patterns.

4.3   Knowledge Discovery and Interpretation of Results

As indicated above, two separate runs were performed using M*i*DAS, one to discover navigational behaviour of targeted visitors and one to detect behaviour of their un-targeted counterpart. Some interesting sequences that were found are shown below, where the two numbers connate support and confidence, respectively.

```
(5.60%, 16.47%) Referrer=kdd | DocName=/products-capri.htm
(22.53%, 66.27%) Referrer=kdd | DocName=/products-emw.htm
(0.93%, 15.91%) Referrer=kdd | DocName=/ , DocName=/products-capri.htm
(2.40%, 40.91%) Referrer=kdd | DocName=/ , DocName=/products-emw.htm


(1.60%, 6.22%) Referrer=other | DocName=/products-emw.htm
(2.27%, 10.76%) Referrer=other | DocName=/ , DocName=/products-emw.htm
(4.27%, 20.25%) Referrer=other | DocName=/ , DocName=/products-capri.htm
```

The first set of chosen sequences shows that visitors who came from the kdnuggets site, either went directly to one of the two products or came to the home page and went to the product pages at a later stage. The second shows the counterpart of all other visitors. The result can be tabularised as follows, where the first value indicates support and the second confidence in percent.

Table 3. Result Summary

Referrer	Easyminer Direct		Easyminer *via* Home page		Capri Direct		Capri *via* Home page	
KDD	22.53	66.27	2.40	40.91	5.60	16.47	3.93	15.91
Other	1.60	6.22	2.27	10.76	< 1.20	n/a	4.27	20.25

The table shows that of all visitors who have come from kdnuggets, 22.5% went straight to the Easyminer home page, whereas only 2.4% came through the MINEit home page to get to the same URL. People from all other referrers with the same destinations only cover 1.6% and 2.3%, respectively. Similar behaviour was found for the Capri page, where 5.6% from kdnuggets went directly to the URL; no sequences were discovered for the given support threshold of 1.2%.

5   Evaluation of Relative Performance

To assess the relative performance of M*i*DAS and study its scale-up properties a range of synthetic data sets were created. The parameters for the data generation program are shown in Table 4.

Table 4. Parameters for Synthetic Data Generation

Parameter	Description
$|N|$	Number of visitors
$|V|$	Average number of visits per visitor
$|P|$	Average number of pages per visit

A permutation of the three parameters has been performed such that $|N|$ has taken on the values 10K, 25K, 50K and 100K, $|V|$ 5 and 10, and $|P|$ 2 and 4, which has led to 16 data sets. The number of visits is picked from a Poisson distribution with mean $\mu = |V|$, and the number of pages is selected from a Poisson distribution with mean $\mu = |P|$. The number of pages per site has been set to 100, the average length of potentially large navigation to 5.

Fig. 11 shows the execution times of the M*i*DAS algorithm for the generated datasets as the minimum support is decreased from 10% down to 0.2%, except for Fig. 11(d) where the minimum support is decreased from 20% down to 1%. As expected, the performance decreases with lower minimum support. The increasing number of visitors shows the scale-up properties of M*i*DAS, which have shown similar behaviour to existing sequential data mining algorithms without web-specific functionality.

The qualitative evaluation has shown that the three types of different pruning methods provide a valuable filtering mechanism in different web mining exercises. The size of the result space can be controlled through the pruning type, where associative pruning produces the least and full pruning the most navigational patterns. The run-time behaviour of M*i*DAS has performed as expected. Because the algorithm requires one pass over the database for creating each tree level (see Section 3.2.2), the execution times depends on the maximum length of a sequence in the log file.

For the purpose of evaluating the relative performance of M*i*DAS, it would have been interesting to distinguish between the run-time behaviour with and without taxonomical domain knowledge. Due to the fact that the domain knowledge incorporation is dealt with at the *a priori* and *a posteriori* stages, respectively, scale-up comparison would not be feasible. That is, a higher degree of domain knowledge incorporation results in more expensive pre- and post-processing, which reduces the discovery phase, and vice versa. An appropriate objective evaluation can be carried out, when domain knowledge is considered in the discovery stage itself (see further work paragraph in Section 7).

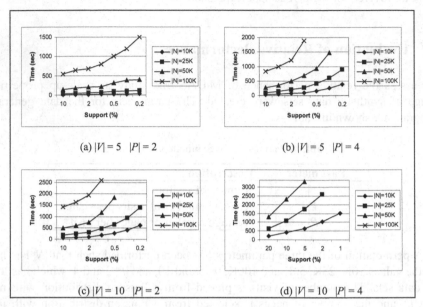

Fig. 11. M*i*DAS Execution Times

6   Related Work

Efforts in the area of discovering sequential marketing intelligence from Internet log files can be sub-divided into two sub-areas. The first tackles the problem of discovering generic sequential patterns, while the second is concerned with the challenge of applying data mining techniques on Internet server data.

6.1   Sequential Patterns

The authors' research has mainly been influenced by that of Agrawal & Srikant [1] and their own extensions [19]. Sequential patterns are discovered, which can be constrained by a number of factors, such as support, minimum and maximum DateTime gaps (between user sessions), sliding DateTime windows (for user session merging) and concept hierarchies. Most of these constructs have been adopted and extended according to electronic commerce requirements. Neither navigational templates nor web topologies can be used in their algorithm, nor is field dependence supported, both features have proven useful in Internet environments. The host of proposed *a priori* and GSP algorithms have difficulties dealing with very large sequence length, which has been resolved in M*i*DAS using depth-dependent pattern trees. Furthermore, the given "contained in" relationship has been proven too limited for some electronic commerce data analyses.

Zaki [21] has parallelised the GSP algorithm using a lattice-based approach and equivalence classes. Although the proposed algorithm has improved the performance of the serial version, it still carries the drawbacks described above.

Somewhat related to sequence discovery is work carried out by Manilla & Toivonen [13, 14, 15] in the field of frequent episode discovery, which can be located between sequential and temporal patterns. An episode contains a set of events and an associated partial order, which can be seen as the equivalent to a sequence. However, their work is concerned with the discovery of frequent episodes in a single event sequence, while our work concentrates on the discovery of sequences across many different online customer sequences.

6.2 Mining Web Logs

Žaïane et al. [20] have applied various traditional data mining techniques to Internet log files in order to find different types of patterns, which can be harnessed as electronic commerce decision support knowledge. The process involves a data cleansing and filtering stage (manipulation of date and time related fields, removal of futile entries, etc.) which is followed by a transformation step that reorganises log entries supported by meta data. The pre-processed data is then loaded into a data warehouse, which has an n-dimensional web log cube as a foundation. From this cube, various standard OLAP techniques are applied, such as drill-down, roll-up, slicing, and dicing. Additionally, artificial intelligence and statistically-based data mining techniques are applied on the collected data which include characterisation, discrimination, association, regression, classification, and sequential patterns. The overall system is similar to ours in that it follows the same process. However, the approach is limited in several ways. Firstly, it only supports one data source — static log files —, which has proven insufficient for real-world electronic commerce exploitation. Secondly, no domain knowledge (marketing expertise) has been incorporated in the web mining exercise, which we see as an essential feature. And lastly, the approach is very data mining-biased, in that it re-uses existing techniques that have not been tailored towards electronic commerce purposes.

Cooley et al. [9] have built a similar, but more powerful architecture. It includes intelligent cleansing (outlier elimination and removal of irrelevant values) and pre-processing (user and session identification, path completion, reverse DNA lookups, et cetera) for Internet log files, as well as the creation of data warehousing-like views [10]. In addition to Žaïane's [20] approach, registration data, as well as transaction information is integrated in the materialised view. From this view, various data mining techniques can be applied; including path analysis, associations, sequences, clustering and classification. These patterns can then be analysed using OLAP tools, visualisation mechanisms or knowledge engineering techniques. Although more electronic commerce-orientated, the approach shares some obstacles of [20]'s endeavour, mainly in the non-incorporation of marketing expertise.

Bhowmick *at al.* [5] have developed a web data warehouse (called WHOWEDA), which is based on their own web data model. From within that environment, various web mining activities can be performed, which are all based on traditional data mining mechanisms and which do not provide any support for domain knowledge incorporation.

Spiliopoulou [17] has developed a sequence discoverer for web data, which is similar to our M*i*DAS algorithm. Their GSM algorithm uses aggregated trees, which are generated from log files, in order to discover user-driven navigation patterns. The mechanism has been incorporated in an SQL-like query language (called MINT), which together form the key components of the Web Utilisation Analysis platform [18].

Borges & Levene [6] have also developed an algorithm to discover user navigation patterns. Their mechanism is based on hypertext probabilistic grammars, which is a subclass of probabilistic regular grammars and uses an entropy measure as an estimator of the statistical properties of each link.

7   Conclusions and Future Work

A new algorithm for discovering sequential patterns from web log files has been proposed that provides behavioural marketing intelligence for electronic commerce scenarios. New domain knowledge types in the form of navigational templates and web topologies have been incorporated, as well as syntactic constraints and concept hierarchies. Multi-dimensional data can be used as input, which allows the representation of hits from multiple attributes. Three different types of "contained in" relationships are supported, which leaves room for typical navigational browsing behaviour on the Internet, such as skipping pages or bookmarking pages for later usage. Also, hit duplicates can be handled, as they reflect browser refresh/reload operations. Finally, all newly proposed mechanisms have been applied in a large-scale electronic commerce data mining project [4] and performance tests on synthetically generated data have shown promising results.

Further work in the area of discovering marketing-driven navigation patterns is twofold. First concentrates on practical issues, which include horizontal and vertical diversification of digital behavioural data (such as Web TV, Internet channels, or wireless mobile devices) and a smoother interface to a web-enabled data warehouse. Second is concerned with the improvement of the algorithmic constituent. In order to leverage the knowledge in concept hierarchies and navigation templates for providing business intelligence, domain knowledge will be incorporated into the discovery phase.

References

1. Agrawal, R., Srikant, R.: Mining Sequential Patterns. Proc. Int'l Conf. on Data Engineering (1995) 3-14
2. Anand, S.S., Bell, D.A., Hughes, J.G.: The Role of Domain Knowledge in Data Mining. Proc. 4th Int'l ACM Conf. on Information and Knowledge Management (1995) 37-43
3. Anand, S.S., Büchner, A.G.: Decision Support using Data Mining. FT Pitman Publishers (1998)
4. Anand, S.S., Büchner, A.G., Mulvenna, M.D., Hughes, J.G.: Discovering Internet Marketing Intelligence through Web Log Mining. Unicom'99
5. Bhowmick, S.S., Madria, S.K., Ng, W.-K., Lim E.P.: Web Mining in WHOWEDA. Some Issues, Proc. PRICAI98 Workshop on Knowledge Discovery and Data Mining (1998)
6. Borges, J., Levene, M.: Data Mining of User Navigation Patterns. Proc. WEBKDD99 Workshop on Web Usage Analysis and User Profiling (1999) 31-36 (same volume)
7. Büchner, A.G., Mulvenna, M.D.: Discovering Internet Marketing Intelligence through Online Analytical Web Usage Mining. ACM SIGMOD Record, 27:4 (1998) 54-61
8. Chen, M.S., Park, J.S., Yu, P.S.: Data Mining for Path Traversal Patterns in a Web Environment. Proc. 16th Int'l Conf. on Distributed Computing Systems (1996) 385-392
9. Cooley, R., Mobasher, R., Srivastava, J.: Web Mining: Information and Pattern Discovery on the World Wide Web. Proc. 9th IEEE Int'l Conf. on Tools with Artificial Intelligence (1997)
10. Cooley, R., Mobasher, R., Srivastava, J.: Data Preparation for Mining World Wide Web Browsing Patterns. Knowledge and Information Systems 1:1 (1999)
11. Han, J., Fu, Y.: Dynamic Generation and Refinement of Concept Hierarchies for Knowledge Discovery in Databases. Proc. KDD'94 (1994) 157-168
12. Ling, C.X., Li, C.: Data Mining for Direct Marketing: Problems and Solutions. Proc. KDD'99 (1998) 73-79
13. Manilla, H., Toivonen, H., Inkeri, A.: Discovery of Frequent Episodes in Event Sequences. Proc. 2nd Int'l Conf. on Knowledge Discovery and Data Mining (1995) 210-215
14. Manilla, H., Toivonen, H.: Discovering generalized episodes using minimal occurrences. Proc. 2nd Int'l Conf. on Knowledge Discovery and Data Mining (1996) 146-151
15. Manilla, H., Toivonen, H., Inkeri, A.: Discovery of Frequent Episodes in Event Sequences. Data Mining and Knowledge Discovery, 1:3 (1997) 259-289
16. Mulvenna, M.D., Norwood, M.T., Büchner, A.G.: Data-driven Marketing. The Int'l Journal of Electronic Commerce and Business Media, 8:3 (1998) 32-35
17. Spiliopoulou, M.: The laborious way from data mining to web mining. Int'l Journal of Computing Systems, Science & Engineering, March (1999)
18. Spiliopoulou, M., Faulstich, L.C., Winkler, K.A.: A Data Miner analyzing the Navigational Behaviour of Web Users. Proc. ACAI'99 Workshop on Machine Learning in User Modelling (1999)
19. Srikant, R., Agrawal, R.: Mining Sequential Patterns: Generalizations and Performance Improvements. Proc. 5th Int'l Conf on Extending Database Technology (1996) 3-17
20. Žaïane, O.R, Xin, M., Han, J.: Discovering Web Access Patterns and Trends by Applying OLAP and Data Mining Technology on Web Logs. Proc. Advances in Digital Libraries Conf. (1998) 19-29
21. Zaki, M.J.: Efficient Enumeration of Frequent Sequences. 7th Int'l ACM Conf. on Information and Knowledge Management (1998) 68-75

Data Mining of User Navigation Patterns

José Borges and Mark Levene

Department of Computer Science, University College London,
Gower Street, London WC1E 6BT, U.K.
{j.borges,mlevene}@cs.ucl.ac.uk

Abstract. We propose a data mining model that captures the user navigation behaviour patterns. The user navigation sessions are modelled as a hypertext probabilistic grammar whose higher probability strings correspond to the user's preferred trails. An algorithm to efficiently mine such trails is given. We make use of the Ngram model which assumes that the last N pages browsed affect the probability of the next page to be visited. The model is based on the theory of probabilistic grammars providing it with a sound theoretical foundation for future enhancements. Moreover, we propose the use of entropy as an estimator of the grammar's statistical properties. Extensive experiments were conducted and the results show that the algorithm runs in linear time, the grammar's entropy is a good estimator of the number of mined trails and the real data rules confirm the effectiveness of the model.

1   Introduction

Data Mining and Knowledge Discovery is an active research discipline involving the study of techniques which search for patterns in large collections of data. Meanwhile, the explosive growth of the World Wide Web (known as the web) in recent years has turned it into the largest source of available online data. Therefore, the application of data mining techniques to the web, called *web data mining*, was the natural subsequent step and it is now the focus of an increasing number of researchers.

In web data mining there are currently three main research directions: (i) mining for information, (ii) mining the web link structure, and (iii) mining for user behaviour patterns. Mining for information focuses on the development of techniques to assist users in processing the large amounts of data they face during navigation and to help them find the information they are looking for, see for example [13]. Mining the link structure aims at developing techniques to take advantage of the collective judgement of web page quality in the form of hyperlinks, which can be viewed as a mechanism of implicit endorsement, see [7]. The aim is to identify for a given subject the authoritative and the hub pages. Authoritative pages are those which were conferred authority by the existing links to it, and hubs are pages that contain a collection of links to related authorities. Finally, the other research direction, which is being followed by an increasing number of researchers, is mining for user navigation patterns. This research focuses on

B. Masand and M. Spiliopoulou (Eds.): WEBKDD'99, LNAI 1836, pp. 92–112, 2000.

techniques which study the user behaviour when navigating within a web site. Understanding the visitors navigation preferences is an essential step in improving the quality of electronic commerce services. In fact, the understanding of the most likely access patterns of users allows the service provider to customise and adapt the site's interface for the individual user [18], and to improve the site's static structure within the underlying hypertext system [21].

When web users interact with a site, data recording their behaviour is stored in web server logs, which in a medium sized site can amount to several megabytes per day. Moreover, since the log data is collected in a raw format it is an ideal target for being analysed by automated tools. Currently several commercial log analysis tools are available [25]; however, these tools have limited analysis capabilities producing only results such as summary statistics and frequency counts of page visits. In the meantime the research community has been studying data mining techniques to take full advantage of information available in the log files. There have so far been two main approaches to mining for user navigation patterns from log data. In the first approach log data is mapped onto relational tables and an adapted version of standard data mining techniques, such as mining association rules, are invoked, see for example [10]. In the second approach techniques are developed which can be invoked directly on the log data, see for example [2] or [23].

In this paper we propose a new model for handling the problem of mining log data which directly captures the semantics of the user navigation sessions. We model the user navigation records, inferred from log data, as a hypertext probabilistic grammar whose higher probability generated strings correspond to the user's preferred trails. Our model has the advantages of being self-contained, compact and based on the well established theory of probabilistic grammars providing a sound foundation for future enhancements such as the study of its statistical properties.

There are two contexts in which such model is potentially useful. On the one hand, it can help the service provider to understand the users needs and as a result improve the quality of its service. The quality of service can be improved by providing adaptive pages suited to the individual user [18], by building dynamic pages in advance to reduce waiting time, or by providing a speculative service which sends, in addition to the requested document, a number of other documents that are expected to be requested in the near future. On the other hand, in a scenario wherein the user's browser is setup to collect personal log data such a model can be useful to the individual web user by acting as a personal assistant integrated with his/her web browser. In fact, having a user's log data characterising his/her interactions with the web allows incremental update of a hypertext probabilistic grammar. Such a grammar would be a representation of the user's knowledge of the web which can act as a memory aid, be analysed in order to infer the user preferred trails for a given subject, or work as a prediction tool to prefetch interesting pages in advance.

Section 2 presents the proposed hypertext grammar model, while Section 3 presents the results of the performed experiments. Section 4 discusses related

work and Section 5 presents a preliminary discussion of recent improvements
to the model. Finally, in Section 6 we give our concluding remarks and discuss
further work.

2   Hypertext Probabilistic Grammars

A log file can be seen as a per-user ordered set of web page requests from which
it is possible to infer the user navigation sessions. In this work we simply define a
user navigation session as a sequence of page requests such that no two consecutive requests are separated by more than X minutes, where X is a parameter
which should be adjusted for the specific characteristics of each web site. In [6]
the authors proposed for X the value of 25.5 minutes which corresponds to $1\frac{1}{2}$
standard deviations of the average time between user interface events. Since then
many authors have adopted the value of 30 minutes. We note however, that more
advanced data preparation techniques, such as those described in [11], could be
used in a data pre-processing stage to fully take advantage of all the information
available in the log files.

The user navigation sessions inferred from the log data are modelled as a
hypertext probabilistic language generated by a *hypertext probabilistic grammar*
(or simply HPG) [16] which is a proper subclass of probabilistic regular grammars [26]. A HPG is a probabilistic regular grammar which has a one-to-one
mapping between the set of non-terminal symbols and the set of terminal symbols. Each non-terminal symbol corresponds to a web page and a production
rule corresponds to a link between pages. Moreover, there are two additional
states, S and F, which represent the start and finish states of the navigation
sessions.

From the set of user sessions we obtain the number of times a page was
requested, the number of times it was the first state in a session, and the number
of times it was the last state in a session. The number of times a sequence of two
pages appears in the sessions gives the number of times the corresponding link
was traversed. The probability of a production from a state that corresponds to
a web page is proportional to the number of times the corresponding link was
chosen relative to the number of times the user visited that page.

The probability of a production from the start state is proportional to the
number of times the corresponding state was visited, implying that the destination node of a production with higher probability corresponds to a state that was
visited more often. We define α as a parameter that attaches the desired weight
to a state being the first in a user navigation session. If $\alpha = 0$ only states which
were the first in a session have probability greater than zero of being in a production from the start state, on the other hand if $\alpha = 1$ all state visits are given
proportionate weight. The intuition behind α is that when $\alpha = 0$ the grammar's
language contains only the strings whose first state was the starting point of a
navigation session, while if $\alpha > 0$ the language contains strings starting in every
grammar's states. Therefore, the value of α should be adjusted according to the
importance given to a state being the first in a navigation session. Finally, the

probabilities of the productions from the start state correspond to the vector of initial probabilities, π, and the probabilities of the other productions correspond to the transition matrix of a Markov chain [14].

In the example shown in Figure 1 we have 6 user sessions with a total of 24 page requests, wherein state A_1 was visited 4 times, 2 of which are the first state in a user session, therefore, since $\alpha = 0.5$ we have $\pi(A_1) = \frac{0.5 \cdot 4}{24} + \frac{0.5 \cdot 2}{6} = 0.25$. Figure 2 shows the grammar inferred from the given set of trails for $N = 1$ and $\alpha = 0.5$. (We freely utilise in our figures the duality between grammars and automata [15].)

Session ID	User trail
1	$A_1 \to A_2 \to A_3 \to A_4$
2	$A_1 \to A_5 \to A_3 \to A_4 \to A_1$
3	$A_5 \to A_2 \to A_4 \to A_6$
4	$A_5 \to A_2 \to A_3$
5	$A_5 \to A_2 \to A_3 \to A_6$
6	$A_4 \to A_1 \to A_5 \to A_3$

Fig. 1. An example set of user's trails

In a HPG the probability of the first derivation step of a string is evaluated against the *support threshold*, θ, and is not factored into the derivation probability. Thus, the support threshold is used to prune out the strings which may otherwise have high probability but correspond to a subset of the hypertext system rarely visited. Moreover, a string is included in the grammar's language if its derivation probability is above the *cut-point*, λ, where the cut-point corresponds to the grammar *confidence threshold*. The values of the support and confidence thresholds give the user control over the quantity and quality of the trails to be included in the rule set. The strings generated by the grammar correspond to user navigation trails, and the aim is to identify the subset of these strings that

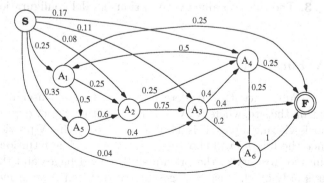

Fig. 2. The hypertext grammar for $N = 1$ and $\alpha = 0.5$

best characterise the user behaviour when visiting the site. Parameters such as *confidence* and *support* are defined as preference measures which rank the generated strings. The algorithm used to mine rules having confidence and support above the specified thresholds is a special case of a directed graph Depth-First Search which performs an exhaustive search of all the strings with the required characteristics, cf. [2].

In Figure 3 we show the rules obtained with different model configurations. From the first two sets of rules we can see how both the number of rules and its average length decreases when the cut-point increases. Note that although A_3 was never the first state in a navigation session both rule-sets include rules starting with it. This occurs because A_3 has a high frequency of traversal and the value of parameter $\alpha = 0.5$ gives a positive weight to that. The third rule-set has a higher support threshold and as a consequence the rules starting in state A_3 are excluded. Finally, rule-set 4 corresponds to a grammar inferred while given the same weight for all traversals, i.e. $\alpha = 1.0$, and consequently rules starting at A_2 and A_3 are included even though these states were never the first in a navigation session.

rule-set 1		rule-set 2		rule-set 3		rule-set 4	
$\alpha = 0.5$						$\alpha = 1.0$	
$\theta = 0.1$				$\theta = 0.15$		$\theta = 0.1$	
$\lambda = 0.2$		$\lambda = 0.3$		$\lambda = 0.3$		$\lambda = 0.3$	
rule	conf.	rule	conf.	rule	conf.	rule	conf.
$A_1 A_2$	0.25	$A_1 A_5 A_2$	0.3	$A_1 A_5 A_2$	0.3	$A_1 A_5 A_2$	0.3
$A_1 A_5 A_3$	0.2	$A_3 A_4$	0.4	$A_4 A_1$	0.5	$A_2 A_3 A_4$	0.3
$A_1 A_5 A_2 A_3$	0.23	$A_4 A_1$	0.5	$A_5 A_3$	0.4	$A_3 A_4$	0.4
$A_3 A_4 A_1$	0.2	$A_5 A_3$	0.4	$A_5 A_2 A_3$	0.45	$A_4 A_1$	0.5
$A_3 A_6$	0.2	$A_5 A_2 A_3$	0.45			$A_5 A_3$	0.4
$A_4 A_1 A_5$	0.25					$A_5 A_2 A_3$	0.45
$A_4 A_6$	0.25						
$A_5 A_3$	0.4						
$A_5 A_2 A_3$	0.45						

Fig. 3. The rules obtained with various model configurations

2.1   The Ngram Model

We use the Ngram concept [8] to determine the assumed user memory when navigating within the site, where N, $N \geq 1$, is called the history depth. Therefore, when the user is visiting a page it is assumed that only the N previously visited pages influence the link he will choose to follow next. The intuition is that the user has a limited memory of the previously browsed pages and that the next choice depends only on the last N pages browsed. In an Ngram model each of the states of the HPG correspond to a sequence of N pages visited.

The drawback of the Ngram model is the increase in the number of states as the history depth increases. For a web site with n pages and for a given history depth N the expected number of grammar states is $n.b^{(N-1)}$, where b is the average number of outlinks in a page. As such, there is a clear trade-off between the modelled user memory (measured by the history depth) and the grammar complexity (measured in the number of states).

Finally, the hypertext grammar model is incremental in the sense that when more log data becomes available it can be incorporated in the model without the need of rebuilding the grammar from scratch. Hence, the HPG is a compact way of keeping the browsing history since the grammar size depends only on the number of pages visited and not on the amount of log data available.

In Figure 4 we present the algorithm used to incrementally build a HPG. We let T be the collection of user navigation sessions and $|T|$ its cardinality, T_i be the ith session in the set and $T_i[j]$ be the jth page of session i. We also let N be the history depth of the grammar, and $StateSet$ be the set of grammar states; the function $StateSet.update()$ updates $StateSet$ with the last inferred state. A $State$ corresponds to N consecutive page requests $State[1], \ldots, State[N]$; the function $shiftLeft()$ performs the assignment $State[i] := State[i+1]$, for $i = 1, \ldots, N-1$. In addition, we let $Productions$ be the set of all grammar productions and the function $Productions.update()$ updates the set with the last inferred production.

```
Algorithm 1 (Build_Grammar (T, N))
1. begin
2.    for i = 1 to |T|
3.       for k = 1 to N do
4.          State[k] = Tᵢ[k];
5.       end for
6.       StateSet.update(State);
7.       for j = N + 1 to |Tᵢ|
8.          LeftState = State;
9.          State.shiftLeft();
10.         State[N] = Tᵢ[j];
11.         StateSet.update(State);
12.         Productions.update(LeftState, State);
13.      end for
14.   end for
15. end.
```

Fig. 4. Incremental algorithm to build the hypertext probabilistic grammar

2.2   The Entropy of a HPG

We propose to use the *entropy* of the HPG as an estimator of the statistical properties of the language generated by the grammar. The entropy is a measure of the uncertainty in the outcome of a random variable and in this context the sample space is the set of all strings generated by the grammar. If we had no information at all about the user interaction with the web the most rational thing would be to assume that all pages had the same probability of being visited and all its links have the same probability of being chosen. The entropy is maximum in this case and there is no point in looking for patterns or trying to predict a random behaviour. On the other hand, if the entropy is close to zero the user behaviour has few uncertainties, and a small set of short rules should contain enough information to characterise his/her behaviour. In conclusion, the intuition behind the estimator is that if the entropy of a probabilistic grammar is close to zero there should be a small set of strings with high probability and if the entropy is high then there should be a large number of strings with similar and low probability.

Assuming a transition with probability one from state F to S a HPG corresponds to an irreducible and aperiodic Markov chain with a stationary distribution vector μ and transition matrix A. Thus, we can estimate the entropy with the following expression $H = H(\pi) + (-\sum_{ij} \pi_i A_{ij} log A_{ij})$ where $H(\pi)$ is included to take into account the randomness of the choice of the initial page, see [12] for detail on the entropy of a Markov chain. Note that we use the vector of initial probabilities π as an estimator of the stationary vector μ, since it is proportional to the number of times each state was visited. The value of H can be normalised to be in the range between 0 and 1 by considering its ratio with the corresponding random grammar. The random grammar is a grammar with the same structure but in which all states have their out-links probabilities according to a uniform distribution.

3   Experimental Evaluation

To assess the performance and the effectiveness of the proposed model experiments were conducted with both random and real data. Tests with random data provide the means of evaluating many different topologies and configurations of a HPG and tests with real data allow us to verify whether or not the model is potentially useful in practice.

The method used to create the random data consisted of four consecutive steps: (i) randomly create a directed graph given the required number of states and the average branching factor, (ii) for each grammar state assign outgoing links weights according with the chosen probability distribution (in the reported experiments we used the Poisson distribution), (iii) verify if the resulting grammar has the required properties, that is, if every state has a path to F and if not add a link to F, (iv) normalise the grammar's weights, that is, calculate the production probabilities.

For the experiments with real data we used log files obtained from the authors of [19]. The log files contain two months of usage from the site:

http://www.hyperreal.org/music/machines/

It should be noted that the data was collected while caching was disabled and that we used the data without cleaning it. We divided each month into four subsets, each corresponding to a week, and for each subset we built the corresponding HPG for several values of the history depth. One of the weeks was discarded because it presented characteristics significantly different from the others, namely in the number of states inferred which was much larger than the number given by its owners in [19]. This last fact indicates that the data should be cleaned; however, since data cleaning was not the aim of the work together with the belief that the probabilistic nature of the model could partially overcome the dirtiness of the data (for example by ignoring misspelled requests) we decided to use the data without cleaning.

3.1   Performance

The first objective of the experiments was to evaluate the algorithm performance and its scalability. The experiments were conducted for several model configurations where the grammar's size, n, varied between 100 and 4000 states, the confidence threshold varied between 0.1 and 0.5. Note that the grammar size depends only on the number of pages in the hypertext system and not on the number of user sessions in the log data. In order to have a measure of support which allows us to compare the results for grammars with different sizes we have decided to define support in a way that takes into account the number of states n, that is $\theta = \frac{x}{n}$ where $x \leq n$. In our experiments we have adopted the value $\theta = \frac{1}{n}$ which means that only trails which have the first state with a frequency of traversal above the average will pass the test. For each configuration 150 runs were performed and the average results taken.

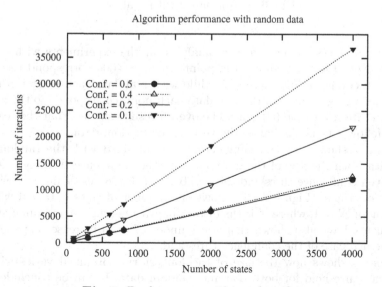

Fig. 5. Performance with random data

Figure 5 shows the variation of the average number of iterations (for the 150 runs) with the grammar size for a fixed confidence. The experiments were performed for various values of the confidence threshold and the results suggest that there is a strong linear correlation between the grammar size and the number of iterations. From Figure 5 it can be also assessed how the performance decreases for lower values of the confidence threshold. The experimental results showed that the performance when measured in CPU time follows a similar trend.

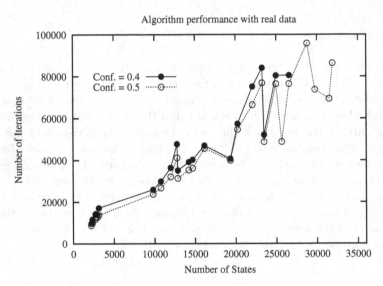

Fig. 6. Performance with real data

Figure 6 shows the performance analysis for the experiments with the real log files. Note that in Figure 6 the points for $n > 4000$ correspond to runs of an Ngram configuration. Moreover, while with real data each point in the plot represents a single run with random data each point corresponds to the average number of iterations for 150 runs. The overall results suggest that the real data results follow a trend similar to the verified for random data.

Figure 7 shows how the number of rules obtained with the random data vary with both the size of the grammar and the confidence threshold. In fact, for a given confidence threshold the number of rules increases linearly with the number of states. (Figure 7 also shows the number of rules obtained with the real data for $N = 1$, where N is the history depth.) For a given grammar size our experiments have also shown that the number of rules increases exponentially with the decrease of the confidence threshold.

Figure 8 shows how the size of the longest rule obtained varies with the confidence threshold for both real and random data. It can be concluded that for high values of confidence we have as a result a small number of short rules

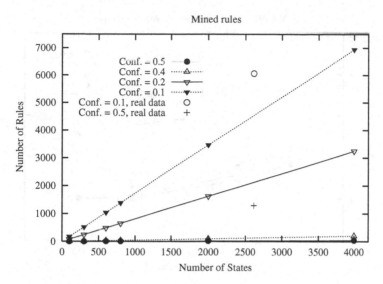

Fig. 7. The number of rules with the grammar size

and for small values of confidence we obtain a large set of longer rules. With the real data even longer rules were obtained but as part of a significantly larger set of rules as is shown in Figure 7. Therefore, there is a clear trade-off between obtaining a manageable number of rules and the desire of having rules with a significant length.

Figure 9 gives some examples of the rules mined from the real data. For each rule we give its probability and the average number of traversals of its links. Figure 10 shows the top-ten pages in the web site, which correspond to the states with the highest initial probability.

3.2 Entropy

In order to verify the utility of the grammar's entropy as an estimator of the statistical properties of the grammar's language we calculated for each grammar size and confidence threshold the correlation between: (i) the entropy and the number of rules, (ii) the entropy and the number of iterations, and (iii) the entropy and the average rule length. Moreover, to assess the effect that both the confidence and support thresholds have on the grammar's entropy we decided to also measure the entropy of a grammar inferred from the set of mined rules, which we call the *posterior grammar*. The posterior grammar is no more than a HPG whose initial input trails are a set of rules mined from its parent grammar. We define PER as the entropy rate of the posterior grammar, and ER is the entropy of the parent grammar but using the vector of initial probabilities of the posterior grammar as the estimator for the stationary vector in the parent grammar.

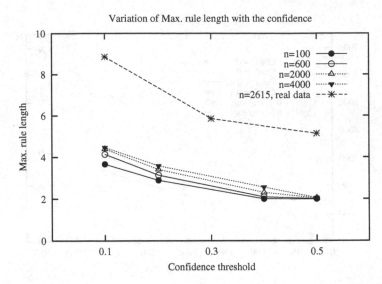

Fig. 8. The size of the longest rule with the confidence

Figure 11 shows the results for grammars with 800 and 2000 states. Each point in the plot represents for a given configuration (size and confidence) the correlation between the number of rules mined and the entropy of the grammar. The results show that both PER and ER present a high correlation (above 0.8 with the number of rules but that PER is a better estimator. The results regarding ER suggest that we can obtain a good estimator for the number of rules from the original grammar provided we find a good estimator for the stationary vector. In fact, the results analysis suggest that the stationary vector has a fundamental importance in the overall quality of the estimator. The experimental results have also shown that the entropy is not a good estimator of the number of iterations or of the average rule length.

We note that the use of estimators from the posterior grammar is justified as an intermediate step in the search for the best way to obtain an estimator from the original grammar. Moreover, in a context where the user has a model that is periodically incremented with new log data the estimators obtained from the posterior grammar in one day can be used as the a priori estimators for the next day's grammar.

Figure 12 shows how the number of mined rules in the real data relates to the entropy in the posterior grammar, note that the logarithm of the number of rules was taken; a similar pattern was obtained for the random data. Note that while in Figure 11 each point represents the correlation between the grammar entropy and the number of rules for a specific grammar topology (for 150 runs), the plot in Figure 12 gives the overall variation of the number of rules with the PER and ER wherein each point corresponds to a single run for a specific topology. In conclusion, our experiments provide strong evidence that while the overall

Rule 1	Conf.= 0.43	Avg. No. Traversals = 44.5	4 pages
/ /ecards/ /ecards/cards/ /ecards/cards/96301			
Rule 2	Conf.= 0.53	Avg. No. Traversals = 11	5 pages
/ /manufacturers/ /manufacturers/Music-and-More/ /manufacturers/Music-and-More/VF11/ /manufacturers/Music-and-More/VF11/info/VF11.review			
Rule 3	Conf.= 0.56	Avg. No. Traversals = 64	5 pages
/categories/drum-machines/samples/ /categories/drum-machines/samples/deepsky_kicks/ /categories/drum-machines/samples/deepsky_kicks/README/ /categories/drum-machines/samples/deepsky_kicks/ /categories/drum-machines/samples/			

Fig. 9. Example of rules mined from the real data

The Top-Ten pages		
Rk.	URL	Prob.
1	/	0.088
2	/manufacturers/	0.050
3	/samples.html	0.026
4	/samples.html?MMAgent	0.023
5	/manufacturers/Roland/	0.020
6	/links/	0.018
7	/Analogue-Heaven/	0.017
8	/categories/software/Windows/	0.016
9	/search.html	0.015
10	/categories/software/	0.014

Fig. 10. Top-Ten Pages

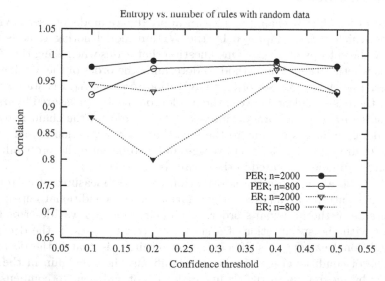

Fig. 11. Correlation between entropy and number of rules with random data

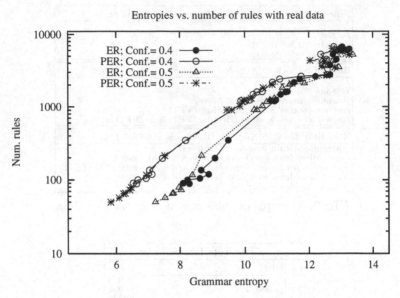

Fig. 12. Correlation between entropy and number of rules with real data

variation presents a regular *log*-linear trend, for a specific grammar topology there is a strong linear correlation between the number of rules and the grammar entropy.

3.3   Ngram Model

The first order Markov chain provides an approximate model of user navigation patterns which can be improved by the *N*gram model noting that as we increase *N* the entropy decreases. One question that arises when using the *N*gram model is whether there is a method to determine the order of the Markov chain that best models a given set of user navigation sessions. As was stated in Section 2.1 there is a tradeoff between the model complexity (measured by its number of states) and its accuracy. Moreover, if the order of the chain is too high the model is uninteresting due to the fact that user navigation sessions within a web site are typically short on average and also because the probability of a very long trail being repeated in the future is not very high.

In [20] the authors use the information theoretic measures of entropy and conditional entropy to analyse the variation of the conditional entropy with the increase of the grammar's order. A similar approach was described in [9] together with the specification of a statistical test to assess if the decrease in the conditional entropy is significant. The intuition is that if the decrease in the value of conditional entropy is not significant then the gain in the model accuracy by moving up in the chain's order is not sufficient to compensate for the additional complexity of the model. In practice the test is difficult to apply

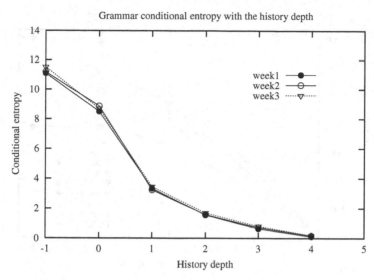

Fig. 13. Variation of the conditional uncertainty with the history depth

because of the extremely large number of degrees of freedom. Note that there is an amount of decrease that is due to the sample size; in fact, the smaller the sample size the faster we expect the conditional entropy to drop. In Figure 13 we show the variation of the conditional entropy with the history depth for the real data used in our experiments. The big drop from $d = 0$ to $d = 1$ shows that there is a big gain in accuracy when considering that the probability of choosing a page depends on the previous page as opposed to considering that the probability of a page is independent of the path. For $d = -1$ the plot shows $log(n)$ which corresponds to a model where the choice probabilities are uniformly distributed.

In Figure 14 we show the increase in the grammar's number of states with the history depth. The values obtained are much lower than the worst case, $n.b^{(N-1)}$, and that might be explained by the insufficient amount of data available.

4 Related Work

Some authors have recently proposed the user of a first order Markov model for predicting user requests on the WWW. In [1] a first order Markov model is proposed to implement a prefetching service to reduce server load. The model is build from past usage information and the transition probabilities between pages are proportional to the number of times both pages were accessed in a predefined time window. Note that the use of the time window results in having transitions with probability greater than zero between pages that were never accessed consecutively. The experiment results show the method to be effective

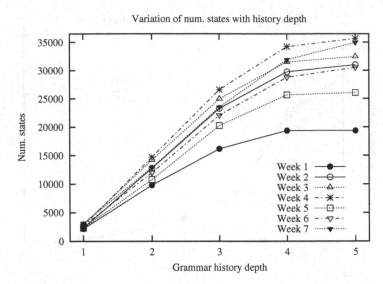

Fig. 14. Variation of the grammar size with the history depth

in reducing both the server load and the service time. A method is proposed in [17] wherein a dependency graph is inferred and dynamically updated as the server receives requests. There is a node for every requested page and an arc between two nodes exists if the target node was requested within x accesses after the source node, the arc's weight is proportional to the number of such requests. This method also doesn't guarantee transitions only between consecutive requests. The simulations performed with log data show that a reduction in the retrieval latency can be achieved. In [20] the authors present a study of the quality of a kth order Markov approximation as a model of predicting user surfing patterns. Using information theoretic measures they conclude that the best compromise between the model accuracy and its complexity occurs with the first order Markov model. Moreover, they show that the model probabilities are more stable over time for lower orders models. This work, however, is concentrated on assessing the predictive power of the model as opposed to providing the analyst with a tool to identify the relevant patterns.

The use of data mining techniques to analyse log data was first proposed by [10] and [27]. In [10] the log data is converted into a set of maximal forward references, a form which is amenable to being processed by existing association rules techniques. Two algorithms are given to mine the rules, which in this context consist of large itemsets with the additional restriction that the references must be consecutive in a transaction. In our opinion the procedure used to build the maximal forward references tends to over evaluate the links close to the root of the resulting traversal tree. In [27] a method is proposed to classify web site visitors according to their access patterns. Each user session is stored in a vector that contains the number of visits to each page and an algorithm is given to find clusters of similar vectors. The clusters obtained with this method do not take into account the order in which the page visits took place.

In [18] the authors challenged the AI community to use the log data to create adaptive web sites and in [19] they present a technique which automatically creates index pages from the log data, i.e., pages containing collections of links which the user navigation behaviour suggests are related. In our previous work, [2], we proposed to model the log data as a directed graph with the arcs weights interpreted as probabilities that reflect the user interaction with the site, and we generalised the association rule concept. The authors of [22] propose to use log data to predict the next URL to be requested so the server can generate in advance web pages with dynamic content. A tree which contains the user paths is generated from the log data and an algorithm is proposed to predict the next request given the tree and the current user session. Although this method is very accurate in the way it represents the navigation sessions inferred from log data it is not very compact since for every path stored all its suffixes are duplicated. In [24] the authors propose a log data mining system composed of an aggregation module and a data mining module for the discovery of patterns with predefined characteristics. The aggregation module infers a tree structure from the data in which the mining is performed by a human expert using a mining query language. However, no performance studies were reported and the use of a query language to find patterns with predefined characteristics may prevent the user finding unexpected patterns. In [5] an approach is proposed to find marketing intelligence from internet data. An n-dimensional web log data cube is created to store the collected data and domain knowledge is incorporated in order to reduce the pattern search space. In [4] an algorithm is proposed to extract navigation patterns from the data which conform to specified navigation templates. This model does not store the log data in a compact form and that can be a major drawback in sites generating large daily log files.

Finally, [28] propose the integration of data warehousing and data mining techniques to analyse web records, and [11] study cleaning and preparation techniques which convert log data into user navigation sessions in a form amenable to processing by the existing data mining techniques.

5   Heuristics for Mining High Quality Patterns

We are currently working on the specification of new algorithms to improve the quality of the results relative to the deterministic DFS (Depth-First Search) used in the experiments reported herein. In fact, as was shown in section 3.1, the exhaustive computation of all grammar strings with probability above the cut-point has the drawback of potentially returning a very large number of rules for small values of the cut-point. Note that if the user wants to find longer rules the threshold needs to be set low. This fact led us to the study of heuristics which allow us to compute a subset of the rule set while being able to control both its size and quality. In the following sections we briefly describe the ideas behind the heuristics we are developing; a complete description can be find in [3].

5.1   The Iterative Deepening Fine Grained Heuristic

Our first approach is based on the iterative deepening concept wherein the rule set is incrementally augmented until it is close enough to the desired set. We call this method the *iterative deepening fine grained* approach. A measure of the distance between the currently explored and the final rule set is provided by the error, and by setting its desired value the user has control over the number of rules to be returned. Informally, the error is defined as the amount of probability left to explore, and it can be estimated by the sum of the probabilities of the trails that are not yet final. Moreover, at each stage the trails chosen to be augmented are those which will lead to the trails with higher probability; in such a way we maintain a high quality rule set.

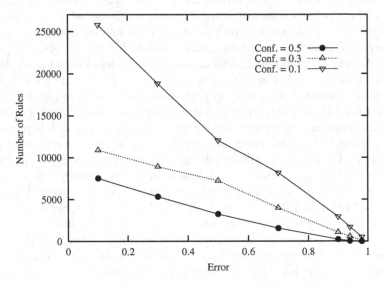

Fig. 15. Results of the iterative deepening fine grained heuristic

Figure 15 shows the variation of the number of rules with the user specified error for a random grammar with 10000 states and average branching factor of 3, similar results were obtained for other configurations. Note that when the error is zero the resulting rule set is the same as the one given by the exhaustive computation done by the DFS. Since the variation is close to linear the proposed heuristic gives the user good control over the number of rules. A more detailed explanation together with extensive experimental results can be found in [3].

5.2   The Inverse Fisheye Heuristic

The second approach aims at providing the user with a method that gives a relatively small set of long rules. We propose the use of a dynamic threshold which imposes a very strict criterion for small rules and becomes more permissible when the trails get longer. We call this method *inverse fisheye* and with it, the early stages of the exploration are performed with the threshold value set high implying that only the best trails will pass the evaluation. In the subsequent stages the threshold has its value progressively reduced in a manner which keeps it proportional to the exploration depth allowing the trails to be further explored. Moreover, the user has to specify the maximum exploration depth since there is no guarantee that the algorithm terminates, specially when the cut-point decreases at a higher rate than the trail probability.

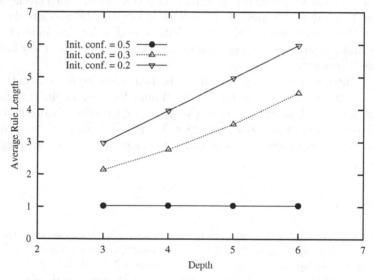

Fig. 16. Results of the inverse fisheye heuristic

Figure 16 shows how the average rule length varies with the exploration depth for a random grammar with 1000 states and average branching factor of 5, similar results were obtained for other configurations. The preliminary results suggest that by setting the initial confidence and the intended depth of exploration the user can have control over both the size of the rule set and its average rule length. Again, more detail of the heuristic and the experimental results can be found in [3].

6 Concluding Remarks

We have proposed a model of hypertext to capture user preferences when navigating through the web. We claim that our model has the advantage of being compact, self contained, coherent, and based on the well established work in probabilistic grammars providing it with a sound foundation for future enhancements including the study of its statistical properties. In fact the size of the model depends only on the number of pages and links in the web site being analysed and not on the amount of data collected.

The set of user navigation sessions is modelled as a hypertext probabilistic grammar, and the set of strings which are generated with higher probability correspond to the navigation trails preferred by the user. An algorithm to efficiently mine these strings is given. Extensive experiments with both real and random data were conducted and the results show that, in practice, the algorithm runs in linear time in the size of the grammar. Moreover, the entropy of the posterior grammar is shown to be a good estimator of the number of rules output from our algorithm, and the experiments with real data confirm the effectiveness of our algorithm. Our model has potential use both in helping the web site designer to understand the preferences of the site's visitors, and in helping individual users to better understand their own navigation patterns and increase their knowledge of the web's content.

A brief introduction was provided to the heuristics we are currently studying which aim to improve the quality of mining for user navigation patterns. Moreover, we intend to further study the use of information theoretic measures and their relation to the model properties. We are also planning to incorporate relevance measures of web pages in order to assist the user in locating useful information.

References

1. Azer Bestavros. Using speculation to reduce server load and service time on the www. In *Proc. of the fourth ACM International Conference on Information and Knowledge Management*, pages 403–410, Baltimore,MD, 1995. 105
2. J. Borges and M. Levene. Mining association rules in hypertext databases. In *Proc. of the fourth Int. Conf. on Knowledge Discovery and Data Mining*, pages 149–153, August 1998. 93, 96, 107
3. José Borges and Mark Levene. Heuristics for mining high quality user web navigation patterns. Research Note RN/99/68, Department of Computer Science, University College London, Gower Street, London, UK, October 1999. 107, 108, 109
4. Alex G. Büchner, M. Baumgarten, S.S. Anand, Maurice D. Mulvenna, and J.G. Hughes. Navigation pattern discovery from internet data. In *Proc. of the Web Usage Analysis and User Profiling Workshop*, pages 25–30, San Diego, California, August 1999. 107
5. Alex G. Büchner, Maurice D. Mulvenna, Sarab S. Anand, and John G. Hughes. An internet-enabled knowledge discovery process. In *Proc. of 9th International Database Conference*, pages 13–27, Hong Kong, July 1999. 107
6. Lara D. Catledge and James E. Pitkow. Characterizing browsing strategies in the world wide web. *Computer Networks and ISDN Systems*, 27(6):1065–1073, April 1995. 94
7. Soumen Chakrabarti, Byron E. Dom, David Gibson, Jon Kleinberg, Ravi Kumar, Prabhakar Raghavan, Sridhar Rajagopalan, and Andrew S. Tomkins. Mining the

link structure of the world wide web. *IEEE Computer*, 32(8):60–67, August 1999. 92

8. E. Charniak. *Statistical Language Learning*. The MIT Press, 1996. 96

9. Christopher Chatfield. Statistical inferences regarding markov chain models. *Applied Statistics*, 22:7–20, 1973. 104

10. M.-S. Chen, J. S. Park, and P. S. Yu. Efficient data mining for traversal patterns. *IEEE Trans. on Knowledge and Data Eng.*, 10(2):209–221, March/April 1998. 93, 106

11. R. Cooley, B. Mobasher, and J. Srivastava. Data preparation for mining world wide web browsing patterns. *Knowledge and Information Systems*, 1(1):5–32, February 1999. 94, 107

12. T. Cover and J. Thomas. *Elements of Information Theory*. John Wiley & Sons, 1991. 98

13. M. Craven, D. DiPasquo, D. Freitag, A. McCallum, T. Mitchell, K. Nigam, and S. Slattery. Learning to extract symbolic knowledge from the world wide web. In *Proc. of the 15th National Conf. on Artificial Intelligence*, pages 509–516, July 1998. 92

14. W. Feller. *An Introduction to Probability Theory and Its Applications*. John Wiley & Sons, second edition, 1968. 95

15. J. Hopcroft and J.Ullman. *Introduction to Automata Theory, Languages, and Computation*. Addison-Wesley, 1979. 95

16. M. Levene and G. Loizou. A probabilistic approach to navigation in hypertext. *Information Sciences*, 114:165–186, 1999. 94

17. Venkata N. Padmanabhan and Jeffrey C. Mogul. Using predictive prefetching to improve world wide web latency. *Computer Communications Review*, 26, 1996. 106

18. Mike Perkowitz and Oren Etzioni. Adaptive web sites: an AI challenge. In *Proc. of Fifteenth International Joint Conference on Artificial Intelligence (IJCAI-97)*, pages 16–21, Nagoya, Japan, August 1997. 93, 107

19. Mike Perkowitz and Oren Etzioni. Adaptive sites: Automatically synthesizing web pages. In *Proc. of the Fifteenth National Conference on Artificial Intelligence (AAAI-98)*, pages 727–732, Madison, Wisconsin, July 1998. 98, 99, 107

20. Peter L.T. Pirolli and James E. Pitkow. Distributions of surfers' paths through the world wide web: Empirical characterizations. *World Wide Web*, 2:29–45, 1999. 104, 106

21. L. Rosenfeld and P. Morville. *Information Architecture for the World Wide Web*. O'Reilly, 1998. 93

22. S. Schechter, M. Krishnan, and M. D. Smith. Using path profiles to predict http requests. *Computer Networks and ISDN Systems*, 30:457–467, 1998. 107

23. M. Spiliopoulou, L. C. Faulstich, and K. Wilkler. A data miner analyzing the navigational behaviour of web users. In *Proc. of the Workshop on Machine Learning in User Modelling of the ACAI99*, Greece, July 1999. 93

24. Myra Spiliopoulou and Lukas C. Faulstich. WUM: a tool for web utilization analysis. In *Proc. of the International Workshop on the Web and Databases (WebDB'98)*, pages 184–203, Valencia, Spain, March 1998. 107

25. R. Stout. *Web Site Stats: tracking hits and analyzing traffic*. Osborne McGraw-Hill, 1997. 93

26. C. S. Wetherell. Probabilistic languages: A review and some open questions. *Computing Surveys*, 12(4):361–379, December 1980. 94

27. T. W. Yan, M. Jacobsen, H. Garcia-Molina, and U. Dayal. From user access patterns to dynamic hypertext linking. In *Proc. of the 5th Int. World Wide Web Conference*, pages 1007–1014, 1996. 106
28. O. R. Zaïane, M. Xin, and J. Han. Discovering web access patterns and trends by applying olap and data mining technology on web logs. In *Proc. Advances in Digital Libraries Conf.*, pages 12–29, Santa Barbara, CA, April 1998. 107

Making Web Servers Pushier

Bin Lan[1], Stéphane Bressan[1], Beng Chin Ooi[1], and Y. C. Tay[2]

[1] Department of Computer Science, National University of Singapore
Lower Kent Ridge, Singapore 119260
{lanbin,steph,ooibc}@comp.nus.edu.sg
http://www.comp.nus.edu.sg/~{lanbin,steph,ooibc}
[2] Department of Mathematics, National University of Singapore
Lower Kent Ridge, Singapore 119260
mattyc@leonis.nus.edu.sg

Abstract. The success of the World Wide Web measured in terms of the number of its users and of the resulting traffic increase is only commensurate to the patience required when sitting in front of one's computer, waiting for a document to be down-loaded. If one could identify the typical access patterns for a set of documents on a Web server, the server could use or extend the existing protocols to accordingly pre-fetch or push documents to the browsers and proxy servers.

In this paper, we present and evaluate a strategy for making Web servers "pushier". Which document is to be pushed is determined by a set of association rules mined from a sample of the access log of the Web server. Once a rule of the form *"Document A → Document B"* has been identified and selected, the Web server decides to push "Document2" if "Document1" is requested. The strategy is individual user oriented while not ignoring the aggregate perspective. We evaluate the effectiveness and the cost of such a strategy for two architectures: a two tier "Web server / Web browser" architecture, and a three tier "Web server / proxy server / Web browser" architecture. We consider different settings in the architectures as well as refinements of the strategy taking into account the size of the documents.

1 Introduction

The unexpected and unprecedented success of the World Wide Web as a global information and communication infrastructure is probably largely due to the initial simplicity of its underlying protocols and languages. All one needs to create a reasonably good-looking Web page is a text editor, the knowledge of a few basic Hyper-Text Mark-up Language (HTML) tags, and the opportunity to upload files into a Web server. Similarly, the Hyper-Text Transfer Protocol (HTTP) is one of the simplest practical client-server protocol.

The ransom of success (as traffic increases) as well as the ransom of simplicity (of HTTP and its implementations) is to be paid by the World Wide Web user waiting for the document she requested to be loaded in her favorite browser. Many authors (e.g. [17,7,14,13,16]) have foreseen the opportunity to reduce the

B. Masand and M. Spiliopoulou (Eds.): WEBKDD'99, LNAI 1836, pp. 112–125, 2000.
© Springer-Verlag Berlin Heidelberg 2000

latency for World Wide Web users by identifying and leveraging access patterns and devising pre-fetching or pushing strategies for the servers. Indeed, it seems that access patterns can be anticipated from the structure of the hypertext documents ("She will follow the link"), *or* learned from access logs maintained by most Web servers *or* from client-side Web Agent(e.g., WebACE[8]).

Figure 1 depicts a simplified Web-client/server architecture with a simple request/response scenario. Our work stems from the hypothesis that the pushing of documents from the server to the client's cache can reduce the latency. Let us imagine that the sequence of requests of figure 1 (document A, document B, document C) could be predicted by the server as soon as it receives the first request (document A). We propose that the server pushes documents B and possibly C to the client (its cache) taking advantage of the delay between the successive requests (e.g. the user reading the requested document). The resulting interaction, illustrated on figure 2, shows the potential for latency reduction in such a scenario.

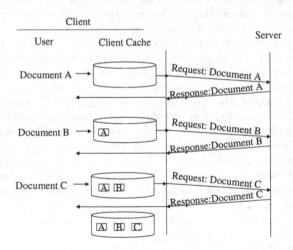

Fig. 1. Client-server traditional interaction

In this paper, we present and evaluate a strategy for making Web servers "pushier". Which document is to be pushed is determined by a set of association rules mined from a sample of the access log of the Web server. Once a rule of the form "*Document A → Document B*" has been identified, the Web server decides to push "Document B" if "Document A" is requested. This strategy can be applied recursively. If we can identify *Document A → Document B,Document B → C*, ..., the Web server can push *B, C,...* with A.

We evaluate the effectiveness and the cost of such a strategy for two architectures: a two tier "Web server / Web browser "architecture and a three tier

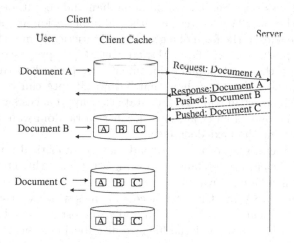

Fig. 2. Client-server push interaction. If the client asks for Document A, and we know that $A \rightarrow B$, $B \rightarrow C$,..., we push Document $B, C, \ldots$ with A. The dashed line shows that the server pushes the document(s), which the user may likely request in the near future

"Web server / proxy server / Web browser" architecture. We consider different settings in the architecture as well as possible refinements of the strategy.

In Section 2, we briefly survey related and comparable approaches. In Section 3, we give an overview of our approach by presenting the association rule mining technique we use as well as the various scenarios we consider in our study. In Section 4, we discuss the methodology we followed for our experiments and present the empirical results substantiating the positive argument in favor of our proposal.

2   Related Work

Client-server environments naturally lead to the consideration of pushing and pre-fetching strategies aiming at improving the efficiency of the service by decreasing the latency for the clients [2,12,18,19]. Franklin et al. [2], for instance, study the balance between push and pull for data broadcast. In the case of the World Wide Web, it seems natural to look for access patterns that may help in making appropriate pushing decisions.

A lot of information about the possible next document is potentially present in either the hyper-document structure, the access log file, or in other access statistics one Web server could realistically maintain. For instance, as reported in [7], Bestravos calculates from the access log the probability p[i,j] of a document D_j to be requested within a time interval t after a document i is requested. This approach incurs a 10% bandwidth overhead for a 23% reduction in document miss-rate. Similarly, Padmanabhan and co-authors [17] exploit the maintenance by their Web server of statistical information about such document inter-dependencies in the form of a graph: the statistically most likely next document is then pushed to the client. Markotos et al. [16] proposed an even simpler strategy where the most popular documents are pushed to the most frequent clients. The reported results show that a 40% hit rate can be obtained at the cost of a 10% increase in traffic. Other statistical approaches have been proposed such as the one by Cunha et al., in [11], where a random-walk model is used to try and determine the next document.

Other characteristics of the workload may be of critical importance for the design of an efficient pre-fetching or pushing strategy. Arlitt et al [6,5] were able to identify ten different invariants in a representative set of six access log files (including the NASA and ClarkNet access log files which we use for this study). They conjecture that their observation apply to most workload. Most important for our study, they show that the file size distribution is heavy tailed and that that daily patterns are representative. As we will see, we could verify that the SF100 access log, which we use in our study, complies with their conjecture.

In [15], we propose the use of an association rules mining technique for the pre-fetching of Web document from the server's disk into the server's cache. The results showed that this technique can effectively anticipate the requests for future documents. In this paper, we study the use of a similar technique for pushing documents between servers and browsers or proxies to decrease the latency for Web users.

3   The Approach

3.1   Mining Association Rules from Access Logs

The access log is a chronological list of entries recording which document (identified by its URL and characterized by its size) was requested by which agent (identified by the IP address of the client machine [1]). For our purpose agents, i.e. machines, will also be considered to be users. We call *transaction* the chronological list of entries for a given agent and for a fixed and given period of time (we call the *transaction's window*). A transaction is a projection of a portion of the access log. Looking at all the transactions in the access log, we construct rules of the form $D_i \rightarrow D_j$, where D_i and D_j are documents (URLs). The intuitive interpretation of such rules is that document D_j is likely to be requested by the same user sometimes after document D_i has been requested and there is no other request between the requests for D_i and D_j, since it is usually the case according to the log. The measure of the viability of such a rule is the confidence which is defined by the ratio support $(D_i D_j)/$ support(D_i). support(D_i) is the total number of occurrences of document D_i in the transactions over the total

---

[1] The assumption that an IP identifies a user may not hold up in a large environment. However, it is made because we can not access the clients, where cookies etc. can be used to separate the access streams.

number of transactions. Similarly as we note D_iD_j a sequence in a transaction containing document D_i *immediately* followed by document D_j, support (D_iD_j) is the total number of occurrences of the a sequence D_iD_j in the transactions over total number of transactions.

The process of discovering all association rules *Document A → Document B* can be decomposed into two subprocesses:

- We first find all document D whose support(D) is above *minimum support*. Such documents can be considered as *popular documents*.
- We then mine the association rule $D_i → D_j$ for the popular documents only. From all possible rules we eliminate those whose confidence is below a predefined threshold(*minimum confidence*).

It is worth noting that the rule mining in the paper is different from traditional rule mining[4,3] and other Web rule mining[10,9].

- The transactions are identified by the host(or IP address), which is provided by the Web server access log. In other words, it is user oriented, while not ignoring the aggregate perspective.
- The items in the transaction are time-ordered. In other words, the order among the requests is relevant and taken into account.
- We mine the rules of the form $A → B$ to predict that a user will request Document B *immediately* after she asks for Document A. In other words, the confidence of $A → B$ is the probability of the user request for B after she requests for A, and no other document is requested between A and B.

3.2   Enabling Servers to Push Relevant Documents

Upon request for a document D_i from a given agent, if rules of the form $D_i → D_j$ has been mined, the server pushes the document D_j according to the one rule with the highest confidence. Ties are resolved arbitrarily. In other words for each D_i, we only keep a rule $D_i → D_j$ with highest confidence. Pushing the document means enclosing the additional document into a multi-part response to the initial request or, in the future, sending an un-requested response in a persistent connection. If the rule we have mined is representative of the access pattern of a typical user, we can expect document D_j to be requested in the near future. In the occurrence of such an event, the client (browser or proxy, as we will see) will find the document available in its cache, reducing the latency.

This strategy can be applied recursively. If there is a rule $D_j → D_k$ with maximum confidence, we can push D_k with both D_i and D_j in the same connection, and so on. A parameter of our strategy is therefore the *push-length*, which is the maximum number of objects pushed with D_i applying successive association rules. A push-length of 0 corresponds to the standard protocol. A more aggressive strategy using a large push length unfortunately incurs a higher cost in bandwidth consumption, i.e. a traffic increase.

As one may suspect that the size of the documents pushed matters as it increases the traffic and therefore the cost, we also experimented with a strategies that take into account the size of the documents. We propose a second strategy, which uses "size-weighted" rules. Instead of the confidence C alone, we take into account S, the size of D_j, in order to select a rule $D_i \rightarrow D_j$. We consider a function f(C, S), which is monotonically increasing with C and monotonically decreasing with S. For the sake of simplicity, in this paper, we choose

$$f(C, S) = \frac{C}{S}$$

Upon request for a document D_i from a given agent, if rules of the form $D_i \rightarrow D_j$ has been mined, the server pushes the document D_j such that the corresponding rule has the highest value for f(C,S).

3.3 Scenarios

We consider three different scenarios for this study.

In our first scenario, we simulate a situation where the clients are Web browsers for which the local caches (disk and main memory) are partially disabled, i.e. the browsers are memory-less. However, the cache still keeps the documents pushed in anticipation until the agent sends another request . The Web server decides to try and anticipate requests from individual clients by pushing documents according to the mined association rules.

In our second scenario, we take into account the fact that the previously fetched documents are kept into the cache of the browsers. Notice that it is reasonable to consider that the cache is sufficiently large to keep all requested and pushed documents over the entire the time period between the consecutive activations of the access knowledge miner, allowing us to ignore the specifics of a replacement policy.

Finally, we consider a third architecture where the web browsers are accessing the Web server through a proxy server providing caching facilities. Again, it is reasonable to consider that the cache provided by the proxy is sufficiently large. We also assume that every 100 agents share one proxy. The new aspect of this latter scenario is that documents requested by one browser or consequently pushed are in the cache of the proxy and are available to other browsers.

For each of the three scenarios we evaluate the two techniques described above:

- $f(C, S)$=C
  In the simplest case, we decide push documents according to the association rules with the highest confidence.
- $f(C, S) = \frac{C}{S}$
  In this case, both the confidence of the rule and the size of the document to be pushed are taken into account.

4   Experiments

This section includes two part: first, we describes the experimental methodology in Section 4.1; second, we present the results in Section 4.2.

4.1   Methodology

The Data. In order to evaluate our proposed techniques, we simulate them using three real-life access logs.

- SF100 is a campus-wide Web course intended for first year students at the National University of Singapore. The hyper-document is hierarchically structured in chapters and sections very much like a traditional textbook. The log sample we considered contains $1,477,046$ request over two and a half month period from July 1997 to October 97.
- The NASA Kennedy Space Center's access log contains $3,461,612$ requests collected over two months between July 1995 and October 1995.
- The ClarkNet is a commercial Internet service provider in the Baltimore (Washington D.C.) region. Its log contains $3,328,587$ requests collected over a period of two weeks between August and September 1995.

Table 1 summarizes the characteristics of these three data sets. Figure 3 recalls the observation of [6,5] concerning the file distribution of the NASA and ClarkNet logs and shows that the conjecture also holds for SF100. An important underlying hypothesis for our experiments is the periodicity of the access pattern. Again, for NASA and ClarkNet it has been shown by the study of [6,5]. Figure 4 shows the burstiness across one time scale. It shows a full week of SF100 data, in which daily usage pattern can be observed. The patterns suggest strong evidence of daily periodicity of SF100 data.

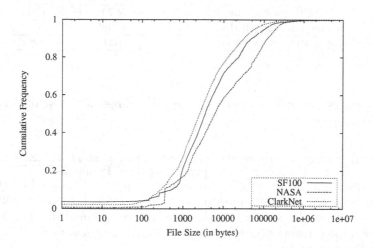

Fig. 3. Distribution of File Sizes. The file size distribution is heavy-tailed; the tail of the distribution is Pareto with $0.40 < \beta < 0.63$

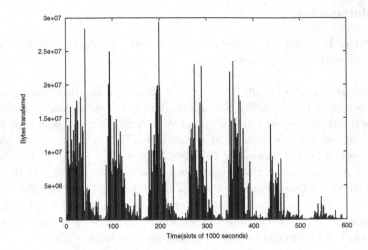

Fig. 4. Server Workload at one Time Scale (SF100 Data). A daily usage pattern can be observed in a full week of SF100 data

Table 1. Access Logs Characteristics

Item	SF100	NASA	ClarkNet
Access Log Duration	2.5 months	2 months	2 weeks
Access Log Start Date	July 23/97	Jul 1/95	Aug 28/95
Access Log Size(MB)	137.0	355.8	327.5
Total Requests	1477046	3461612	3328587
Ave Requests/Day	32156	56748	237756
Bytes Transferred(MB)	19524	62489	27647
Avg Bytes/Day(MB)	433.9	1024.4	1974.8

The Metrics. In order to evaluate the effectiveness and cost of our strategy, we use two metrics:

1. hit rate
$$\frac{\texttt{total number of requests serviced from pushed documents}}{\texttt{total number of requests initially needed}}$$
It represents the capacity of our strategy to predict the useful documents. If request is serviced from pushed documents(i.e., *hit*), the user will wait less time because the copy of the document is near to him/her. Therefore it also shows the percentage of the cases when users wait *less* time.

2. traffic increase
$$\frac{\texttt{total send size with push-total send size without push}}{\texttt{total send size without push and cache disabled}}$$

Notice that we compare the traffic to the traffic when the cache is disabled. As a result, all the plots are comparable across the three scenarios. We recall

that the values obtained for a push-length of 0 correspond to the disabling of
the association rule (no rule is used), i.e. the standard protocol.

Other Settings. Graph 4 shows the **daily pattern** for the workload of SF100,
which is part of the argument that SF100 has the periodicity of one day. Because
of the daily periodicity we could confirm from the NASA and ClarkNet access
logs and observe on the SF100, we decided to define the **transactions' window**
to be **one day**.

The **minimum support** and **minimum confidence** are set as **10%** and
1%, respectively. The (average) number of popular files and association rules
is very small comparing to the number of objects, which is shown in Table 2.
Incidentally we remark that for each of the popular document we mine few (1-2)
association rules.

Table 2. Size of popular files and association rules

Data Set	Number of Popular Files	Number of Association Rules
SF100	272.4	554.1
NASA	157.8	244.6
ClarkNet	213.9	390.2

To study the performance when **push-length** varies, there are six different
push lengths **0, 1, 2, 4, 8, 16** in the following experiments.

4.2   Results

Figures 5, 6 and 7 show the results for three different scenarios using two different
techniques: using simple association rules and weighting the association rule by
the size of the pushed document. The figures plot the **hit-rate percentage** as
a function of the **traffic increase in percentage**. [2] The successive points on
each plot represent the successive push lengths (0 to 16 from left to right).

Figures 8 separately plots the **traffic increase in percentage** as a function
of the **push-length**. The first remark applies to all scenarios and both strategies:
the traffic increase is a linear function of the push length.

Applying Simple Association Rules. In this first experiment, we simply use
the confidence to select association and decide the documents to be pushed. The
plots labeled with "push to browser with cache off", "push to browser with cache

---

[2] That we use *traffic increase in percentage* as a variable aims to show the maximum
hit rate at different loaded network. It is reasonable for a specific workload to get a
higher hit rate in a lightly loaded network than in heavily loaded network.

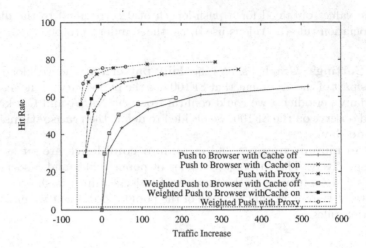

Fig. 5. Hit Rate vs Traffic Increase for SF100

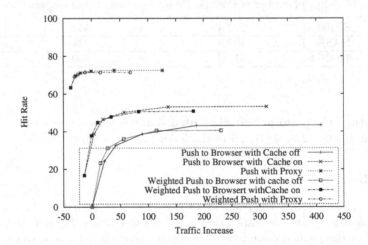

Fig. 6. Hit Rate vs Traffic Increase for NASA

on", and "push with proxy" show the performance in three different scenarios. The first observation is a confirmation that the architecture with proxy is better than the architectures without, and that the use of the cache is an improvement. Then, we notice that the relative performance of the three architectures is maintained by the use of our strategy.

More interestingly, the results show that the pushing strategy (push length > 0) produces a higher hit rate than the strategy without pushing (push length=0). The hit rate can reach about 80%, 70% and 60% for SF100, NASA and ClarkNet workloads, respectively. In other words, the strategy we propose is effective.

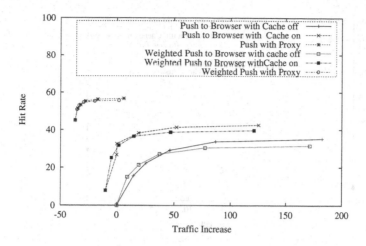

Fig. 7. Hit Rate vs Traffic Increase for ClarkNet

Unfortunately but predictably, the traffic volume also increases as the push-length increases. However, as already remarked, the traffic increase is only linear in the push length. For all plots on figures 5, 6, and 7, we see that the rate of traffic increase is higher than the rate of hit rate increase until a push length of 3 to 4 (at the critical point where the slope equals 1). This, we believe, suggests that lower push-length may be of higher practical interest.

Mozilla: Does Size Matter? The cost of our strategy essentially depends on the incurred traffic increase measured in volume of data transferred. It seems natural to try and take into account the size of the documents to be pushed in order to reduce the cost while trying to maintain the benefit.

For each of the three architectures considered, the plots labeled with "weighted" show the performance for a strategy using the size-weighted confidence. The observation made in the previous sub-section, in the case of a confidence-only selection of association rules, still apply. Moreover, for a given push-length, the new strategy results in a lower traffic increase as smaller documents are pushed. Globally, i.e independently from the push-length, the results are only systematically better (generating a given hit-rate at lower cost in traffic increase) for the SF100 benchmark. For the NASA and ClarkNet benchmarks the improvement only occurs before the critical point with slope 1 (for push-length 3 or 4). As we have already remarked, we believe that such shorter push-lengths will be the most practical in actual implementations. Therefore we can conclude that the size-weighted strategy is a practical improvement.

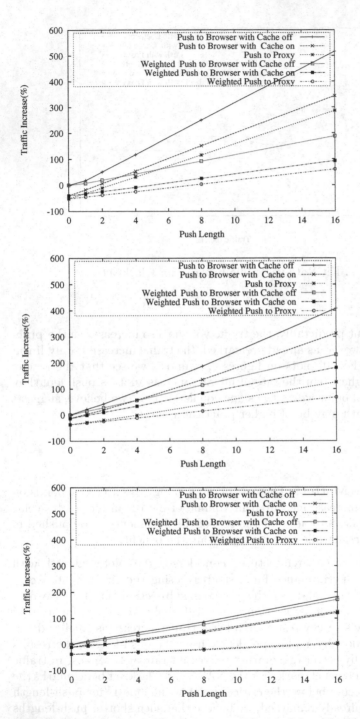

Fig. 8. Traffic increase as a function of the push length. The figures from top to bottom are for SF100, NASA and ClarkNet, respectively

5   Conclusion

We have proposed an original and effective strategy to reducing the latency for Web users. Web server are made "pushier", i.e. anticipate the needs of their clients, browsers or proxies, by pushing un-requested documents. The documents to be pushed are determined by association rules, which have been mined from the access log of the Web server. Our strategy incurs a cost in terms of traffic increase. In the choice of the different parameters of our strategy (mainly the push length), a trade-off is necessary. Our experiments with three representative access logs for existing Web seem to indicate the existence of invariants in the relationship between the cost and the benefit. In particular we remarked that the traffic increase is a linear function of the push length, i.e. the number of documents pushed in anticipation and that the benefit increases at a higher rate than the cost for push-length up to 3 or 4. In a first attempt to reduce the cost, we could successfully improve our strategy by taken the size of the pushed documents into account in the selection decision. We are currently experimenting with a more systematic approach to this idea.

We recognize however that implementing the strategy proposed for existing commercial browsers and proxy servers may not be realistic given the definition and implementation of HTTP. It is likely however that features such as the multi-part/byterange mime type of HTTP/1.1 will soon be better exploited by commercial user-agents. At the same time we also expect more support for push technology to be available in protocols dedicated to channels and live data feeds. Such technology, integrated into Web browsers will be available to implement original pre-fetching and pushing strategies.

We are now experimenting with variants of the basic strategy proposed aiming at reducing the cost and maximizing the benefit by establishing the right combination of parameters: size, push-length, and confidence. At the same time, we are considering the prototyping of a Web server implementing our strategy, extending, for instance, the W3C Jigsaw server[1].

Acknowledgment

We like to thank Arlitt and the Computer Center of National University of Singapore, for respectively making the NASA and ClarkNet, and SF100 data sets available to us.

References

1. Jigsaw - the w3c's web server. http://www.w3.org/Jigsaw/.   124
2. Acharya, S., Franklin, M., and Zdonik, S. Balancing push and pull for data broadcast. In *Proceedings of ACM SIGMOD Conference* (Tuscon,Arizona, May 1997). http://www.cs.umd.edu/project/bdisk/pushpull.ps.   114
3. Agrawal, R., and Srikant, R. Fast algorithms for mining association rules. In *Proc. 1994 Int. Conf. Very Large Data Bases* (Santiago, Chile, Sept. 1994), pp. 487–499. 116

4. Agrawal, R., Imienlinski, T., and Swami, A. Mining association rules between sets of items in large databases. In *Proc. 1993 ACM-SIGMOD Int. Conf. Management of Data* (Washington, D. C., May 1993), pp. 207–216. 116

5. Arlitt, M. F. A performance study of internet Web servers. Master's thesis, University of Saskatchewan, Saskatoon,Saskatchewan, 1996. 115, 118

6. Arlitt, M. F., and Williamson, C. L. Web server workload characterization:the search for invariants. In *Proceedings of the ACM Sigmetrics Conference on Measurement and Modeling of Computer Systems* (Philadelphia,PA, May 1996), pp. 126–137. 115, 118

7. Bestavros, A. Using speculation to reduce server load and service time on the www. In *Proceedings of CIKM'95: The 4th ACM International Conference on Information and Knowledge Management* (Baltimore,Maryland, Nov. 1995). 112, 114

8. Boley, D., Gini, M., K.Hastings, Mobaster, B., and Moore, J. A client-side Web agent for document categorization. *Journal of Internet Research 8*, 5 (1998). 113

9. Chen, M.-S., Park, J. S., and Yu, P. S. Efficient data mining for path traversal patterns. *IEEE Transactions on Knowledge and Data Engineering*, 2 (Mar. 1998), 209–221. 116

10. Cooley, R., Mobasher, B., and Srivastava, J. Web mining: Information and pattern discovery on the World Wide Web. In *Proceeding of the 9th IEEE International Conference on Tools with AI* (Nov. 1997). http://www-users.cs.umn.edu/~cooley. 116

11. Cunha, C. R., and Jaccoud, C. F. B. Determining WWW user's next access and its application to pre-fetching. In *Proceedings of ISCC'97: The second IEEE Symposium on Computers and Communications* (Alexandria, Egypt, July 1997). 115

12. Curewitz, K. M., Krishnan, P., and Vitter, J. S. Practical prefetching via data compression. In *Proceedings of ACM SIGMOD Conference* (Washington, D.C, 1993), pp. 257–266. 114

13. Fan, L., Cao, P., Lin, W., and Jacobson, Q. Web prefetching between low-bandwidth clients and proxies:potential and performance. In *Proceedings of the ACM Sigmetrics Conference on Measurement and Modeling of Computer Systems* (Atlanta, GA, May 1999), pp. 178–187. 112

14. Jacobson, Q., and Cao, P. Potential and limits of Web prefectching between low-bandwidth clients and proxies. In *3rd International Caching workshop* (Manchester, England, June 1998). 112

15. Lan, B., Ooi, B. C., Tay, Y. C., and Goh, C. H. Web server caching and prefetching: A data mining-based approach. http://comp.nus.edu.sg/~lanbin/web-server-caching.ps, 1999. 115

16. Markatos, E. P., and Chronaki, C. E. A Top-10 approach to prefetching on the Web. Technical report, Institute of Computer Science,Foundation for Research & Technology- Hellas(FORTH),Greece, Aug. 1996. http://www.ics.forth.gr/proj/arch-vlsi/www.html. 112, 115

17. Padmanabhan, V. N., and Mogul, J. C. Using predictive prefetching to improve World Wide Web latency. *ACM SIGCOMM Computer Communication Review 26*, 3 (1996), 22–36. 112, 115

18. Palmer, M., and Zdonik, S. B. Fido: A cache that learns to fetch. In *Proceedings of 17th International Conference on Very Large Data Bases* (Barcelona,Spain, Sept. 1991), pp. 255–264. 114

19. Rousskov, A., Soloviev, V., and Tatarinov, I. Static caching. In *NLANR Web Cache Workshop* (Boulder,Colorado, U.S.A, June 1997). 114

Analysis and Visualization of Metrics for Online Merchandising

Juhnyoung Lee, Mark Podlaseck, Edith Schonberg, Robert Hoch,
and Stephen Gomory

IBM T.J. Watson Research Center
P.O. Box 704, Yorktown Heights, NY 10598
{jyl,podlasec,ediths,rhoch,gomory}@us.ibm.com

Abstract. While techniques and tools for Web marketing are being actively
developed, there is much less available for Web merchandising. This paper
contributes to the area of Web usage analysis for E-commerce merchandising.
First, we categorize areas of analysis for Web merchandising such as product
assortment, merchandising cues, shopping metaphors, and Web design features.
Second, we define a new set of metrics for Web merchandising, which we call
micro-conversion rates. These new metrics provide capabilities for examining
data about sales and merchandising in online stores, and also provide detailed
insight into the effectiveness of different Web merchandising efforts by
answering related business questions. Third, we present a set of novel
visualizations that explore patterns in micro-conversions in online stores
reflecting in customer responses to various Web merchandising efforts.
Through an empirical study using look-to-buy data from an online store, we
demonstrate how the proposed visualizations can be used to understand the
shopping behavior in an online store and the effectiveness of various
merchandising tactics it employs. Finally, we discuss the types of data required
for this kind of visual analysis of online merchandising, and briefly describe
how the data can be collected and integrated in an E-commerce site.

1 Introduction

In just a few years, the Internet has evolved into a significant commerce vehicle, that
is, a channel for sales and customer service of virtually every type of business. In
order to maximize their return on investment, Web merchants are finding it necessary
to thoroughly understand the effectiveness of their sites and to take appropriate action
when and where the sites fall short. Web merchants generally analyze their sites'
effectiveness from two perspectives: marketing and merchandising.

Marketing on the Web is narrowly defined as the activities used to acquire
customers to an online store and retain them. Techniques for online marketing include
the use of banner ads and email campaigns. Examples of marketing business
questions include the followings: Which banner ads generate the most traffic and
sales? Which portal sites are pulling in the most qualified traffic? Who are the buyers
referred by a particular ad? Web usage metrics for answering these questions are the
banner ad *clickthrough rate*, which is the percentage of viewers who click on a banner

B. Masand and M. Spiliopoulou (Eds.): WEBKDD'99, LNAI 1836, pp. 126-141, 2000.

ad, and the *conversion rate*, which is the percentage of visitors who purchase from the store. Recently, ad banner *return on investment* (ROI) has become the significant metric for Web marketing. Marketers want to know not only the number of visitors who come to a site from a particular banner ad and purchase from the site, but also how much revenue and profit is generated by these visitors.

Merchandising consists of the activities involved in acquiring particular products and making them available at the places, times, and prices and in the quantity to enable a retailer store to reach its goals [3]. The activities also include how and where to display products, and which products to advertise and promote. Online merchandisers are responsible for product assortment and product display, including promotions, cross-selling and up-selling. In large online stores, merchandisers make adjustments to the Web site content continuously, i.e., weekly or even daily. To assist online merchandisers, there are tools available for content management [8], which facilitate modifying the Web site and also data mining techniques for association rule generation to determine which products are suitable for cross-selling [2]. However, in the area of Web usage analysis, while the needs of reporting and analysis for marketing is being addressed, useful merchandising metrics and tools lag behind. Web page hit counts provide a broad indication of visitor interest. However, keeping track of which products are shown on each Web page can be tedious or impossible, in particular, when page content is highly dynamic and personalized. Furthermore, there is a need to know to what extent interest translates into sales.

This paper focuses on the analysis of merchandising effectiveness in online stores. We define a new set of metrics, which we call *micro-conversion rates*. We show how these metrics provide detailed insight into the success of different Web merchandising, product assortment, and site design strategies. Also, we present novel visualizations of micro-conversion, inspired by the starfield model [1] which is a scatterplot graph, a well-known general-purpose visualization tool useful for finding patterns in multidimensional data. The concept of micro-conversion rates is based on banner ad marketing metrics. More specifically, we view an E-commerce site as a collection of advertisements for individual products in the store. From this perspective, we measure clickthrough rates, conversion rates, and ROI for a broad range of internal Web site features, including cross-sell, up-sell, and promotion. These metrics provide information at the individual product level, as well as on the product attribute and aggregate levels. Our belief is that this kind of information is both actionable and necessary for merchandising success.

The rest of this paper is structured as follows: Section 2 presents a high level set of merchandising usage analysis areas and related business questions. Section 3 defines a new set of metrics for merchandising, referred to as micro-conversion rates. Techniques for visualizing micro-conversion are illustrated and described in Section 4. In Section 5, an empirical study on the starfield visualization technique is described with look-to-buy data from an online store. In Section 6, we discuss the types of data required for this kind of visual analysis of online merchandising, and briefly describe how the data can be collected and integrated from an E-commerce site. In Section 7, related work is evaluated and summarized. Finally, in Section 8, conclusions are drawn and further work is outlined.

2   Analysis of Web Merchandising

Before defining micro-conversion rates, this section first categorizes and describes four primary areas of Web merchandising analysis: product assortment, merchandising cues, shopping metaphor, and Web design features. The first analysis area, *product assortment*, deals with whether the products in an online store appeal to the visitors. If the product assortment is not optimal, the merchants may adjust, for example, brands, quality, selection, inventory or price of the products they carry. Examples of business questions related to product assortment include the following: What are the top sellers for a specific period of time, e.g., this week? What is the conversion rate for a particular department? In what frequencies and quantities are products purchased? What characterizes the products that end up being abandoned? Analyzing the effectiveness of individual products by finding answers to these questions provides some insight into product assortment. However, there may be some other merchandising problems that are resulting in poor sales. Complete understanding requires looking at other metrics and the remaining three areas of analysis, which deal with site design effectiveness.

Merchandising cues are different ways Web merchants present and/or group their products to motivate purchase in online stores. Examples of merchandising cues are cross-sells, up-sells, recommendations, and promotions. A *cross-sell* in an online store is a hyperlink, which refers the visitor to a Web page marketing an item complementary in function to the item marketed on the current Web page. An *up-sell* hyperlink refers the visitor to a Web page presenting a similar but more upscale item. A *recommendation* hyperlink highlights product pages that are likely to be of interest to the shopper based on knowledge of the shopper and the behavior of a larger population. A *promotion* hyperlink refers a visitor to a product page from a "What's Hot" page or a high traffic area such as the "Home" page for informing, persuading and/or reminding the shoppers about a product and/or other aspects of the site. Online merchants need to understand the effectiveness of the merchandising cues in their stores in terms of traffic and sales driven by them. Examples of business questions related to merchandising cues include the followings: How much cross-sells and up-sells contribute to gross revenue? What are the best performing cross-sell pairs? And worst? What is the overall conversion rate for cross-sells? How much do promotions contribute to gross revenue? Which promotions are generating the most sales? At which levels in the site hierarchy are the best promotions located?

Shopping metaphors in an online store are different ways that shoppers use to find products of interest.   Examples include browsing through the product catalog hierarchy, various forms of searching, and configuration for "build-to-order" type products. The effectiveness of different shopping metaphors in the store is a concern for online merchants. Like merchandising cues in online stores, shopping metaphors are associated with hyperlinks on Web pages. This allows one to categorize and group together hyperlinks in an online store by their types of merchandising cue and shopping metaphor. Examples of business questions related to shopping metaphors in online stores include the followings: What generates the most sales value, e.g., search or browsing? How much does search contribute to gross revenue? What is the conversion rate for search?

Table 1. Areas of Web merchandising analysis and sample business questions

Analysis Areas	Business Questions
Product Assortment	What are the top sellers of the week? What is the conversion rate for a particular department? How is a product purchased: purchase frequency and quantity? What characterizes the products that end up being abandoned? How much of the sales of each product are driven by search?
Merchandising Cues	How much do cross-sells contribute to gross revenue? What are the best performing cross-sell pairs? Worst? What is the overall conversion rate for cross-sells? How much do promotions contribute to gross revenue? Which promotions are generating the most sales? Which levels in site hierarchy are the best promotions located at?
Shopping Metaphors	What generates the more sales value: search or browsing? How much does search contribute to gross revenue? What is the conversion rate for search?
Design Features	What are the features of links shoppers most frequently click? What are the features of links shoppers most frequently buy from? What are the parts of page customers most frequently buy from? Do products sell better in the upper left corner?

Other merchandising aspects that can be used to categorize hyperlinks are their design features such as media type (e.g., image or text), font (if text), size, color, location. The effectiveness of Web design features presents another area of analysis for merchandising. Examples of business questions related to Web design features include: What are the features of links customers most frequently click? What are the features of links customers most frequently buy from? What are the parts of Web pages customers most frequently buy from? Do products sell better in the upper left corner? Table 1 summarizes the areas of Web merchandising analysis with some sample business questions for each area.

Just as Web marketing uses banner ads and/or referral sites to attract customers from external sites to an online store, Web merchandising uses hyperlinks and image links within the store to lead customers to click to Web pages selling products. Web merchants employ a variety of merchandising schemes associated with hyperlinks. From this perspective, the problem of tracking and measuring the effectiveness of different merchandising strategies in an online store can be partitioned into three sub-problems:

- classifying each hyperlink by its merchandising purposes,
- tracking and measuring traffic on the hyperlinks and analyzing their effectiveness (e.g., profitability), and
- attributing the profit of the hyperlinks to their merchandising cue type, shopping metaphor type, and design features.

The analysis of the effectiveness of marketing strategies is conducted in a similar way by using the metrics such as clickthrough rates and ad banner ROI described earlier. The only difference is that the originating hyperlinks in marketing efforts are presented and controlled in external sites.

3   Micro-Conversion Rate

Having identified the areas of Web merchandising analysis, we now introduce a set of metrics, referred to as micro-conversion rates, which can be used for measuring the effectiveness of efforts in these merchandising areas. The metrics are based on the conversion rate which is used for measuring online marketing performance. Traditionally, the conversion rate of an online store indicates the percentage of visitors who purchase from the store. While this measure is useful for evaluating the overall effectiveness of the store, it does not help understand the possible factors within the store that may affect the sales performance. The notion of a micro-conversion rate extends this traditional measure by considering the four general shopping steps in online stores, which are:

- product impression: the view of hyperlink to a Web page presenting a product.
- clickthrough: the click on the hyperlink and view the Web page of the product.
- basket placement: the placement of the item in the shopping basket.
- purchase: the purchase of the item - completion of a transaction.

Basic micro-conversion rates are computed for each adjacent pair of these measures, resulting in the first three rates in the following list. In addition, the aggregation of the first three is also interesting. By looking at this look-to-buy rate, online merchants can tell if a product is overexposed or underexposed and take action to change the presentation of the product:

- look-to-click rate: how many product impressions are converted to clickthroughs.
- click-to-basket rate: how many clickthroughs are converted to basket placement.
- basket-to-buy rate: how many basket placements are converted to purchases.
- look-to-buy rate: what percentage of product impressions is eventually converted to purchases.

Note that the first of these, look-to-click rate, is similar to the clickthrough rate used for measuring the amount of traffic on banner ads. Also note that the micro-conversion rates relate the traffic-related measure to sales which happen later in the shopping process.

Table 2. Micro-conversion rates for sample business questions

Product Assortment	Look-to-click	Is a product's exposure optimized for the current level of customer interest?
	Click-to-basket	Is the detailed information about a product appropriate?
	Basket-to-buy	What kinds of products are abandoned in the shopping basket?
Merchandising Cues	Look-to-click	What cross-sells are working best? Worst?
	Click-to-basket	Is a cross-sell more likely to be placed in a shopping basket if the first item has already been placed there?
	Basket-to-buy	Are the customers who responded to a cross-sell any more or less likely to abandon a product in a shopping basket?
Shopping Metaphors	Look-to-click	Are customers finding what they want from the search engine?
	Click-to-basket	Do customers who found a product through the search engine want the same amount of product detail as those that found it by browsing?
	Basket-to-buy	Are the customers who responded to a search result any more or less likely to abandon a product in a shopping basket?
Design Features	Look-to-click	Are visitors clicking more image links than text links?
	Click-to-basket	Are there product links that are misleading?
	Basket-to-buy	Where are the problems in the check-out process?

Table 2 presents sample business questions on merchandising that can be addressed by micro-conversion rates for each analysis area. By precisely tracking the shopping steps with these rates, it is possible to spot exactly where the store loses how many customers. The micro-conversion rates extend the traditional measure by considering the merchandising purposes associated with hyperlinks viewed in the first shopping step, i.e., product impression. In this way, the micro-conversion rate is related to tactics of merchandising, and can be used for evaluating the effectiveness of different merchandising aspects of the store.

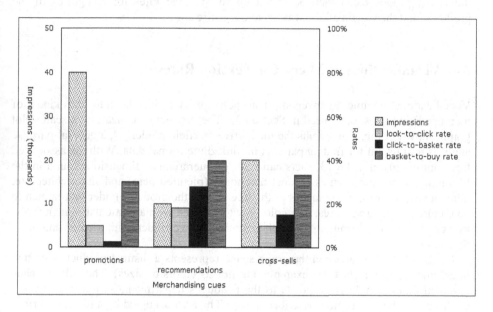

Fig. 1. An example of micro-conversion rates

Fig. 1 illustrates in a bar chart an example of micro-conversion rates for three different types of merchandising cues, i.e., promotions, recommendations, and cross-sells. Visitors are seeing twice as many impressions of promotions (40,000) than cross-sell impressions (20,000), and twice as many cross-sell impressions than those of recommendations (10,000). However, the look-to-click rate for recommendations (18%) is twice as high as for either promotions or cross-sells. Additionally, recommendations are resulting in a relatively high look-to-buy rate (2%). This means that the recommendation engine is relatively effective at personalization. On the other hand, this example shows that promotions in this store are not effective. Of the visitors who place a promoted item in a shopping basket, 30% of them purchase the product. However, the clickthrough rate for promotions is 10% and the click-to-basket rate is only 2.5%, so the look-to-buy rate is 0.075%, which shows poor overall performance, and an over-exposure of the promoted items. Finally, the look-to-buy rate for cross-sells in this example is about 0.5%.

As illustrated in this example, micro-conversion rates can be calculated for individual merchandising cue types, and also, for individual products, individual shopping metaphor types, individual design features, and individual banner ads. As a result, all the individual hyperlinks pointing to product pages in various forms and purposes, internal or external to the site can be analyzed. Unlike the traditional conversion rate, which gives just one number for the entire site, these micro-conversion rates provide insight into a rich set of information pertaining to the analysis areas described in section 2. For instance, they can be computed for individual products to measure the product performance in the site. The rates for individual products can then be rolled up to give the rates for categories of the products, and then again all the way up to the entire site.

4   Visualizations of Micro-Conversion Rates

Visualizations of micro-conversion can help provide insight into the kinds of merchandising questions raised in Section 3. The product visualization, a scatterplot graph, shown in Fig. 2 augments the interactive starfield model [1], a general-purpose analysis tool useful for finding patterns in multidimensional data. With the associated tree controls given in Fig. 3, users can filter on hierarchical dimensions found in the E-commerce domain such as product taxonomy (pictured here) and site architecture. Selection of one or more branches of the tree causes the products under that branch to be pictured in the graph area. The color key associated with a particular branch in the tree can be inherited from a parent (the default) or overridden with a color unique to that child.

Each rectangle or *glyph* in the graph space represents a distinct product (a certain brand and type of T-shirt, for example, but not its colors or sizes). The color of each glyph in this example corresponds to the product's department, as indicated by the color key on the tree control described above. The area occupied by a glyph describes a product's relative significance: width is an indicator of the product's price, and height, its relative (profit) margin.

The x-axis and the y-axis of the starfield graph can represent any two of the micro-conversion rate metrics. In the example in Fig. 2, the user configured the axes to analyze product exposure relative to customer interest ("Are the right products being promoted? How do I optimize the exposure of all my products to maximize my revenue stream?"). The x-axis thus represents raw impressions, that is, the number of times a hyperlink to a product was served. (Product hyperlinks can occur anywhere on the commerce site: the home page, category pages, search result pages, as well as other product pages.) The y-axis represents the percentage of impressions that resulted in a clickthrough (that is, of the number of customers that saw a hyperlink to this product, the percentage that clicked on the link).

The scatterplot graph makes evident the heavy over-promotion of a product represented by the small glyph in the lower right quadrant. While it has had more impressions than almost any other product, its clickthrough is almost the lowest. To make matters worse, it is a low-priced, low-margin product. Its exposure could be reduced by moving its promotion to a less-trafficked page, or eliminating it entirely.

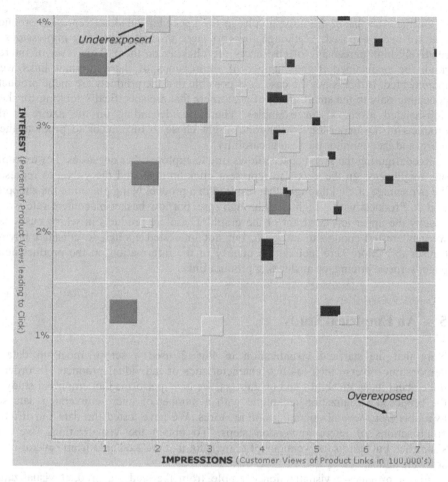

Fig. 2. Product visualization based on the starfield model

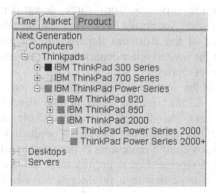

Fig. 3. Tree control

On the other hand, the large glyphs in the upper left quadrant represent products that are under-exposed. Although links to these products have few impressions, a relatively high percentage of customers are clicking on them. This level of interest might be maintained if the number of impressions of these product links were incremented. If that is not the case, it is possible that the products are niche products, appealing only to the small group of customers that are specifically looking for them (left-handed joysticks, for example). Therefore, depending on the nature of the products in the upper-left corner, one might chose to display or to promote them more, and then monitor the results carefully.

Reconfiguring the graph space allows one to explore other questions. For example, one might reassign the x-axis to represent clickthroughs and the y-axis to represent the percentage of clickthroughs that resulted in a product being placed in the shopping basket. Products with a high clickthrough rate, but low basket-placement rate would occupy the upper left quadrant of the graph. These are products in which customers were interested enough to click on, but not interested enough to consider buying. Causes to explore here include the quality of the information on the product detail page, surprise pricing, or misleading product links.

5   An Empirical Study

Note that the starfield visualization in Fig. 2 used a set of mock-up data to demonstrate diverse look-to-click characteristics of individual products. In order to understand its applicability and usefulness, we have performed an empirical study on the proposed visualization technique with a number of micro-conversion data sets available from several operating online stores. We have tested the data for different combinations of micro-conversion steps. To obtain the visualizations, we used simplified but still useful versions of scatterplot that are available from several office software suites.

Fig. 4 provides a visualization example from the study, a product visualization based on a data set of 531,873 hits (minus hits on graphic files) and 7,584 basket placements acquired from an online computer store over a period of one week in 1999. Fig. 4 shows the products from three departments of the online store: Consumer, Business, and Accessory. The number of products in the Consumer department is 55, that of the Business department 30, and that of the Accessory department 157. Data for several other departments in the online store is not shown in this figure for the sake of clarity.

In this figure, bubbles instead of rectangles are used to represent individual products. As in Fig. 2, the size of each bubble describes a product's relative significance. In this case, the diameter of each bubble indicates the price of the product represented. (Data about profit margin of products were not available for this study.) The color of each bubble represents department to which this product belongs The x-axis of the graph represents raw impressions, i.e., the number of times a Web page that containing a hyperlink to a product is served. The y-axis represents the percentage of impressions that resulted in a basket placement, i.e., of the number of visits that saw a hyperlink to this product, the percentage that eventually added this product to the shopping basket. Note that the percentage of impressions leading to basket placements (i.e., look-to-basket rate), not the raw orders, is used to normalize the data over a fixed range, that is, between 0 and 100.

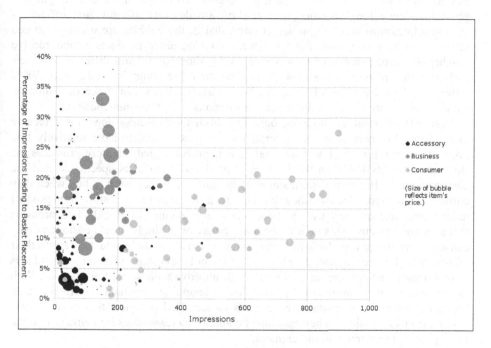

Fig. 4. Scatterplot of look-to-basket rates of an online store

Fig. 4 illustrates that the look-to-basket rates of products from three different departments show vastly different characteristics. There are several possible causes. Either the store displays the products differently, resulting in products from some departments shown to more visitors than others do, or the shopping behavior of visitors is different for the various departments of products. Identifying the shopping behavior of customers and what is important for customers of different departments, Web merchandisers can upgrade the Web design and merchandising schemes to adjust for different characteristics of individual departments.

First, we observed that most of the Consumer products receive high number of impressions, i.e., between 180 and 900, compared with products of other departments. It may be the case that the store promotes Consumer products more in high-trafficked pages to lure the customers to the Consumer department. It is also speculated that the customers of the Consumer department browse more and review more information about products than those of other departments do. Web merchandisers of the Consumer department can use this information to improve their Web design and sales. For example, they may want to improve product information in the department because it is what the customers of the department look for. Also, unlike the Business products (as will be explained later), well-presented impressions are particularly important for the Consumer products.

It is important to note that the look-to-basket rates of the Consumer products generally increase as their impressions increase, i.e., overall average about 3% increase in look-to-basket rate for each impression. Also important is that, despite this general tendency, the Consumer products show a wide range of individual differences in their impressions and look-to-basket rates, that is, the bubbles are widely scattered across both x- and y-axis. For example, two Consumer products which receive roughly the same number of impressions (615), show significant difference in their look-to-basket rates: one has about 21%, and the other about 7%, i.e., about 300% difference. Based on this observation, Web merchandisers can make decisions on which products are better candidates for promotions and/or recommendations.

Unlike the Consumer products, only few from the Business department receive more than 200 impressions. In general, the Business products have relatively low impressions, but high look-to-basket rates. It is probable that the store promotes the Business products less than the Consumer products. Also, it is speculated that the customers of the Business department already know what they want to buy when they come to the store. Hence, they do not tend to browse the store for product information. Instead, they use tools such as search engines to quickly find products that they want to buy. This unique shopping behavior of the Business customers may cause the relatively high look-to-basket rates of the Business products, despite their relatively high price (indicated by the size of the bubbles). Again, Web merchandisers of this department can use this information to improve their sales. For instance, Web merchandisers may want to improve their shopping mechanisms (other than browsing) to help the Business purchasers rapidly find products they want to buy under various conditions. They may also be able to increase sales by marketing to the more potential customers in the segment.

There are more products in the Accessory department than in the other two departments, but most of them are low-priced as their size indicates. Most receive relatively small number of impressions, probably because the store does not heavily promote the Accessory products. It is interesting to note that several high-priced Accessory products show both low impressions and low look-to-basket rates, while most low-priced Accessory products show relatively high look-to-basket rate. This indicates that when shopping for accessory items, customers become more sensitive to price.

In this case study, we have suggested various possible interpretations of the data in this visualization. Ultimately, the merchandisers who know their own products are best qualified to assign meaning and take action. The role of visualization tools is to help the merchandisers understand data by displaying complex data in a clear way.

6   Data Requirements

In this section, we briefly describe several data requirements for the proposed starfield visualizations for E-commerce. While some source data are readily available from most E-commerce sites, others are not and need to be collected with some special tools. Also, the collected data has to be integrated to compute the micro-conversion rates before visualizing them to provide insight into the merchandising effectiveness of online stores.

First, the visualization of merchandising effectiveness based on micro-conversion rates requires the combination of the site traffic data (i.e., access requests) and sales data. In most E-commerce sites, the two types of data are typically stored in separate storage systems in different structures: the traffic data in Web server logs in a file format, and the sales data in the database of the commerce server. The commerce server database also contains information about customers and products (including product taxonomy) that may be useful and interesting to visualize with micro-conversion rates. It is important to tie together data from the two different sources with a common key and to construct an integrated database system or a data mart system for business visualization.

Second, computing micro-conversion rates also requires product impression data. Capturing product impression data involves tracking content of served Web pages, which is more challenging when Web pages are dynamic. Currently, the standard Web server logging mechanism does not capture the content of Web pages. One possible method is to enhance the Web server logging as a way to dynamically parse the content of served Web pages and extract useful data such as product impressions and information on hyperlink types. The ability of dynamically scanning Web pages as they are served is critical for tracking Web usage, because more and more Web pages are dynamically created from databases and contain personalized and adaptive content. A simple example of a dynamically created Web page is a search result page commonly found in online stores.

Finally, it is important to classify and identify hyperlinks by their merchandising purposes, so that later to attribute the profit of the hyperlinks to their merchandising cue type, shopping metaphor type, and design features. For this purpose, Web pages and hyperlinks in an online store need to be tagged with semantic labels describing their merchandising features. Semantic labels of a hyperlink may include, for example, a product label, a cross-sell or promotion label, and a tag indicating where the product is being displayed. Such semantic labels for hyperlinks in a site may be explicitly provided in a form of meta-data during the site creation. If this is not the case, semantic labels need to be inferred from various sources such as the file name and/or path portion of URLs, types, values and orders of parameters in URLs of dynamic Web pages, and the location of a hyperlink in the page.

E-Commerce Intelligence (ECI) is an ongoing project at IBM T. J. Watson Research Center. The architectural goal of the ECI project is to provide an analysis environment that is rich in data expressed in terms that are comfortable for the business analysts to answer the business questions. To achieve this goal, data from disparate sources such as Web servers, commerce servers and enterprise data systems needs to be combined into a single analysis environment that places various E-commerce activities into their business context. Fig. 5 illustrates the ECI data mart architecture. It shows the types of source and target data of the data mart system, and the steps in transforming source to target data. During the data transformation process, data from various sources is cleansed, normalized, integrated, and then loaded into a multidimensional data model for use by business analysts, who seek answers to their business questions by using techniques such as data mining and

OLAP (On-Line Analytical Processing). The visualization of micro-conversions with the starfield model is a reporting and analysis metaphor provided by the ECI system.

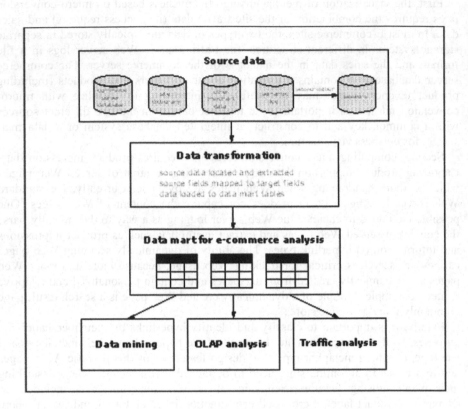

Fig. 5. E-Commerce Intelligence data mart system architecture

7   Related Work

There are several commercial services and software tools for evaluating the effectiveness of Web advertising such as banner ads, in terms of traffic and sales driven by them [7]. They use metrics such as clickthrough rates and ad banner ROI. The objective of these tools is different from our work; they focus on understanding the effectiveness of advertising, while our work focuses on the effectiveness of merchandising. The techniques used for Web advertising tracking tools are not directly applicable to tracking and measuring the merchandising effectiveness in online stores.

There are several commercial Web server log analysis tools available [11]. Most of these Web log analysis tools generate reports mainly on Web traffic and system measurements. It is difficult, though not impossible, to report on the effectiveness of specific marketing and merchandising efforts because those tools primarily rely on information in Web server logs which are hard to interpret and extract data useful for measuring the business efforts.

Recently, Web usage analysis by applying data mining techniques to Web server logs has been actively studied [5, 6]. Some of the data mining algorithms that are commonly used in the studies are association rule generation, sequential pattern generation, and clustering. Also, there has been some work done on loading Web usage data into a data cube structure in order to perform both data mining and traditional OLAP operations such as roll-up and drill-down of the data [4]. These studies formally defined generic data hypercubes for Web usage data and provided designs for exploratory analysis and reporting. Some of the work showed how data mining techniques are used on the data model in electronic commerce scenarios. While these studies and our work share similar objectives of finding interesting aspects of Web usage of an online store which are potentially useful for improving marketing and merchandising strategies on the site, they address different types of business questions and may be used in a complementary way.

Interactive starfield visualizations were studied to explore Web server log data in [9]. The study argued that these visualizations provide capabilities for examining data that exceed those of traditional Web log analysis tools, by combining two-dimensional displays of access requests, color and size coding for additional attributes, and facilities for zooming and filtering. While the study introduced a series of interactive starfield visualizations to explore Web traffic data across various dimensions, it used only Web server log data as its data source. In comparison, the work presented in this paper envisions how interactive starfield visualizations can be used to explore commerce server data and how they can be interpreted to provide insight into merchandising effectiveness of online stores.

8   Concluding Remarks

This paper has presented a set of Web usage analysis requirements in the area of online merchandising. It also presented the details of tracking and analyzing the effectiveness of merchandising in online stores by using the novel concept of micro-conversion rate. Then we presented techniques for visualizing the micro-conversions, which can be used to rapidly answer merchandising questions. Through an empirical study, we demonstrated how the proposed starfield visualizations could be used to understand the shopping behavior in an online store and the effectiveness of various merchandising schemes it employs. We also discussed the types of data required for this kind of visual analysis of online merchandising, and briefly described how the data can be collected and integrated from an E-commerce site.

The ideas presented in this paper are currently being implemented in a business intelligence system that manages and integrates diverse data from an E-commerce site, and provides capabilities for examining and exploring the data. As part of this effort, we have designed a data model, and developed a number of software tools for collecting and managing E-commerce data. Those components are required to prepare data that will be shown in the visualizations presented in this paper.

We extend our work on visualization of E-commerce data with a number of other data visualization ideas including parallel coordinates which map multi-dimensional data into a two-dimensional display. Unlike the starfield model, parallel coordinates places axes parallel rather than perpendicular to each other, allowing many axes to be placed and seen [10]. This mapping procedure has unique geometric properties and useful relationships to the original space.

Our work for analyzing online store merchandising presented in this paper can be extended in many ways to address different questions on both business and system effectiveness of online stores. First, the idea of classifying hyperlinks, labeling them with semantic vocabularies, and aggregating them, can be generalized and applied to other types of business questions in areas such as online marketing and operation. One example is clustering customers by their shopping behavior measured by types of hyperlinks they click. In this case, hyperlinks in an online store need to be categorized and labeled to distinguish characteristics of shoppers' behavior. Also, the metrics for merchandising effectiveness presented in this work can be adjusted and extended for the use in new shopping paradigms in the Internet such as online auction and dynamic pricing. Finally, the approach of data visualization-based exploratory analysis used in this work can be combined with a different but complementary approach, that is, data mining. Data mining can help sample data clusters interesting for visualization, and/or find patterns in navigation paths and identify product associations.

References

1. C. Alhberg and B. Schneiderman, "Visual Information Seeking: Tight Coupling of Dynamic Query Filters with Starfield Displays," *ACM CHI Conference on Human Factors in Computing Systems*, 1994, 313-317.
2. S. Anand, J. Hughes, D. Bell, and A. Patrick, "Tackling the Cross-Sales Problem Using Data Mining," *Proc. Of the 1st Pacific-Asia Conference on Knowledge Discovery and Data Mining*, 1997, 331-343.
3. B. Berman and J. R. Evans, *Retail Management: A Strategic Approach*, 7th Edition, Prentice-Hall, Inc., 1998.
4. A. G. Büchner and M. Mulvenna, "Discovering Internet Marketing Intelligence through Online Analytical Web Usage Mining," *SIGMOD Record*, 27(4):54-61, December 1998.
5. M. S. Chen, J. S. Park, P. S. Yu, "Data Mining for Traversal Patterns in a Web Environment," *Proc. of the 16th International Conference on Distributed Computing Systems*, 1996.
6. R. Cooley, B. Mobasher, and J. Srivastava, "Data Preparation for Mining World Wide Web Browsing Patterns," *Journal of Knowledge and Information Systems*, 1(1), 1999.
7. S. V. Haar, "ROI Shows Marketers The Money," *InteractiveWeek*, March 22, 1999, http://www.interactive-week.com.
8. M. E. Hardie, J. C. McCarthy, M. MacKenzie, and R. Scheier-Dolberg, "Content Management Crisis," *The Forrester Report*, Volume One, Number Eleven, January 1997.
9. H. Hochheiser, and B. Schneiderman, "Understanding Patterns of User Visits to Web Sites: Interactive Starfield Visualizations of WWW Log Data," *Technical Report*, CS-TR-3989, Department of Computer Science, University of Maryland, 1999.
10. A. Inselberg, "The Plane with Parallel Coordinates," *The Visual Computer* 1, 1985, 69-91.
11. T. Wilson, "Web Site Mining Gets Granular," *InternetWeek*, March 29, 1999, http://www.internetwk.com.

Improving the Effectiveness of a Web Site with Web Usage Mining

Myra Spiliopoulou[1], Carsten Pohle[1], and Lukas C. Faulstich[2*]

[1] Institute of Information Systems, Humboldt-University Berlin
Spandauer Str. 1, D-10178 Berlin, Germany
myra@wiwi.hu-berlin.de
cpohle@snafu.de
[2] Institute of Computer Science, Free University Berlin
Takustraße 9, D-14195 Berlin, Germany
faulstic@inf.fu-berlin.de

Abstract. For many companies, effective web presence is indispensable for their success to the global market. In recent years, several methods have been developed for measuring and improving the effectiveness of commercial sites. However, they mostly concentrate on web page design and on access analysis. In this study, we propose a methodology of assessing the quality of a web site in turning its users into customers. Our methodology is based on the discovery and comparison of navigation patterns of customers and non-customers. This comparison leads to rules on how the site's topology should be improved. We further propose a technique for dynamically adapting the site according to those rules.

1 Introduction

Effective presence in the web is for many companies the key to success in the global market. This key has two dimensions: content and form. The evaluation of a web site in promoting the business objectives of its owner should take both dimensions into account.

Much research has been devoted to offering the right content, ranging from the discovery of semantically related documents to the identification of products being purchased together. In this study, we concentrate on the second issue, the evaluation of a site's form. Methods of measuring the quality of web *page* design have been proposed by [8,9,10] and others. However, the quality of a web *site* is not only determined by exciting web pages. A web site is a network, in which users should be assisted in finding information or products in a way that is *intuitive to them*. To improve the quality of this network, we need the feedback of the users on how they perceive it.

Although user feedback can be obtained directly via questionnaires and studies based on experimental settings, this approach is not appropriate for most

---

* Supported by the German Research Society, Berlin-Brandenburg Graduate School on Distributed Information Systems (DFG grant no. GRK 316)

B. Masand and M. Spiliopoulou (Eds.): WEBKDD'99, LNAI 1836, pp. 142–162, 2000.

sites, due to cost considerations and due to the time overhead involved. Moreover, since most sites change often, it is not feasible to repeat an experiment whenever a change takes place. On the other hand, indirect user feedback is already available for each site. Web servers record the activities of users in a site to a quite fine level of detail. Data mining is the appropriate methodology for analyzing these activities, gaining insights on how the users perceive the site and identifying necessary improvements in the site's form.

Sequence mining [1,13,18] is the appropriate paradigm for analyzing the behaviour of users in a site. However, the original paradigm for discovering frequent sequences is not adequate, because these sequences reflect the navigational behaviour of users only partially. In [17,15], we have proposed the miner WUM [1] that shifts the focus from frequent sequences to navigation patterns.

WUM offers a powerful, template-based language for guiding the miner in the discovery of patterns that have statistical or structural properties of interest for the expert. However, the site owner rather thinks in terms of business goals and of requirements on how the site should be used to achieve a business goal. Translating them into constraints on statistical properties is not straightforward.

Hence, in this study, we use WUM as a basis for a more business-oriented approach to web usage analysis. In particular, we propose the comparative analysis of navigation patterns of customers and non-customers, in order to improve the site's efficiency in turning non-customers into customers. To this purpose, we analyze the differences between their navigation patterns and find the pages that must be redesigned in order to conform to the perception of potential customers.

In the next section we describe how navigation patterns are discovered by our web utilization miner WUM. In section 3, we describe and extend a model measuring the efficiency of a web site in turning visitors to customers into a model for comparing the corresponding efficiency of individual *pages* on the basis of typical navigation patterns. We then describe how navigation patterns of customers and non-customers are compared and how improvement hints can be drawn from the comparison. Section 5 describes how the results of the analysis can be put to practice by processing the discovered patterns and building links according to them. Section 6 reports on the current state of our work and on future activities.

2   Discovering Navigation Patterns with WUM

WUM is a web utilization miner for the discovery of representative or otherwise interesting patterns in a web server log. It has been developed in the Institute of Information Systems, Faculty of Economics of the Humboldt-University Berlin.

2.1   A Brief Overview of WUM

The architecture of WUM is depicted in Fig. 1. In this picture, we would like to stress the close interaction of the human analyst and the mining software. The

---
[1] http://wum.wiwi.hu-berlin.de

white arrows indicate data input to and output from WUM. The black arrows indicate instructions from the analyst and mining results to her.

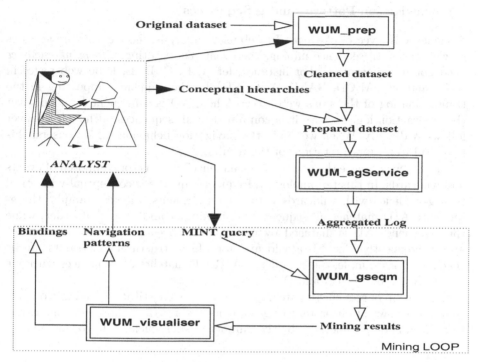

Fig. 1. The environment and modules of WUM

The upper part of the figure shows the data preparation steps. The module WUM_prep undertakes data cleaning, which encompasses the removal of entries considered undesirable or irrelevant for further analysis, such as image retrievals, failed requests and entries of already known robots. WUM_prep also makes efforts of identifying and removing programmable software agents by detecting their non-human behaviour, e.g. consecutive accesses on the same page or adjacent page requests at a speed incompatible to human perception of page content.

WUM_prep is also responsible for organizing the page requests into user sessions, according to different sessioning criteria. A thorough description of this module can be found in [16]. The sessions produced by WUM_prep are transformed by the WUM_agService into sequence objects and stored in a compact tree (trie) structure, the "Aggregated Log" [17]. The sequences comprising the Aggregated Log are merged on common prefix, and each tree node is annotated by its occurence number within the sequence/branch and by the number of sequences having the same prefix upto this node. This number is actually the number of web site visitors that reached the corresponding web page across the path of pages depicted in the tree branch leading to it. Hence, the Aggregated Log offers a first overview of how users enter and move into the web site. Their actual navigation patterns are discovered by the miner WUM_gseqm.

2.2   Navigation Patterns and g-Sequences

A sequence is a vector of events. In web usage analysis, those events are accesses to web pages. In sequence mining, the events constituting a *frequent sequence* need not be adjacent [1]. For instance, let A, B, C, D, E, F be web pages in a site and let {ABCD, BAED, ABCEFD} be the sequences appearing in the transaction log of the site's web server. Then, AD is a frequent sequence over the transaction log, because it is contained in all sequences, although D never follows A directly. When we study the navigation behaviour of web users, this may lead to misinterpretations of the results.

In [15], we propose the notion of "g-sequence" as a vector composed of events and wildcards. In this terminology, a frequent sequence is conceptually identical to a g-sequence with wildcards between its elements. In our example, the g-sequence A*D matches all sequences containing A and D in that order, while the g-sequence AD is matched by no sequence, because the two pages never appear adjacently. The * is a wildcard, for which structural constraints can be specified. For example, the g-sequence A*[1;2]D matches all sequences with one or two events between A and D.

The group of sequences matching a g-sequence constitute a "navigation pattern". The navigation pattern of g-sequence B*[1;5]D is shown in Fig. 2 as a tree. Each node is annotated by the number of subsequences up to this node.

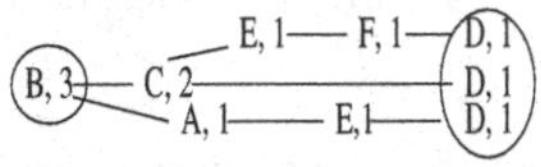

Fig. 2. The navigation pattern of the g-sequence B*[1;5]D

A conventional sequence miner returns all frequent g-sequences of arbitrary length. WUM rather discovers all navigation patterns that satisfy a template with a fixed number of variables, subject to more arbitrary constraints on the variable's statistics and the template's structure. For example:

```
SELECT t FROM NODE AS x y, TEMPLATE x *[1;5] y AS t
WHERE x.support >= 3 AND ( y.support / x.support ) >= 0.5
```

This mining query, expressed in the language MINT [17], asks for all g-sequences, such that (i) the event bound to x appears in at least 3 sequences and (ii) the event bound to y appears in at least 50% of *those sequences* after the event bound to x. The g-sequence B*[1;5]D satisfies this query. WUM returns as result B*[1;5]D *and* its navigation pattern of Fig. 2.

The complete theory on g-sequences and navigation patterns appears in [15]. For the data preparation phase and the detailed description of the mining language, the reader is referred to [17].

3   Comparing the Navigational Behaviour of User Groups

Frequent navigation patterns give indications on how the site is being used. They can reveal cases of semantically related pages that are not yet linked. Long paths between already linked pages might indicate disoriented users. However, this information is still not sufficient for building a successful web site. To improve a site's quality, we need to compare the behaviour of users exploring the site in a way conforming to the site's objective goals (e.g. product purchase) to those that do not. Here, we propose a model for the comparative analysis of the types of users accessing the site.

3.1   Types of Site Users

Berthon et al classify the users of a site into "short time visitors", "active investigators" and "customers" [4]. A short time visitor is a user staying in the site for only a short while. An active investigator stays longer and explores the site. Some active investigators become customers, in the sense of buying products or making use of the offered services. Some customers remain loyal to the site and return again to it. The ratio of active investigators to all users measures the site's "contact efficiency"; the ratio of customers to active investigators measures its "conversion efficiency" [4]. Our goal is to maximize these ratios.

For our analysis, this classification has two disadvantages. First, we cannot recognize a customer revisiting the site as such, unless either (i) she purchases something again, or (ii) there is an authentication service recording her visits. Second, a user already familiar with the site might be misclassified as a short term visitor, because she does not need to study the contents of each page thoroughly.

We use a variation of this classification, by specifying the types of users more explicitly. A "short time visitor" is a user who visits only one page of the site, the page by which she reached the site. All other users are "active investigators". This definition is appropriate for many commercial sites, where the acquisition of goods and of information about them requires the active involvement and engagement of the visitor.

A "customer" is an active investigator that has performed a task conformant to the site's objective goals, such purchasing a product, registering herself as user of a service or downloading some free software. Thus, our definition of customer is also applicable for non-commercial sites, which nevertheless observe their visitors as potential customers, even if the goods are offered without imbursement. For brevity, we call an active investigator that is not a customer a "non-customer".

Since we allow for multiple groups of customers, characterized by different navigation patterns, we take account of the fact that experienced customers behave differently than ones unfamiliar with the site.

3.2   Patterns Reflecting Contact Deficiencies

To compute the contact efficiency of a site, we just enumerate its users and extract its active investigators [4]. To *improve* the contact efficiency, we must compare the behaviour of the active investigators to the behaviour of short time users. For this, we discover all patterns that consist only of the first page being accessed and all those containing at least one more page. We issue two queries:

```
SELECT t FROM NODE AS x, TEMPLATE # x AS t
SELECT t FROM NODE AS x y, TEMPLATE # x y AS t
```

where the # symbol denotes that the variable x should be bound to the first page of a navigation path [17]. The application expert may add constraints and restrict the discovery to frequently accessed pages only.

The first query returns all first pages accessed by users. The second query returns those of them, from which one further access has taken place. In both queries, the first pages are bound to the variable x. Pages appearing only in the first query should be subjected to careful *page* redesign.

Similarly, pages bound to x in both queries but rarely leading to a further access are candidates for redesign. WUM supports the analyst in inspecting these pages by its visualization module [16]. From the graphical representation of the result, the analyst can check whether the number of accesses to the first page is equal or close to the total number of accesses among the paths emanating from this page. Pages with a large gap between those two numbers have a potential for increasing the contact efficiency.

3.3   Patterns Revealing Conversion Deficiencies

To compute the conversion efficiency of the site, we simply divide the number of customers by the number of active investigators on the site [4]. To improve this value, we must compare the navigation patterns of customers to those of non-customers. The members of each of the two groups form subgroups that differ in navigation style, explorative impetus and need for assistance. We can assume that members of each subgroup are present in each of the main groups. Hence, by discovering each typical navigation pattern of customers and finding its differences to the most similar ones of non-customers, we can extract concrete hints on how the web site should be improved. The task of the improvement is then to make the behaviour of the non-customers similar to the behaviour of the customers.

To this task, we first filter the web server log to remove the accesses of short time visitors. We then generalize from the contents of the individual web pages to more general concepts. These can be product types as in market basket analysis, document descriptors, or query parameters for automatically generated web pages. This issue is discussed in [3].

The active investigators are either customers or non-customers. We split the preprocessed log into the log of customers and the log of non-customers. Pattern discovery is performed in each log separately and according to the same statistical and structural constraints. Then, the navigation patterns discovered in the two logs must be compared.

Comparing Navigation Patterns. A mining result is a g-sequence and its navigation pattern, both annotated with statistical data. This makes the comparison of mining results difficult: For example, the sequence ABC contains AB and is thus a refinement of the AB; however, the support of AB is obviously higher than that of ABC.

However, the goal of our comparison is not an ultimate qualitative ordering of the patterns but the identification of comparable groups of patterns. Hence, we use the following rules for comparisons:

R_1 *Two patterns are comparable if their g-sequences have at least the first n values in common.* The analyst may set this n to a small number, like 1 or 2, if she suspects that customers and non-customers access completely different pages. Otherwise, she may set n to the length of each g-sequence, so that only patterns of g-sequences containing the same URLs are comparable.

R_2 *Within each pattern, only frequent path fragments (i.e. subsequences) are considered for comparisons, while infrequent fragments are removed.* An intuitive lowerbound would be the support threshold used to discover frequent patterns in the whole customer, resp. non-customer log. This lowerbound applies to fragments *in the context of the pattern* only and is appropriate for removing fragments that occur rarely.

With these rules in mind, we establish the collections of patterns to be compared as follows:

Phase I.

1. The miner discovers the g-sequences $g_1, \ldots, g_k$ in the *customer log* and the g-sequences $ng_1, \ldots, ng_m$ in the *non-customer log*.
2. For each g-sequence g_i, a MINT query describing the structure and URLs of its first n variables is issued against the non-customer log. The result is a g-sequence ng_i with the same URLs as g_i but with different statistics.
   The same is done for each ng_j against the customer log.
3. All pairs of g_i, ng_i g-sequences whose ratio of confidence for the common prefix is below a noise threshold, are removed. Hence, only g-sequences are retained, which depict behavioural differences among customers and non-customers.
4. A set of potentially comparable results is built: $\mathcal{R} = \{((g_i, CP_i), (ng_i, nCP_i))\}$ where g_i and ng_i are the retained g-sequences and CP_i, resp. nCP_i are their navigation patterns.
5. For each navigation pattern in $\mathcal{R}$, we remove all path fragments that are rare *within the pattern* (cf. rule (R_2)).
6. From each pair $((g_u, CP_u), (ng_u, nCP_u)) \in \mathcal{R}$, we extract all pairs of individual paths (x, y), forming a set $\mathcal{R}'$.

To compare the individual paths, we introduce the statistic measure of "successor-confidence" as the ratio of accesses between each node a in a path and its predecessor a': $SC(a, a') \equiv SC$.

Phase II. For a non-customer path y, the following cases may occur:

1. There is a customer path $x \cdot x'$, where x contains the same URLs as y but has lower support.
   We compare the successor-confidence for each pair of consecutive pages in y and in $x \cdot x'$, until we find the first page in y that shows a lower SC value towards its predecessor than the respective pair of pages in $x \cdot x'$. This predecessor page should be redesigned.
2. There is a customer path $x \cdot x'$, where x contains the same URLs as y but has higher support.
   We find the non-customer paths of the form $y \cdot y'$ and we compare each y' to x' in terms of content. Of interest is each common page a with different followup pages $a_{y'}$ in y' and $a_{x'}$ in x', such that the SC value of $a_{y'}$ is larger than that of $a_{x'}$. For each such page, its connection to $a_{x'}$ appearing in the customer pattern should be reconsidered, since non-customers apparently prefer another page to it.
3. There is a customer path $x_1 \cdot x \cdot x_2$, where x contains the same URLs as y.
   We find the non-customer paths of the form $y_1 \cdot y \cdot y_2$, such that y_1 has no counterpart among the customer paths. Each such path fragment y_1 indicates a route that needs improvement. For instance, users who enter the site at a page other than the official welcome-page might experience difficulties in getting oriented and, consequently, perceive the pages they access in another context than intended by the designer.

Finally, non-customer paths with no comparable customer paths can be observed as reflections of users that perceive the site in a completely different way than assumed by the site designer. If there are many such users, special adjustments of the site for them might be considered.

4   Experiments

We have experimented with our proposed methodology on the SchulWeb site (http://www.schulweb.de). This web site accommodates the largest and most comprehensive database of German high schools in the web. SchulWeb is organized like an online catalog with fill-in forms, in which the web site visitor specifies the criteria to be satisfied by the schools of interest. The result is a dynamically generated list of schools, obtained by querying the SchulWeb database server. The visitor browses through this list, which may be more than one page long, and eventually selects a school by clicking at its home page or at its description, as provided by the SchulWeb.

The SchulWeb site offers many more services beyond the search for schools. However, this service is very important, because it is accessed by a large user community. The current design of the site reflects the importance of this service and should be improved, if necessary, to better conform to the visitors' needs. Hence, our pre-processing and experiments concern the use of school search services in the SchulWeb.

4.1   Customers in the SchulWeb

To apply our concepts on the web server log of the SchulWeb, we have first adapted the notions of customer to the objective goals of the SchulWeb site. In particular, a customer is an active investigator who has reached a school *and* studied the information on this school for a considerable amount of time. This includes users that shifted over to the web site of a school and never (or much later) returned to the SchulWeb, but excludes users who only briefly inspect a school page and immediately shift their interest to another school. Then, we define as "non-customers" those active investigators that are not customers.

In subsection 3.1, we have defined an active investigator as a visitor that accessed at least two pages. This is appropriate for studying the contact efficiency of a web site as a whole. In our experiments, though, we have concentrated on only one of the services offered by the SchulWeb. To exclude visitors interested in other services, we have restricted the notion of active investigator to users that have posed a query to retrieve schools. Thus, the ratio of active investigators to visitors does not reflect the contact efficiency of the site, but only the percentage of users that are interested in this particular service. Its value is 17%.

4.2   Establishment of Concept Hierarchies

To compare the navigational behaviour of customers and non-customers, we must abstract from the concrete queries posed by the users to the querying mechanisms exploited and the criteria employed by the one and the other group. We have therefore established a set of concept hierarchies, which are depicted in Fig. 3. According to those concept hierarchies, we abstract a URL, which actually is a CGI script invocation, into strings comprised of names of concepts. The concept hierarchies are thoroughly described in [3].

According to the hierarchy in the upper part of the figure, a URL describes either an individual school or a list of schools, which is produced as the result of a user query. A school description can be either composed of data from the SchulWeb database or be the homepage of the school in their own local site. A list of schools, being a query result, consists of one or more pages; we distinguish between the first page and any consecutive one. Note that the page design is such that a list of schools also contains the query form, with which the user can pose a new (or refining) query.

On the lower right part of Fig. 3, we see that schools and queries on them are categorized by country, distinguishing among Germany, Austria, Switzerland and Rest of the World. When a SchulWeb visitor poses queries, she must first select the country of interest.

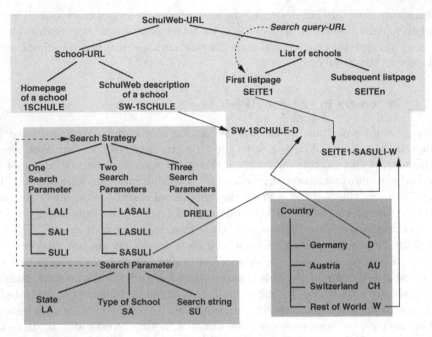

Fig. 3. Concept hierarchies for the SchulWeb usage data

The supported query parameters are depicted in the two interrelated hierarchies on the lower left part of the figure: state within the country ("Bundesland" in German, abbreviated into LA), type of school ("Schulart" in German, abbreviated into SA) or a textual string that the user types in ("Suchkriterion" in German, with abbreviation SU). The parameters can be combined, resulting into search strategies with one, two or three parameter specifications, whose acronyms are shown in the figure.

In the shaded part of the figure, we see two example string composed by the concepts, to which the actual CGI script invocations have been abstracted. When we refer to "URLs" in the following, we mean those concept combinations rather than the concrete URLs they stand for.

4.3   Preparation of the Web Server Log

The preprocessing phase for web usage mining involves several steps, which aim at the reconstruction of the users' activities in the site. Heuristics to perform these steps in the general case are discussed by Cooley et al [6]. For the purposes of this study, we concentrate on the particular steps needed to build the customer log and the non-customer log.

In a first step, we have used the concept hierarchies of Fig. 3 to transform the individual CGI script invocations into abstract strings, thus mapping queries into

search strategies and requests for individual schools into requests for a SchulWeb
school description or a school home page.

We have then built preliminary user sessions on the basis of host identifier
and on an upper limit for the time spent on each web page. From these sessions, we distinguished active investigators and short time visitors, customers
and non-customers. It is recognized that the host identifier is not adequate to
distinguish among different users. However, the advanced heuristics proposed
in [6] for sessioning could not be applied here, because the form-based structure
of the SchulWeb makes it correspond to an almost fully connected graph.

We have then removed all preliminary sessions not containing at least one
query, i.e. a URL with a "???LI" in its name (cf. Fig. 3). Thus, only the part of the
log composed of active investigators' sessions has been retained for further processing. We partitioned this dataset into the customer log and the non-customer
log by using an upper time limit on the stay at a school's homepage, i.e. at
a URL of the form "1SCHULE-???". According to our definition for a Schul-
Web customer in subsection 4.1, a lengthy stay on a school's homepage signals a
strong interest and is taken as equivalent to product selection by a conventional
customer. Hence, sessions containing such a long duration stay were moved to
the customer log. The remaining ones formed the non-customer log.

Within the customer log, we have split sessions into a part leading to the
homepage of the selected school and a part of consecutive visits. The latter part
of the session corresponds to the activities of returning customers who conduct
further searches using their experience from previous visits. Since a session may
contain the homepages of more than one schools, we have renamed the URL
that classifies a user as customer into "SUCCESS". As a consequence, the non-
customer log does not contain any URLs with that name, although it may well
contain accesses to the homepages of schools.

Finally, we have shrinked sessions in both logs by removing adjacent accesses
to the same URL. Such accesses have many causes, namely (i) reloading of the
same CGI script, (ii) formulation of a new query using the same search strategy
as for the previous one, so that the two CGI scripts are abstracted to the same
string and (iii) retrieval of the 2nd, 3rd etc page of a list of schools, which are all
abstracted to the string "???-SEITEn-???" (SEITE stands for page on German).

By the end of the data preparation, the customer log contained 615 sessions,
while the non-customer log contained 464 ones.

4.4   Customers' Frequent Short Paths

We studied the behaviour of customers that need only a small number of steps
to reach the desired school page. We have formulated the following MINT-query
that returns the navigation patterns with zero to four nodes after the first web
page of the SchulWeb is visited and until the desired school is reached.

```
SELECT t FROM NODE AS a b, TEMPLATE # a [0;4] b AS t
WHERE a.support >= 30
AND ( b.support / a.support ) >= 0.2
```

AND b.url = "/SUCCESS"

The first variable a of this query is not bound to any URL. The second one b is bound to the pseudo-URL named "SUCCESS". The wildcard [0;4] determines the allowed number of steps between the first and last page. To prevent the retrieval of rare patterns, we have placed two statistic thresholds. The number of visitors of the first page (variable a) should be no less than 30 (almost 5% of the total number of sessions in this log). Further, the confidence with which the SUCCESS page has been reached should be at least 20%.

WUM returned 5 navigation patterns. One of the patterns, starting at the German SchulWeb homepage, accounted for more than 50% of the sessions in the log and showed a confidence of ca. 77%. Hence, more than half of the SchulWeb customers start at its German homepage and rapidly locate a school of interest to them. This pattern is important, not only because it occurs often but also because the homepage is the usual starting point for novice users.

In Fig. 4, we show part of this navigation pattern of the above query. In particular, we show the subpatterns, in which the second page was a query to the SchulWeb using as (sole) search parameter the federal state, in which schools of interest are located. This single-parameter search strategy (acronym: LALI) is very popular, selected by almost one third of the users within this pattern.

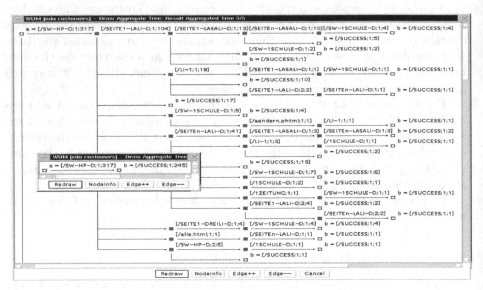

Fig. 4. Part of a navigation pattern

The other 4 result patterns had as first page a search query, formulated by combining different search parameters according to the concept hierarchies of Fig. 3. Since users are unlikely to type in the URL of a search query, we can assume that they reach the querying service via a bookmark they placed on it during a previous visit. Thus, they have accessed the SchulWeb before and are experienced in using it. The confidence of the SUCCESS page in these patterns ranged from 73% to 85%.

For our comparative investigations, we have concentrated on the subpattern of Fig. 4 for the following reasons: (a) The homepage of the SchulWeb is the page expected to be accessed first by novice users. Since these users might need the most assistance, it is reasonable to first concentrate on them. (b) The search strategy LALI, which specifies the federal state as sole search criterion, is the most popular first-choice strategy, as verified by another set of experiments [3]. Hence, the behaviour of customers and non-customers with respect to this search strategy is important for improving the SchulWeb towards the latter.

4.5   Comparing Customer and Non-Customer Patterns

The customer pattern we have selected for comparisons is described by the g-sequence SW-HP-D·SEITE1-LALI-D·[0;3]·SUCCESS, where we have used "·" as the separator between the components. To obtain comparable patterns according to rule R_1 in subsubsection 3.3, we have issued the following MINT query towards the non-customer log:

```
SELECT t FROM NODE AS a b c, TEMPLATE # a b [0;3] c AS t
WHERE a.url = "/SW-HP-D"
AND b.url = "/SEITE1-LALI-D"
```

This mining query has three variables. The first two are bound to the URLs SW-HP-D and SEITE1-LALI-D, while the last one is free to become bound to any page reached from the above two pages in at most 4 further steps. Since no SUCCESS pages exist in the non-customer log, we want to know which pages are mostly reached instead. The result of this query is one pattern per binding of variable c. We have summarized these patterns into one, corresponding to the g-sequence SW-HP-D·SEITE1-LALI-D·[0;4], which cannot currently be expressed in MINT.

After obtaining the patterns of the customer g-sequence
g_1 =SW-HP-D·SEITE1-LALI-D·[0;3].SUCCESS
and the non-customer g-sequence ng_1 =SW-HP-D·SEITE1-LALI-D·[0;4]
we proceeded with the extraction of comparable results, according to a slightly simplified version of the algorithm presented in subsection 3.3.

1. The suffix SUCCESS was removed from the paths in the customer pattern, since it has no counterpart in the non-customer pattern.
2. The common prefix of g_1 and ng_1 is SW-HP-D·SEITE1-LALI-D. The confidence of selecting the search strategy LALI after visiting the German homepage of the SchulWeb is 32.81% for customers and 51.30% for non-customers. The difference between these values is quite large (ratio: circa 0.7), so that a be-havioural difference between customers and non-customers can be assumed, according to the requirements in the second step of Phase I in 3.3.

3. All rare path fragments were removed from g_1 and ng_1. As "rare" we termed the path fragments followed by only one user.
4. Path fragments starting at pages that describe an unclassifiable search strategy have been removed. Such pages occur, because in some cases the SchulWeb server does not record all parameters used in the CGI script invocation.

During the elimination of the rare path fragments, we realized that there were many more such fragments in the pattern of ng_1 than in the pattern of g_1. In particular, the customer pattern contained only one rare path fragment immediately after SEITE1-LALI-D, while the non-customer pattern contained 10 such fragments, accounting for more than 10% of the non-customers that have accessed the first two web pages of this pattern. This means that customers persisted on continuing their search, while non-customers turned to other services of the SchulWeb, at least temporarily.

After the removal of rare and unclassifiable path fragments, an one-to-one comparison among the remaining subpatterns was possible, as can be seen from Fig. 5(a) and (b): The subpatterns 1 and 2 we compared are marked with the same colours/shades in both figures. We have also marked a customer path fragment (subpattern-3) that has no counterpart in the non-customer pattern but deserves special attention.

One remarkable difference between g_1 and ng_1 is the absence of a path involving the DREILI search strategy in the non-customer pattern. This strategy combines the specification of a federal state, a type of school and a search string (e.g. contained in the school's name) and consecutively leads to the most focussed type of search supported by the SchulWeb. Of course, the DREILI strategy is only appropriate for users that know quite precisely what they want, so it is not used frequently. On the other hand, all users that exploited this strategy became customers with a confidence of 100% (cf. Fig. 5(a)). Thus, one of the possible improvements to the SchulWeb would be an online help on how this strategy can be used even for not very precise searches.

The path fragments having SEITE1-LASALI-D as the third page show a quite similar successor confidence, being 12.50% in the customer pattern and 14.14% for non-customers. This page indicates a refinement of the search strategy by specifying one more parameter, namely the type of a school (currently, a selection among three types is supported). However, in the next step, the successor confidence of the SEITEn-LASALI-D is 76.92% for customers but only 28.57% for non-customers. This page indicates the continuation of a rather long list of results. While customers browse through the long list, non-customers give up.

The same observation is made when comparing the path fragments having SEITEn-LALI-D as the third page. The successor confidence is approximately 10% lower for non-customers than for customers. This indicates again that the non-customers are users not willing to browse through long lists of results; instead, they turned to other SchulWeb services, as indicated by the many rare paths in the non-customer pattern.

To summarize our results, active investigators that do not become customers show two interesting types of action, or more precisely of its absence: they do not

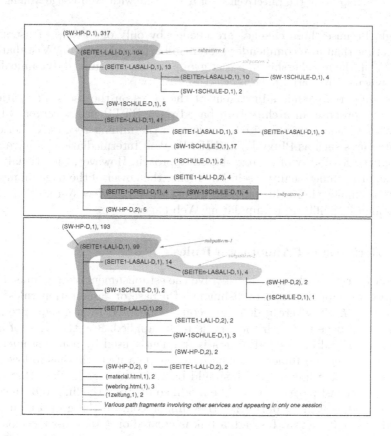

Fig. 5. Part of the customer pattern of g_1 (a) and of the respective non-customer pattern of ng_1 (b)

browse into long lists, but they also do not use the ideal strategy for considerably narrowing the search. Given the fact that this latter strategy involves typing text, a reason for its lesser popularity may be unfamiliarity with this kind of search. This indicates that this group of users needs search parameters that narrow the search but do not require text typing. Such a parameter could be the name of the city where the school should be located; this criterion is currently supported but requires typing of text. It could be modified into a parameter with values selected from a list.

5 Improving a Web Site by Dynamic Rule-Based Links

The results of our comparative study of navigation patterns can lead to extensive re-design of the site. In many cases, though, only some pages need to be modified or linked, especially if the site consists of static pages instead of generic forms. Permanently changing the original web pages is not always appropriate, though, because those changes are needed by only one group of users. Moreover, other than in recommender systems like Third Voice [19], Vistabar [14] or Pharos [5], the membership in a user group is here determined dynamically from the navigation pattern of the user.

To support dynamic adjustment of the pages on the users' navigation patterns, we propose an architecture based on a HTTP proxy server, which establishes an adaptive web site according to the mining results. Generic proxy architectures such as Pluxy [7] and IBM's Web Intermediaries [2] have demonstrated the feasibility of a proxy-based approach. However, the crucial point is not the proxy functionality itself, but rather the power of the page manipulation methods employed. To this purpose we use the HyperView system [11,12] which offers high flexibility in manipulating Web pages.

5.1   Derivation of Annotation Rules

We concentrate on changes that involve the establishment of new links. For such changes, we propose the establishment of a base of "annotation rules" having the form g,A→B, where g defines a context denoted by a g-sequence and the URL A of a page to which the rule is to be applied. B is the URL of a target page that should be pointed to. g·A is frequently used by non-customers, while g·B is a frequent customer g-sequence. To guide a user who has followed g and now requests A, a link to page B should be added to page A. Note that in static redesign, the last page of g would be modified to stress the link to B. In contrast, dynamic adjustment avoids links that might confuse the group of users that would choose B anyway. Instead, a link is created on A to stress the existence of B as an alternative route.

These annotation rules are derived from the comparative analysis, after the inspection by the analyst. The derivation itself cannot be automated, since the designer must decide which patterns would lead to permanent changes of the site, and when dynamic adjustment should be preferred.

In our architecture, annotation rules are encoded in RDF[2] and stored in our architecture on a "metadata server" (see next section). In Fig. 6 we present an example of an annotation rule. This rule specifies that page A=product4711.html is to be annotated with a link to a page B=product9827.html if the user has followed a path from the company's home page via at least one intermediate page and the promotional page pro991014.html before.

In the context of the SchulWeb, a rule could specify that a page of the form ???-LASALI-??? is to be annotated with a link to the query form ???-DREILI-??? if the user has reached ???-LASALI-??? after invoking ???-LALI-???. In that case, the user first performed a query on schools of a federal state (strategy LALI). She then attempts to refine the search by additionally specifying the school type (strategy LASALI). The rule would then prescribe that the user's attention should be drawn to the possibility of determining all three search criteria (strategy DREILI) to perform a more focussed search. Since the

---

[2] The *Resource Description Framework* (see <http://www.w3.org/RDF>).

```
<rdf:RDF
  xmlns:rdf="http://www.w3.org/1999/02/22-rdf-syntax-ns#"
  xmlns:ar="http://hyperview.org/annotation-rules/">
  <rdf:Description about="http://www.foo.com/products/product4711.html">
    <ar:Rule>
      <ar:Context>
        <rdf:Sequence>
          <rdf:li resource="http://www.foo.com/"/>
          <rdf:li>
            <ar:Wildcard min=1>
          </rdf:li>
          <rdf:li resource="http://www.foo.com/promotion/pro991014.html"/>
        <rdf:Sequence>
      </ar:context>
      <ar:Link>
        <ar:Target resource="http://www.foo.com/products/
                                            product9827.html"/>
        <ar:Label>See also our new product X</ar:Label>
      </ar:Link>
    </ar:Rule>
  </rdf:Description>
</rdf:RDF>
```

Fig. 6. Example of an annotation rule in RDF encoding.

original query form always contains all three search criteria, a new form would be needed though, in which the suggested criterion is somehow highlighted.

5.2   Applying Annotation Rules with the HyperView System

We adapt the Web site linkage to the annotation rules by coupling the original web site with a proxy server that applies those rules. We use the HyperView system as proxy server, coupled with a metadata server that maintains the annotation rules. This architecture is depicted in Fig. 7. We can see that the original site is left unchanged. WUM is used to discover the navigation patterns reflecting the behaviour for customers and non-customers in the site. The patterns are compared as described in section 3.

The HyperView server operates as a proxy: It intercepts a HTTP request for a page of the original Web site, retrieves it in its original form and then adapts it on the fly according to the user's browsing history and information from the metadata server. It then forwards the adapted page to the user. The challenge in this context is in maintaining state, in order to verify the annotation rules.

To adapt the web pages for each user, the HyperView server builds and maintains the users' sessions using the same heuristics as the data preparation module of W UM [17]. Then, for each page request, it retrieves the annotation rules whose

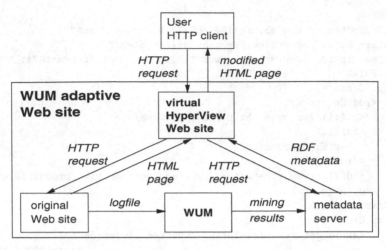

Fig. 7. Building an adaptive web site with WUM and HyperView

LHS matches the pages requested thus far, and applies them to the requested page before transmitting it to the user.

Applying an annotation rule g,A→B implies modifying the requested page A to stress the connection to B. The new or updated link must be labeled by a description of the target page. The metadata server might offer this information as part of the annotation rule. Otherwise, the label can be extracted by the HyperView server's mechanism for data extraction from web documents [12,11].

Framing. We call the simplest method for page annotation "framing": A HTML frame is created around the original page A and the desired link is placed in it. This has the advantage that the original page is preserved, while still adding the new link. However, the effectiveness of this approach may be low since the new environment does not reflect the importance of the new link.

Link insertion. A better method is to automatically embed the link in the original page, probably labeling and surrounding it with further material from B. HyperView provides a rule-based language, HVQL, with which the dynamically formed page can be expressed as a "view", which extracts and combines data from both pages A and B. This approach has the advantage of incorporating the desirable path to B into page A, at the cost of a higher specification effort. It may well happen, that the pages need to be partially redesigned to remain intuitive.

View adaptation. A third solution is possible if the original Web site is itself a virtual Web site built with HyperView: HyperView dynamically generates pages as views over semistructured data extracted from the underlying site(s) on the fly. In that case, it suffices to modify the views defining the virtual Web site in order to take the annotation rules from the metadata server into account.

This approach is particularly appropriate for web sites that are not static by nature, like the SchulWeb site of our experiments. Many web sites, especially online catalogs of products, services or document collections, are simply interfaces integrating information from multiple underlying servers. HyperView has been designed to establish such a web site as a "virtual site" that can be changed and improved dynamically. Then, the views defining the virtual Web site can be modified directly to take the annotation rules from the metadata server into account. Thus, the original Web site itself is turned into an adaptive Web site.

6   Current Status and Future Work

In this work, we have proposed the comparative study of the navigation behaviour of customers and non-customers in order to assess and improve the quality of a commercial web site. We increase the efficiency of the site in motivating site users to become customers, by identifying comparable navigation patterns of customers and non-customers. We detect the pages at which they deviate from each other and adjust them dynamically, according to the behaviour pattern of each user.

We use the Web Utilization Miner WUM to discover navigation patterns that reflect the behaviour expressed and the assistance needed by the site users. We focus on the differences between patterns of customers and non-customers. We introduce a notion of comparability among patterns based on the structure of frequent paths within them. By identifying the pages at which comparable patterns of the two groups deviate from each other, we obtain valuable indications on shortcomings of the web site design and concrete hints for improving it. Our preliminary experiments show that our principles are valid and applicable even to non-commercial sites who regard the users of their services as customers that should be assisted and kept satisfied.

Some of the discovered adaptions of the site topology depend on the user, so that dynamic linking is preferable to site redesign. To this purpose, we propose the coupling of the web site with a metadata server and a proxy server based on the HyperView paradigm for building dynamic views over sites. The metadata server retains the mining results in the form of annotation rules that describe which links should be dynamically presented in which context. The proxy HyperView server retrieves the rules and builds the links on demand. Our future work includes the establishment of an experimental environment for testing our approach.

This study is a first step in exploiting the behaviour differences among groups of users to improve a web site. Our comparisons concentrate on different navigational behaviour and selection of different search options in fill-in forms. However, sites designed for exploration via forms lend themselves to a much larger spectrum of changes, whose goal is to improve the search palette in terms of options and intuitiveness. For this type of sites, we are currently extending our quality criteria and the methodology of inspecting them during data mining.

Our ongoing work includes optimizations of the algorithm performing the comparisons, by employing heuristics to reduce the paths being tested, as well as a better support for the postprocessing of the results. Moreover, we anticipate that users can also be grouped by interests and demographics. We intend to combine such user clusters with groups formed by people having similar navigation behaviour and compare their activities in the site.

References

1. Rakesh Agrawal and Ramakrishnan Srikant. Mining sequential patterns. In *Proc. of Int. Conf. on Data Engineering*, Taipei, Taiwan, Mar. 1995. 143, 145
2. R. Barrett and P. P. Maglio. Intermediaries: New places for producing and manipulating web content. In *Seventh International World Wide Web Conference (WWW7)*, 1998. 157
3. Bettina Berendt and Myra Spiliopoulou. Analysing navigation behaviour in web sites integrating multiple information systems. to appear, 2000. 147, 150, 154
4. Pierre Berthon, Leyland F. Pitt, and Richard T. Watson. The world wide web as an advertising medium. *Journal of Advertising Research*, 36(1):43–54, 1996. 146, 147
5. Vincent Bouthors and Olivier Dedieu. Pharos, a collaborative infrastructure for web knowledge sharing. In *ECDL'99*, 1999. To appear. 157
6. Robert Cooley, Bamshad Mobasher, and Jaidep Srivastava. Data preparation for mining world wide web browsing patterns. *Journal of Knowledge and Information Systems*, 1(1), 1999. 151, 152
7. Olivier Dedieu. Pluxy: un proxy Web dynamiquement extensible. In *Proceedings of the 1998 NoTeRe colloquium*, October 1998. 157
8. Xavier Drèze and Fred Zufryden. Testing web site design and promotional content. *Journal of Advertising Research*, 37(2):77–91, 1997. 142
9. Xavier Drèze and Fred Zufryden. Is internet advertising ready for prime time? *Journal of Advertising Research*, 38(3):7–18, 1998. 142
10. John Eighmey. Profiling user responses to commercial web sites. *Journal of Advertising Research*, 37(2):59–66, May-June 1997. 142
11. Lukas C. Faulstich. Building HyperView web sites. Technical Report B 99-09, Inst. of Computer Science, Free University Berlin, 1999. 157, 159
12. Lukas C. Faulstich and Myra Spiliopoulou. Building HyperView wrappers for publisher web-sites. In *2nd European Conf. on Digital Libraries (ECDL'98)*, LNCS 1513, Heraclion, Greece, Sept. 1998. Springer Verlag. Extended version to appear in the IJODL Special Issue "In the Tradition of Alexandrian Scholars". 157, 159
13. Heikki Mannila and Hannu Toivonen. Discovering generalized episodes using minimal occurences. In *Proc. of 2nd Int. Conf. KDD'96*, pages 146–151, 1996. 143
14. Hannes Marais and Krishna Bharat. Supporting cooperative and personal surfing with a desktop assistant. In *Proceedings of the ACM Symposium on User Interface Software and Technology*, Asynchronous Collaboration, pages 129–138, 1997. 157
15. Myra Spiliopoulou. The laborious way from data mining to web mining. *Int. Journal of Comp. Sys., Sci. & Eng., Special Issue on "Semantics of the Web"*, 14:113–126, Mar. 1999. 143, 145, 146
16. Myra Spiliopoulou, Lukas Faulstich, C., and Karsten Winkler. A Data Miner analyzing the Navigational Behaviour of Web Users. In *Proc. of the Workshop on Machine Learning in User Modelling of the ACAI'99 Int. Conf.*, Creta, Greece, July 1999. 144, 147

17. Myra Spiliopoulou and Lukas C. Faulstich. WUM: A Tool for Web Utilization Analysis. In *extended version of Proc. EDDT Workshop WebDB'98*, LNCS 1590, pages 184–203. Springer Verlag, 1999.   143, 144, 145, 146, 147, 158
18. Ramakrishnan Srikant and Rakesh Agrawal. Mining sequential patterns: Generalizations and performance improvements. In *EDBT*, Avignon, France, Mar. 1996. 143
19. Third Voice. About third voice. http://www.thirdvoice.com/about/index.htm, 1999.   157

Discovery of Interesting Usage Patterns from Web Data

Robert Cooley*, Pang-Ning Tan, and Jaideep Srivastava**

Department of Computer Science and Engineering
University of Minnesota
{cooley,ptan,srivasta}@cs.umn.edu

Abstract. *Web Usage Mining* is the application of data mining techniques to large Web data repositories in order to extract usage patterns. As with many data mining application domains, the identification of patterns that are considered *interesting* is a problem that must be solved in addition to simply generating them. A necessary step in identifying interesting results is quantifying what is considered uninteresting in order to form a basis for comparison. Several research efforts have relied on manually generated sets of uninteresting rules. However, manual generation of a comprehensive set of evidence about beliefs for a particular domain is impractical in many cases. Generally, domain knowledge can be used to automatically create evidence for or against a set of beliefs. This paper develops a quantitative model based on *support logic* for determining the interestingness of discovered patterns. For Web Usage Mining, there are three types of domain information available; *usage, content*, and *structure*. This paper also describes algorithms for using these three types of information to automatically identify interesting knowledge. These algorithms have been incorporated into the Web Site Information Filter (WebSIFT) system and examples of interesting frequent itemsets automatically discovered from real Web data are presented.

1 Introduction and Background

The World Wide Web continues to expand at an amazing rate as a medium for conducting business and disseminating information. Even with evolving standards and technology, the ability to thoroughly analyze the usage of a Web site remains, and will grow, as an important capability for Web administrators. Design of a Web site centers around organizing the information on each page and the hypertext links between the pages in a way that seems most natural to the site users, to facilitate their browsing. For small sites, an individual Web designer's intuition along with some straightforward usage statistics may be adequate for predicting and verifying the users' browsing behavior. However, as the size and complexity of a Web site increases, the statistics provided by existing Web log analysis tools [1,2,3] may prove inadequate, and more sophisticated

---

* Supported by NSF grant EHR-9554517
** Supported by ARL contract DA/DAKF11-98-P-0359

B. Masand and M. Spiliopoulou (Eds.): WEBKDD'99, LNAI 1836, pp. 163–182, 2000.
© Springer-Verlag Berlin Heidelberg 2000

types of analysis will be necessary. *Web Usage Mining*, which is the application of data mining techniques to large Web data repositories, adds powerful techniques to the tools available to a Web site administrator for analyzing Web site usage.

Web Usage Mining techniques developed in [8,9,11,16,19,25,27,30] have been used to discover frequent itemsets, association rules [5], clusters of similar pages and users, sequential patterns [15], and perform path analysis [9]. Several research efforts [17,13] have considered usage information for performing *Web Content Mining* [10]. An overview of some of the challenges involved in Web Content Mining is given in [28].

The notion of what makes discovered knowledge interesting has been addressed in [14,18,20,26]. A common theme among the various criteria for interestingness is the concept of *novelty* or *unexpectedness* of a rule. Results that were previously known by the data analyst are not considered interesting. In Web Usage Mining, as with many data mining domains, thresholds for values such as *support* and *confidence* are often used to limit the number of discovered rules to a manageable number. However, high thresholds rarely discover any knowledge that was not previously known and low thresholds usually result in an unmanageable number of rules. The approach advocated by [14,18] is to identify a set of *beliefs*, and use the set as a filter for identifying interesting rules. Rules that confirm existing beliefs are deemed uninteresting.

In a more general sense, both the discovered knowledge and any expectations defined from domain knowledge can be considered as pieces of evidence providing support *for* or *against* a particular belief. There can be multiple sources of evidence pertaining to any given belief about a domain, some of them possibly contradictory. Also, as pointed out in [14], evidence about some of the beliefs is likely to be imprecise or incomplete, requiring a framework with fuzzy logic [29] capabilities. A framework based on Baldwin's *support logic* [6] can be defined, which is specifically designed to handle reasoning about multiple sources of evidence with both boolean and fuzzy logic and includes an explicit accounting of ignorance regarding a belief. The framework is built around defining *support pairs* for every piece of evidence.[1]

Another problem that exists with the identification of interesting results is the generation of an initial set of evidence about beliefs from domain knowledge. Both [14] and [18] rely on manually generated sets of evidence. For [18], beliefs are only defined as interesting if there is conflicting evidence, so unless a fairly comprehensive set is created, many interesting results can be missed. [14] has a broader definition of interestingness that includes results that provide evidence about a belief not covered by domain knowledge. However, without a comprehensive set of evidence from domain knowledge, this method will end up misclassifying many results.

---

[1] In order to avoid confusion with the standard data mining definition of support, Baldwin's support pairs will be referred to as *evidence pairs* for the rest of this paper.

The Web Usage Mining domain has several types of information available that can be used as surrogates for domain knowledge. Using this information, a large and fairly comprehensive set of evidence can be automatically generated to effectively filter out uninteresting results from the Web Usage Mining process.

The specific contributions of this paper are:

- Development of a general quantitative model of what determines the interestingness of discovered knowledge, based on Baldwin's support logic framework [6].
- Development of an approach for the automatic creation of an initial set of evidence about a belief set.
- Development of specific algorithms for automated discovery of interesting rules in the Web Usage Mining domain.
- Presentation of results from a Web Usage Mining system called the Web Site Information Filter (WebSIFT) system, using data collected from an actual Web site.

The rest of this paper is organized as follows: Section 2 defines the different types of Web data and information abstractions suitable for usage mining. Section 3 develops a general support logic based framework for defining and combining evidence about a domain. A formal definition of interestingness is also given in this section. Section 4 describes algorithms that can be used for automatically identifying interesting frequent itemsets and Section 5 presents an overview of the WebSIFT system. Section 6 summarizes some results from tests of the WebSIFT system on a Web server log. Finally, section 7 provides conclusions.

2   Data Sources and Information Abstractions

Web Usage Mining analysis can potentially use many different kinds of data sources, as discussed in [21]. This paper classifies such data into the following broad types:

- **Content:** The *real* data in the Web pages, i.e. the data the Web page was designed to convey to the users. This usually consists of, but is not limited to text and graphics.
- **Structure:** The data which describes the organization of the content. *Intra-page* structure information includes HTML or XML tags of various kinds, the sequence in which they appear, etc. The principal kind of *inter-page* structure information is hyper-links connecting one page to another.
- **Usage:** The data that describes the pattern of usage of Web pages, such as IP addresses, page references, and the date/time of accesses. This information can be obtained from Web server logs.

The World Wide Web Committe (W3C) Web Characterization Activity [4] has defined several data abstractions that are useful for Web Usage mining, such as *page view*, *server session*, and *click stream* that are based on the data types listed above. A page view is defined by all of the files that contribute to the client-side presentation seen as the result of a single mouse "click" of a user. A click-stream is then the sequence of page views that are accessed by a user. A *user session* is the click-stream of page views for a single user across the entire Web. Typically, only the portion of each user session that is accessing a specific site can be used for analysis, since access information is not publicly available from the vast majority of Web servers. The set of page-views in a user session for a particular Web site is referred to as a *server session* (also commonly referred to as a *visit*). The term *user episode* refers to a subset of page views in a user session. In addition, Web pages can be classified into various types based on their content, structure and other attributes. For example, the ratio of the number of links in a page to the number of text units (say words) can be used as a measure for classifying pages into various types such as *navigational*, *content*, or *hybrid*. This issue is discussed in detail in [11].

Various kinds of analyses can be performed on these abstractions to extract knowledge useful for a variety of applications. A specific type of analysis is to make assertions about the aggregate usage behavior of all users who visit pages of a Web site. For example, the assertion can be made that a pair of pages that have structural proximity (due to hyperlinks between them) and/or content proximity (since they have information on closely related topics), are *likely* to be visited together *often*. Analysis of structure and content information can be used to make the initial assertion, and subsequent analysis of usage data can be used to examine the truth of such an assertion.

Note that in the above assertion, words such as *likely* and *often* are used rather than *will* and *always*. In an inductive analysis scenario with many sources of uncertainty, the first set of words more accurately captures the nature of assertions that can be made, making standard predicate logic too brittle a reasoning framework. Hence, the framework of *support logic* [6] is used for analysis, as described in the next section.

3 Evaluation of Beliefs in a Support Logic Framework

3.1 Measures of Interestingness

The ultimate goal of any data mining effort is to provide the analyst with results that are interesting and relevant to the task at hand. [26] defines two types of interestingness measures - *objective* and *subjective*. *Objective* measures rate rules based on the data used in the mining process. Thresholds on *objective* measures such as confidence, support, or chi-square [7] are invaluable for reducing the number of generated rules, but often fall well short of the goal of only reporting rules that are of potential interest to the analyst.

For *subjective* measures of interestingness, [26] defines two criteria to evaluate rules and patterns. A rule is *unexpected* if it is "surprising" to the data analyst, and *actionable* if the analyst can act on it to his advantage. The degree to which a rule is *actionable* depends on its application. Consider the use of association rules to restructure a Web site. Since the topology or content of a Web site can be modified based on any discovered information, all rules are *actionable* for this application. [18] formally defines the unexpectedness of a rule in terms of its deviation from a set of beliefs. [14] has a broader definition of interestingness that includes discovered rules that are not specifically covered by an initial set of beliefs. In other words, a rule that doesn't contradict an existing belief, but points out a relationship that hadn't even been considered is also interesting. While both [14] and [18] give examples of small sets of manually generated beliefs, neither addresses the issue of automated generation of a realistic belief set from a large amount of data.

3.2   Support Logic

A more general way to look at the problem of identifying the interestingness of discovered patterns is to consider each piece of information in terms of the evidence it gives *for* or *against* a given logical statement (belief). Baldwin's *support logic* [6,23], which is an implementation of the Dempster-Schafer theory of evidence [24], provides a framework for this point of view. For a belief $\mathcal{B}$, evidence collected for or against $\mathcal{B}$ can be used to form an *evidence pair*, $[e_n, e_p]$, where:

$$e_n = \text{necessary evidence in support of } \mathcal{B} \tag{1}$$
$$e_p = \text{possible evidence in support of } \mathcal{B} \tag{2}$$
$$(1 - e_p) = \text{necessary evidence in support of } \neg\mathcal{B} \tag{3}$$
$$(1 - e_n) = \text{possible evidence in support of } \neg\mathcal{B} \tag{4}$$
$$(e_p - e_n) = \text{uncertainty of } \mathcal{B} \tag{5}$$

The values of e_n and e_p must satisfy the constraints:

$$e_n + (1 - e_p) \leq 1 \tag{6}$$
$$e_n \geq 0, e_p \geq 0 \tag{7}$$

Figure 1 shows the concepts that map to each region of a belief scale, given e_n and e_p. If e_n and e_p are equal, the situation reduces to probabilistic uncertainty. When e_n and e_p are not equal, the difference between the values represents the amount of ignorance about a belief. Note that ignorance, or lack of evidence, is fundamentally different than uncertainty. The uncertainty of a fair coin flip coming up heads is known to be 0.5. However, not enough is known about many real life situations to attach a definitive probabilistic value. Instead of assigning a default probability, Dempster-Schafer theory allows the assignment of an interval indicating that there is missing evidence about a particular belief. Another way to think of ignorance is the lack of confidence in the probabilistic values assigned

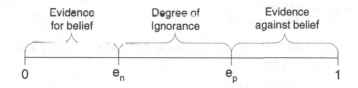

Fig. 1. Evidence Pair Values for a Belief

to a belief. As an example, assume that evidence has been collected about the belief $B(X,Y)$, that Web pages X and Y are related. If all of the evidence is in support of $B(X,Y)$ and one is completely confident in the evidence, the evidence pair is $[1,1]$. On the other extreme, if all of the evidence is against $B(X,Y)$, the evidence pair is $[0,0]$. If the data leads to a 25% degree of belief that $B(X,Y)$ is true,and a 40% degree of belief that $B(X,Y)$ is false, then $[0.25, 0.6]$ would represent the appropriate evidence pair. This says that the degree of ignorance about $B(X,Y)$ is 35%. Finally, if there is no evidence pertaining to $B(X,Y)$, the evidence pair is $[0,1]$, giving a complete lack of confidence, or a degree of ignorance of 100%. Independent of the type of the source for generating an evidence pair, pairs can be combined per Baldwin's *support logic programming calculus* [6] to obtain a single evidence pair per belief. The basic rules are as follows:

If $B{:}[e_{1n}, e_{1p}]$ AND $B{:}[e_{2n}, e_{2p}]$ are two independent evidence pairs from different sources about belief B, then conclude $B{:}[e_n, e_p]$, where

$$e_n = [e_{1n}e_{2n} + e_{1n}(e_{2p} - e_{2n}) + e_{2n}(e_{1p} - e_{1n})]/K \tag{8}$$
$$1 - e_p = [(1 - e_{1p})(1 - e_{2p}) + (e_{1p} - e_{1n})(1 - e_{2p}) +$$
$$(e_{2p} - e_{2n})(1 - e_{1p})]/K \tag{9}$$
$$K = 1 - e_{1n}(1 - e_{2p}) - e_{2n}(1 - e_{1p}) \tag{10}$$

All beliefs have a default evidence pair value of $[0,1]$ until some data is introduced that pertains to that belief. As subsequent data relevant to a belief is analyzed, the evidence pair can be updated using equations 8, 9, and 10. For any data mining domain, the rules that are generated can be used to initialize a set of evidence pairs. A second set of evidence pairs can be generated from domain knowledge or from another knowledge discovery algorithm. Building on the support logic framework, an interesting result can be defined as either a belief with a combined evidence pair that is significantly different from one of the original evidence pairs, or original evidence pairs that are significantly different from each other. "Significantly different" can be determined by setting a threshold value, $\mathcal{T}$, for differences in both e_n and e_p. A formal definition of interesting can be defined as follows[2]:

For a belief, $\mathcal{B}$ with an interestingness pair $\mathcal{I}(n_i, p_i)$, where

$$n_i = |e_n^{(x)} - e_n^{(y)}| \tag{11}$$
$$p_i = |e_p^{(x)} - e_p^{(y)}| \tag{12}$$

$\mathcal{B}$ is interesting if:

$$\mathcal{T} \leq \sqrt{n_i^2 + p_i^2} \tag{13}$$

In the definition above, the x and y superscripts designate values from different evidence pairs. Since the interestingness of a belief is defined by a real-value, an ordering among interesting beliefs can also be established. In the simplest case, all evidence is either 100% for a belief, 100% against a belief, or there is no evidence about a belief. This leads to nine different "boundary" cases that can occur when comparing evidence generated from two separate sources. These are shown in Table 1, along with the three types of comparisons that can be made. For the two cases where the evidence pairs are in complete disagreement, the combined evidence pair is "Null." This is because completely contradictory evidence can not, and should not be automatically reconciled. Comparing one of the original evidence sources with the combined evidence identifies beliefs with conflicting evidence along with evidence only represented in the other source as interesting. This is useful when one set of evidence is considered to be established or "known" and a second set of evidence is "new." By comparing the known evidence pairs to the combined evidence pairs, all of the previously unknown and conflicting results will be labeled as interesting. If the two evidence sources are directly compared, all beliefs that have evidence from only one of the sources will be declared interesting in addition to any conflicting beliefs. This may be desirable for situations when both sources of evidence are considered to be new. By setting an appropriate threshold $\mathcal{T}$ and choosing which evidence pairs will be compared, any combination of the following situations can be automatically labeled as interesting:

- Beliefs with conflicting evidence.
- Beliefs with evidence from source 1 but not source 2.
- Beliefs with evidence from source 2 but not source 1.

Note that the definitions of interestingness from both [18] and [14] are included in this framework.

3.3   Generation of Belief Sets for Web Usage Mining

For Web Usage Mining, there are two additional sources from which evidence pairs can be automatically created; the content and structure data (as discussed

---

[2] While this definition uses the familiar L2-norm, other norms could be substituted as appropriate.

Table 1. Comparison of Boolean Evidence Pairs from Separate Sources

Evidence			Interestingness ($\mathcal{T} = 1$)		
Source 1	Source 2	Combined	Source 1 vs. Combined	Source 2 vs. Combined	Source 1 vs. Source 2
[0,0]	[0,0]	[0,0]	No	No	No
[0,0]	[0,1]	[0,0]	No	Yes	Yes
[0,0]	[1,1]	Null	Yes	Yes	Yes
[0,1]	[0,0]	[0,0]	Yes	No	Yes
[0,1]	[0,1]	[0,1]	No	No	No
[0,1]	[1,1]	[1,1]	Yes	No	Yes
[1,1]	[0,0]	Null	Yes	Yes	Yes
[1,1]	[0,1]	[1,1]	No	Yes	Yes
[1,1]	[1,1]	[1,1]	No	No	No

Table 2. Examples of Web Usage Information that can be Automatically Flagged as Interesting

Source 1	Source 2	Interesting Belief Example
General Usage Statistics	Site Structure	The head page is not the most common entry point for users
General Usage Statistics	Site Content	A page that is designed to provide content is being used as a navigation page
Frequent Itemsets	Site Structure	A frequent itemset contains pages that are not directly linked
Usage Clusters	Site Content	A usage cluster contains pages from multiple content clusters

earlier, evidence can also be manually generated by a domain expert). The task of reconciling conflicting evidence from the content and structure data falls under the category of *Web Content Mining*, which is beyond the scope of this paper. The assumption is that content and structure data can be used as surrogates for the Web site designer's domain knowledge. Links between pages provide evidence in support of those pages being related. The stronger the topological connection is between a set of pages, the higher the value of e_n is set for the evidence pair. Evidence pairs based on the site content can also be automatically generated by looking at content similarity, and assigning values of e_n and e_p based on the calculated "distance" between pages. Table 2 gives some examples of the types of interesting beliefs that can be identified in the Web Usage Mining domain using the framework described in the previous section.

4   Filtering of Knowledge Based on Interestingness

4.1   Evidence from Structure Information

The use of structure information to guide the knowledge discovery process in Web Mining has been discussed by several authors [16,19,21,25]. Most of their work is focused on using the site structure to perform clustering on Web pages or user path profiles. However, the utilization of structure information during knowledge analysis (in particular, for automated filtering of uninteresting results) has been largely ignored.

There are several ways to accommodate structure information into the filtering phase of a Web Mining system. This section introduces one approach for incorporating structural evidence into the support logic framework for filtering uninteresting frequent itemsets. The goal is to obtain a structural evidence pair $E^{(s)} = [e_n^{(s)}, e_p^{(s)}]$ that will represent the belief that a set of pages are related. Any suggested approach for quantifying $E^{(s)}$ must satisfy the following minimum requirements :

- **Consistency:** The values of $e_n^{(s)}$ and $e_p^{(s)}$ are subjected to the constraints given in equations 6 and 7 (Namely, the values are between 0 and 1, and the sum of $e_n^{(s)} + e_p^{(s)}$ is not greater than 1).
- **Reducibility:** The structural evidence pair for a large itemset can be calculated from the evidence pairs of its constituent itemsets. Furthermore, the rules for combining the evidence pair for the smaller itemsets must be consistent, i.e. the combined evidence pair for the larger itemset must be the same irrespective of the order in which the itemsets are combined.
- **Monotonicity:** The necessary structural evidence, $e_n^{(s)}$, should increase monotonically as the number of links connecting the pages within an itemset increases.
- **Connectivity:** If the graph representing an itemset is connected, its $e_n^{(s)}$ should be large compared to one that is not connected (when both graphs contain the same number of links and vertices).

One method for calculating $e_n^{(s)}$ that meets the requirements listed above is to use a combination of the following two parameters: the link factor and connectivity factor. Link factor (lfactor) is a normalized measure for the number of links present among the pages in an itemset.

$$\text{lfactor} = \frac{L}{N(N-1)} \tag{14}$$

where N is the number of pages in the itemset and L is the number of direct hyperlinks between them. The denominator ensures that the consistency requirement is satisfied. Furthermore, one can verify that both monotonicity and reducibility requirements are obeyed by the lfactor measure.

The connectivity requirement can be captured in a simple way by introducing a connectivity factor (cfactor) which is defined as

$$\text{cfactor} = \begin{cases} 1, & \text{if } G(I) \text{ is connected;} \\ 0, & \text{otherwise.} \end{cases} \tag{15}$$

where G(I) is the graphical representation for itemset I. The necessary evidence can now be defined as :

$$e_n^{(s)} = \text{lfactor} \times \text{cfactor} \tag{16}$$

$e_p^{(s)}$ can be set anywhere between $e_n^{(s)}$ and 1, depending on the desired degree of ignorance. The experiments described in Section 6 use $e_n^{(s)} = e_p^{(s)}$.

4.2 Evidence from Usage Information

Mined results in the form of frequent itemsets can be used to provide evidence for pages being related. In order to derive an evidence pair from a frequent itemset, a single measure of the strength of the relationship between the pages is needed. This is normally done by breaking an N item frequent itemset up into N separate association rules, and reporting the confidence for each rule. However, this method results in several rules about the same set of pages, all with potentially different confidence levels. Since the order and number of page accesses for a user session have been removed from frequent itemsets, this expansion of the discovered rules does not make sense. A measure other than support that can be calculated for frequent itemsets is the *coverage*. The coverage of a rule is the fraction of the total number of transactions that contain *at least one* of the items in the itemset (as opposed to support, which measures the fraction of transactions that contain *all* of the items). Support, $\mathcal{S}$, and coverage, $\mathcal{C}$, for a frequent itemset with items i_1 through i_n are defined as follows, where Count(predicate) is the number of transactions containing the predicate, and N_T is the total number of transactions:

$$\mathcal{S} = \frac{\text{Count}(i_1 \wedge i_2 \ldots \wedge i_n)}{N_T} \tag{17}$$

$$\mathcal{C} = \frac{\text{Count}(i_1 \vee i_2 \ldots \vee i_n)}{N_T} \tag{18}$$

Notice that both support and coverage are highly dependent on the total number of transactions. By taking the ratio of support to coverage, this dependency is eliminated. The support-to-coverage ratio (SCR) gives a single measure of the strength of a frequent itemset that is independent of the total number of transactions in the database. Essentially, the SCR is the support of a frequent itemset when only considering the transactions that contain at least one item in the itemset. The SCR for a frequent itemset can be calculated using the algorithm shown in Table 3, which is called after the completion of each level of a frequent itemset generation algorithm, such as Apriori [5] (or one of its variants). The Table 3 algorithm is based on the fact that for any frequent itemset, the

Table 3. SCR Algorithm

```
Algorithm SCR
1. let F = {I₁, I₂, · · · , Iₙ} denote the discovered frequent itemset
2. cover = 0
3. for level l = 1 to n
4.     lcount = CountSum(itemsets ⊆ F)
5.        cover = cover + (−1)^{l+1} * lcount
6. SCR = Count(F)/cover
7. end;
```

supports or counts for all of the contributing subset itemsets have already been calculated.

For a given frequent itemset, the SCR provides evidence for, and (1-SCR) provides evidence against a set of pages being related to each other. Therefore, a simple evidence pair for usage evidence that does not take any degree of ignorance into account is [SCR,SCR].

4.3   Evidence Combination

The remaining issue before using the support logic calculus to combine the structural and usage evidence is scaling. Since the two sets of evidence are derived in different manners from different sets of data, the scales do not necessarily match. For the usage data, a factor that has not been considered in the generation of the evidence pairs is user attrition. Several studies summarized in [22] have found that the mean path length of user sessions is typically about 3 pages with a heavy tailed distribution. Therefore, as the number of pages in a belief increases, the less likely it is that a corresponding frequent itemset will be discovered, simply because of user attrition. However, the strength of the corresponding domain evidence pair does not necessarily decrease as the size of the set increases. In order to account for this, one set of evidence pairs needs to be scaled based on the size of the page set. The WebSIFT information filter simply uses the number of pages in the set as its scaling factor as follows:

$$\text{sfactor} = n \tag{19}$$

Once the evidence pairs are scaled, the evidence combination rules presented in Section 3 are used to calculate the combined evidence pairs. Either the mined or domain evidence pair can be taken as the "existing" evidence to be compared with the combined evidence. The algorithm for creating, combining, and comparing evidence pairs is shown in Table 4.

Table 4. Frequent Itemset Filter Algorithm

Algorithm Filter
1. for each F in the discovered frequent itemsets
2. $\quad e_p^{(m)} = e_n^{(m)} = \text{SCR}(F) * \text{sfactor}(F)$
3. $\quad e_p^{(s)} = e_n^{(s)} = \text{lfactor}(F) * \text{cfactor}(F)$
4. $\quad [e_p^{(c)}, e_n^{(c)}] = \text{BaldwinCombine}(e_p^{(m)}, e_n^{(m)}, e_p^{(s)}, e_n^{(s)})$
5. $\quad$ let x = m or s per user input
6. $\quad$ If $\text{Interest}(e_p^{(x)}, e_n^{(x)}, e_p^{(c)}, e_n^{(c)}) \geq \mathcal{T}$
7. $\quad\quad$ Add F to InterestingSets
8. end;

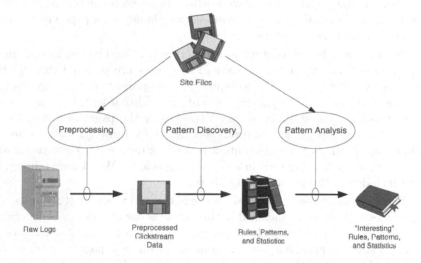

Site Files

Preprocessing   Pattern Discovery   Pattern Analysis

Raw Logs   Preprocessed   Rules, Patterns,   "Interesting"
               Clickstream   and Statistics   Rules, Patterns,
               Data   and Statistics

Fig. 2. High Level *Web Usage Mining* Process

5 The WebSIFT System

The WebSIFT system[3] divides the Web Usage Mining process into three main
parts, as shown in Figure 2. For a particular Web site, the three server logs -
access, referrer, and agent (often combined into a single log), the HTML files,
template files, script files or databases that make up the site content , and any
optional data such as registration data or remote agent logs provide the information to construct the different information abstractions defined in Section 2.
The preprocessing phase uses the input data to construct a server session file
based on the methods and heuristics discussed in [11]. In order to preprocess a
server log, the log must first be "cleaned", which consists of removing unsucess-
ful requests, parsing relevant CGI name/value pairs and rolling up file accesses

---

[3] Based on the WEBMINER prototype [10].

into page views. Once the log is converted into a list of page views, users must be identified. In the absence of cookies or dynamically embedded session IDs in the URIs, the combination of IP address and user agent can be used as a first pass estimate of unique users. This estimate can be refined by using the referrer field, as described in [11]. The click-stream for each user is divided up into sessions based on a simple thirty minute timeout. Finally, path completion is performed by again looking at the referrer information for each request. These steps are shown in Figure 3.

The preprocessing phase of the WebSIFT system allows the option of converting the server sessions into *episodes* prior to performing knowledge discovery. In this case, episodes are either all of the page views in a server session that the user spent a significant amount of time viewing (assumed to be a content page), or all of the navigation page views leading up to each content page view. The details of how a cutoff time is determined for classifying a page view as content or navigation are also contained in [11].

Preprocessing for the content and structure of a site involves assembling each page view for parsing and/or analysis. Page views are accessed through HTTP requests by a "site crawler" to assemble the components of the page view. This handles both static and dynamic content. In addition to being used to derive a site topology, the site files are used to classify the pages of a site. Both the site topology and page classifications can then be fed into the *information filter*. While classification of the site content is really a data mining process in its own right, because it is being used in a supporting role for Web Usage mining, it has been included in the preprocessing phase.

The knowledge discovery phase uses existing data mining techniques to generate rules and patterns. Included in this phase is the generation of general usage statistics, such as number of "hits" per page, page most frequently accessed, most common starting page, and average time spent on each page. Clustering can be performed on either the users or the page views. The discovered information can then be fed into various pattern analysis tools. The current implementation includes the information filter, an association rule graph/visualization tool, and querying of the results through SQL. The WebSIFT system has been implemented using a relational database, procedural SQL, and the Java programming language. Java Database Connectivity (JDBC) drivers are used to interface with the database. Although algorithms have been identified and tested for individual portions of the system, only the generation and filtering of frequent itemsets, association rules, and general statistics is fully automated at this time.

6   Experimental Evaluation

The experiments described in this section were performed on Web server logs from February 1999 at the University of Minnesota Department of Computer Science and Engineering Web site; http://www.cs.umn.edu/.

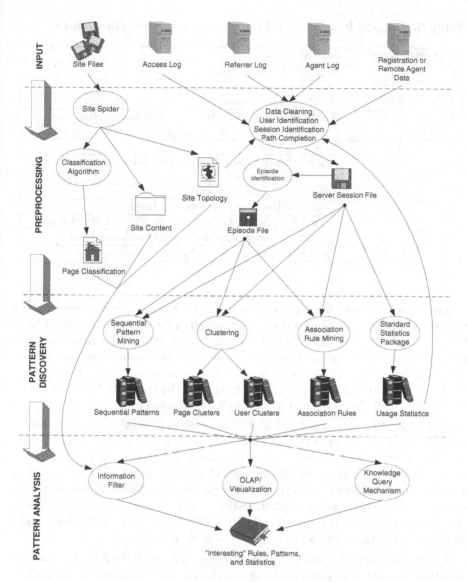

Fig. 3. WebSIFT Architecture

6.1   Preliminary Experiments

To test the feasibility of filtering discovered rules based on site structure, two simple preliminary tests were run. All of the discovered itemsets were assigned an evidence pair of [1,1] (100% belief that the pages are related), and sets of pages without a frequent itemset were assigned an evidence pair of [0,0]. Any frequent itemset that represented a set of pages not directly connected by hypertext links was declared to be potentially interesting. This is analogous to the boundary

Table 5. Frequent Itemsets with Usage Evidence but no Structural Evidence

#	Mined Support(%)	Related Pages
1	0.10	/Research/, /tech_reports/
2	0.10	/employment/, /newsletter/
3	0.10	/faculty/, /newsletter/
4	0.10	/icra99/ICRA99-Index.htm, /icra99/Notice.html, /icra99/TechnProgram.htm, /icra99/advanceprogram2.htm
5	0.10	/new/, /sem-coll/
6	0.10	/reg-info/98-99_schedule.html, /reg-info/ss1-99.html, /reg-info/ss2-99.html
7	0.11	/Research/Agassiz/, /faculty/
8	0.11	/icra99/Notice.html, /icra99/best.html
9	0.11	/icra99/Proceeding-Order.htm, /icra99/Registration.htm
10	0.22	/grad-info/, /grad-info/97-98-grad-handbook.html
11	0.25	/grad-info/, /grad-info/96-97-grad-handbook.html

case of one source providing evidence for a belief with no corresponding evidence from the second source . The second test took all of the connected pairs of pages that had sufficient individual support, and looked for corresponding frequent itemsets. Pairs of pages that did not have a corresponding frequent itemset were also declared to be interesting. This is the boundary case where there is conflicting evidence. These tests are referred to as the BME (Beliefs with Mined Evidence) and BCE (Beliefs with Conflicting Evidence) in [12].

The processed log consisted of 43,158 page views divided among 10,609 user sessions. A threshold of 0.1% for support was used to generate 693 frequent itemsets, with a maximum set size of six pages. There were 178 unique pages represented in all of the rules. Both methods described in the previous section were run on the frequent itemsets. The first method resulted in 11 frequent itemsets being declared as potentially interesting, and the second method resulted in 10 missing page pairs being declared as potentially interesting. Tables 5 and 6 show the interesting results identified by each algorithm.

Of the frequent itemsets shown in Table 5, the two including the graduate handbook (numbers 10 and 11) are of note because these pages are out-of-date. A page with the 1998-99 graduate handbook exists, and the links from the /grad-info/ page to the older handbooks have been removed. However, since the pages were not actually removed from the site and other pages in the site reference them (or users have old bookmarks), the older handbooks are still accessed. The supports of these itemsets are 0.25% and 0.22% respectively. Had the support threshold been set higher to limit the total number of itemsets discovered, the rules would have been missed.

In Table 6, the fourth pair of pages is of note because the first page functions solely as an entry page to a particular research group's pages. However, the link from the first page is flashing and located fairly low on the page. This indicates

Table 6. Itemsets with Conflicting Evidence

#	Web Pages
1	/Research/Agassiz/agassiz_pubs.html, /Research/Agassiz/agassiz_people.html
2	/Research/GIMME/tclprop.html, /Research/GIMME/Nsync.html
3	/Research/airvl/minirob.html, /Research/airvl/loon.html
4	/Research/mmdbms/home.shtml, /Research/mmdbms/group.html
5	/newsletter/kumar.html, /newsletter/facop.html
6	/newsletter/letter.html, /newsletter/facop.html
7	/newsletter/letter.html, /newsletter/kumar.html
8	/newsletter/newfac.html, /newsletter/facop.html
9	/newsletter/newfac.html, /newsletter/kumar.html
10	/newsletter/newfac.htm, /newsletter/letter.html

a design problem since not all of the visitors from the first page are visiting the second.

6.2   Interesting Frequent Itemsets

For this set of experiments, the processed log consisted of 31,584 page views divided among 8175 user sessions. A threshold of 0.1% for support was used to generate 1345 frequent itemsets, with a maximum set size of nine pages. There were 363 unique pages represented in all of the rules. The usage and structure evidence pairs were calculated and combined as described in Section 4. Figure 4 shows the number of rules that are declared to be interesting for a range of thresholds.

Notice that at an interestingness threshold of 0.1, only about 300 of the 1345 discovered rules are declared to be interesting. This indicates that the methods for calculating evidence pairs for usage and structure evidence result in similar values for most of the itemsets.

Two lists of potentially interesting rules were identified by comparing the structure evidence with the combined evidence, and then comparing the usage evidence with the combined evidence. The lists of potentially interesting frequent itemsets are shown in Tables 7 and 8. Table 7 basically contains pages that are used together less than would be expected from the structure of the site (using an interestingness threshold value of 0.4). The first two rules are of note because /Research/arpa/ and /Research/cais/ aren't actually HTML pages, but are only directories, which might explain why they are not accessed as often as expected. The results presented in this table are consistent with the theoretical arguments presented in the previous section. Table 8 contains rules with pages that aren't directly connected by links but have relatively high support (with the threshold set at 0.5). Despite not having directly connected hyperlinks, these pages are somewhat related by their common URL structure. This is an artifact of the choice of a binary cfactor for computing the structural evidence pair. A cfactor that assigns non-zero values for pages that are close to each other but

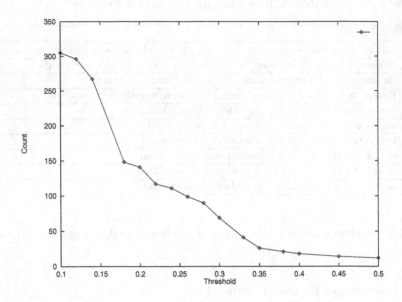

Fig. 4. Number of Interesting Itemsets with Different Threshold Values

not directly connected would most likely filter out many of the rules listed in Table 8. Nevertheless, both tables verify the ability of WebSIFT's information filter to identify rules with conflicting evidence in accordance with the support logic framework.

7   Conclusions

Using the support logic model, this paper has developed a general framework for determining the interestingness of mined knowledge. The framework leverages the power of a robust logic system based on fuzzy logic and evidential reasoning, that is capable of reasoning about evidence from multiple sources about a given belief. Both reinforcing and conflicting pieces of evidence can be handled. In addition, automated methods for generating evidence in support of beliefs have been defined and tested for the Web Usage Mining domain.

Future work will include the incorporation of content data and development of information filter algorithms for use with sequential patterns and clusters of pages and users. In addition, tests will be run with various degrees of ignorance built into the calculated evidence pairs.

Table 7. Interesting Frequent Itemsets Comparing Structure Evidence with Combined Evidence

#	Structure Evidence	Combined Evidence	Interestingness	Related Pages
1	(0.5,0.5)	(0.092,0.092)	0.577	/Research/,/Research/arpa/
2	(0.5,0.5)	(0.083,0.083)	0.589	/Research/,/Research/cais/
3	(0.5, 0.5)	(0.196,0.196)	0.430	/Research/airvl/loon.html, /Research/airvl/minirob.html
4	(0.5,0.5)	(0.096,0.096)	0.572	/contact-info.html, /systems-staff/contact-info.hml
5	(0.5,0.5)	(0.179,0.179)	0.453	/help/,/help/configure/
6	(0.5,0.5)	(0.146,0.146)	0.500	/help/,/help/security/
7	(0.5,0.5)	(0.128,0.128)	0.523	/help/,/help/setup/cs-setup.html
8	(0.5,0.5)	(0.139,0.139)	0.510	/help/,/help/software/
9	(0.5,0.5)	(0.190,0.190)	0.439	/help/,/help/support.html
10	(0.5,0.5)	(0.185,0.185)	0.445	/help/,/help/web/
11	(0.5,0.5)	(0.179,0.179)	0.453	/newsletter/, /newsletter/kumar.html
12	(0.5,0.5)	(0.128,0.128)	0.526	/newsletter/, /newsletter/relations.html
13	(0.5,0.5)	(0.141,0.141)	0.508	/newsletter/, /newsletter/robfac.html

References

1. Funnel web professional. http://www.activeconcepts.com. 163
2. Hit list commerce. http://www.marketwave.com. 163
3. Webtrends log analyzer. http://www.webtrends.com. 163
4. World wide web committee web usage characterization activity. http://www.w3.org/WCA. 165
5. R. Agrawal and R. Srikant. Fast algorithms for mining association rules. In *Proc. of the 20th VLDB Conference*, pages 487–499, Santiago, Chile, 1994. 164, 172
6. J. F. Baldwin. Evidential support logic programming. *Fuzzy Sets and Systems*, 24(1):1–26, 1987. 164, 165, 166, 167, 168
7. S. Brin, R. Motwani, and C. Silverstein. Beyond market baskets: Generalizing association rules to correlations. In *ACM SIGMOD International Conference on Management of Data*, 1997. 166
8. Alex Buchner and Maurice D Mulvenna. Discovering internet marketing intelligence through online analytical web usage mining. *SIGMOD Record*, 27(4):54–61, 1998. 164
9. M.S. Chen, J.S. Park, and P.S. Yu. Data mining for path traversal patterns in a web environment. In *16th International Conference on Distributed Computing Systems*, pages 385–392, 1996. 164
10. Robert Cooley, Bamshad Mobasher, and Jaideep Srivastava. Web mining: Information and pattern discovery on the world wide web. In *International Conference on Tools with Artificial Intelligence*, pages 558–567, Newport Beach, 1997. IEEE. 164, 174
11. Robert Cooley, Bamshad Mobasher, and Jaideep Srivastava. Data preparation for mining world wide web browsing patterns. *Knowledge and Information Systems*, 1(1), 1999. 164, 166, 174, 175

Table 8. Interesting Frequent Itemsets Comparing Usage Evidence with Combined Evidence

#	Usage Evidence	Combined Evidence	Inter- estingness	Related Pages
1	(0.409,0.409)	(0,0)	0.579	/Research/airvl/people.html, /Research/airvl/postdoc.html
2	(0.5,0.5)	(0,0)	0.707	/Research/arpa/, /Research/neural/
3	(0.391,0.391)	(0,0)	0.553	/employment/fac-positions/soft-sys.html, /employment/msse/
4	(0.370,0.370)	(0,0)	0.524	/employment/msse/, /employment/temporary/
5	(0.643,0.643)	(0,0)	0.909	/employment/other/naog.html, /employment/other/ncs.html
6	(0.393,0.393)	(0,0)	0.556	/help/configure/, /help/offsite/cs-offsite.html
7	(0.435,0.435)	(0,0)	0.615	/icra99/TechnProgram.htm, /icra99/advanceprogram.htm
8	(0.391,0.391)	(0,0)	0.553	/icra99/best.html, /icra99/bestk.html
9	(0.474,0.474)	(0,0)	0.670	/labs/1-214.html, /labs/downtime/
10	(0.474,0.474)	(0,0)	0.670	/labs/1-260.html, /labs/2-216.html
11	(0.5,0.5)	(0,0)	0.707	/labs/1-260.html, /labs/downtime/
12	(0.409,0.409)	(0,0)	0.579	/labs/2-216.html, /labs/downtime/
13	(0.556,0.556)	(0,0)	0.786	/labs/CCIE/cost.html, /labs/CCIE/description.html
14	(0.707,0.707)	(0,0)	1.000	/reg-info/ss1-99.html, /reg-info/ss2-99.html
15	(0.583,0.583)	(0,0)	0.825	/sem-coll/cray.html, /sem-coll/seminar/seminar.html

12. Robert Cooley, Pang-Ning Tan, and Jaideep Srivastava. Discovery of interesting usage patterns from web data. Technical Report TR 99-022, University of Minnesota, 1999. 177

13. T. Joachims, D. Freitag, and T. Mitchell. Webwatcher: A tour guide for the world wide web. In *The 15th International Conference on Artificial Intelligence*, Nagoya, Japan, 1997. 164

14. Bing Liu, Wynne Hsu, and Shu Chen. Using general impressions to analyze discovered classification rules. In *Third International Conference on Knowledge Discovery and Data Mining*, 1997. 164, 167, 169

15. H. Mannila, H. Toivonen, and A. I. Verkamo. Discovering frequent episodes in sequences. In *Proc. of the First Int'l Conference on Knowledge Discovery and Data Mining*, pages 210–215, Montreal, Quebec, 1995. 164

16. Olfa Nasraoui, Raghu Krishnapuram, and Anupam Joshi. Mining web access logs using a fuzzy relational clustering algorithm based on a robust estimator. In *Eighth International World Wide Web Conference*, Toronto, Canada, 1999. 164, 171

17. D.S.W. Ngu and X. Wu. Sitehelper: A localized agent that helps incremental exploration of the world wide web. In *6th International World Wide Web Conference*, Santa Clara, CA, 1997. 164

18. Balaji Padmanabhan and Alexander Tuzhilin. A belief-driven method for discovering unexpected patterns. In *Fourth International Conference on Knowledge Discovery and Data Mining*, pages 94–100, New York, New York, 1998. 164, 167, 169

19. Mike Perkowitz and Oren Etzioni. Adaptive web sites: Automatically synthesizing web pages. In *Fifteenth National Conference on Artificial Intelligence*, Madison, WI, 1998. 164, 171

20. G. Piatetsky-Shapiro and C. J. Matheus. The interestingness of deviations. In *AAAI-94 Workshop on Knowledge Discovery in Databases*, pages 25–36, 1994. 164

21. Peter Pirolli, James Pitkow, and Ramana Rao. Silk from a sow's ear: Extracting usable structures from the web. In *CHI-96*, Vancouver, 1996. 165, 171

22. James E Pitkow. Summary of www characterizations. In *Seventh International World Wide Web Conference*, 1998. 173

23. A. L. Ralescu and J. F. Baldwin. Concept learning from examples and counter examples. *International Journal of Man-Machine Studies*, 30(3):329–354, 1989. 167

24. G. Schafer. *A Mathematical Theory of Evidence*. Princeton University Press, 1976. 167

25. Cyrus Shahabi, Amir M Zarkesh, Jafar Adibi, and Vishal Shah. Knowledge discovery from users web-page navigation. In *Workshop on Research Issues in Data Engineering*, Birmingham, England, 1997. 164, 171

26. A. Silberschatz and A. Tuzhilin. What makes patterns interesting in knowledge discovery systems. *IEEE Transactions on Knowledge and Data Eng.*, 8(6):970–974, 1996. 164, 166

27. Myra Spiliopoulou and Lukas C Faulstich. Wum: A web utilization miner. In *EDBT Workshop WebDB98*, Valencia, Spain, 1998. Springer Verlag. 164

28. Shivakumar Vaithaynathan. Data mining on the internet - a kdd-98 exhibit presentation. http://www.epsilon.com/kddcup98/mining/, 1998. 164

29. L. A. Zadeh. A theory of approximate reasoning. *Machine Intelligence*, 9:149–194, 1979. 164

30. O. R. Zaiane, M. Xin, and J. Han. Discovering web access patterns and trends by applying olap and data mining technology on web logs. In *Advances in Digital Libraries*, pages 19–29, Santa Barbara, CA, 1998. 164

Author Index

Lecture Notes in Artificial Intelligence (LNAI)

Lecture Notes in Computer Science